Binding and Loosing

K. NEILL FOSTER
WITH PAUL L. KING

BINDING & LOOSING

Exercising Authority over the Dark Powers

CHRISTIAN PUBLICATIONS, INC.
CAMP HILL, PENNSYLVANIA

CHRISTIAN PUBLICATIONS, INC.
3825 Hartzdale Drive, Camp Hill, PA 17011
www.christianpublications.com

Faithful, biblical publishing since 1883

Binding and Loosing
ISBN: 0-87509-852-5
© 1998 by Christian Publications, Inc.
All rights reserved
Printed in the United States of America

05 06 07   7 6 5 4

Cover illustration by Justin Kay

CONTENTS

Part III
Binding and Loosing:
The Theological Factors

Part IV
Binding and Loosing:
The Exegetical Factors

Part V
Binding and Loosing:
The Pragmatic Factors

Part VI
Binding and Loosing:
The Conclusion of the Matter

TRUE-LIFE INCIDENTS

ILLUSTRATION

FOREWORD

Exactly what did Jesus mean when He said to His disciples, "Whatever you bind on earth will be bound in heaven, and whatever you loose on earth will be loosed in heaven" (Matthew 18:18)?

K. Neill Foster, whose preaching has taken him to some of the world's darkest places, has no doubt as to what Jesus meant. In our Savior's promise he sees victory over the forces of Satan. Binding and loosing is part of the spiritual warfare in which every believer is to be engaged. When *we* bind, God binds too. When *we* loose, God looses too.

The author has a Ph.D. from the School of World Mission in Pasadena and currently presides over his denomination's publishing house as Executive Vice-President/Publisher. He has preached in English, French and Spanish to audiences throughout much of the world.

You owe it to yourself to hear him through—you'll find it an interesting read. He cites many of his own experiences. He has sought and included input from other people as well. Rich in anecdote, this text will hold your attention.

If the author wins you to his point of view, there will be one more believer engaged in this important ministry.

H. Robert Cowles,
Editor, *The Alliance Life*, 1971-1983;
Publisher, Christian Publications, Inc., 1983-1988

INTRODUCTION

ARLY IN OUR YEARS in Christian ministry, my wife and I participated in various summer conventions all over North America (I more than she). During those days we interacted with hundreds of Christian workers who converged annually on the campgrounds as speakers, musicians and counselors.

Most were people of the highest integrity, men and women whose lives and ministries evidenced a personal knowledge of and love for God. But there were a few whose ministries turned out to be, shall we say, compromised by conflicting currents. Such was the case with a certain morning speaker. Although the administrative team had no idea what was amiss, they intuitively knew something was wrong after only a message or two. They called the offending speaker "on the carpet" not once but twice during the conference days in the hope that he could explain the problem. He couldn't—or wouldn't. His answer was noncommittal.

With nothing concrete to go on, they allowed him to continue his public speaking schedule but held the camp meeting in an iron grip. Though ordinarily there was a great deal of freedom and participation at the various gatherings, they now forbade spontaneous expressions, such as congregational participation in prayer and testimony, because of what was perceived to be a current of evil emanating from a source they could neither fathom nor identify.

One morning, toward the end of the week, the speaker in question took his place behind the rustic pulpit on the platform of the big tent.

"During the night," he said, "I received a word from the Lord." The message he proceeded to share was loaded with double meanings, potentially both spiritual and sensual, sounding much like something that might come from the Song of Solomon.

Already uneasy with this man's ministry and after listening to his "word from the Lord," my inner alarm bells started to ring when he further suggested that he was going to open the meeting for testimonies.

As I sat on my chair on the grass to the right of the platform, my response was a silent but intuitive and instant no. Without uttering a word, I forbade the spontaneous sharing the speaker had just announced. Apparently what I was binding on earth had already been bound in heaven, for without explanation and without further elaboration, the man began to preach. There had been only a split second between his announcement of the testimony time and his invitation to the congregation to open their Bibles to a certain passage.

To this day, I doubt that he knows why he did not proceed with his intended plan. But we know. He had been bound in the name of the Lord Jesus Christ.

What was the problem that was unleashing those evil spiritual currents? On the final day of the camp it was revealed that the speaker had fallen into adultery on the way there. The woman involved was also on the grounds for the entire week. The Song of Solomon-like "prophecy" was revealed for what it was—a seductive message directed at his partner.

I had believed in the principles of binding and loosing for many years and had published some material on the subject.[1] My wife and I had also practiced it. We liked how it worked. Yet, if pressed, I no doubt would, in times past, have admitted that my views could have been part of a private interpretation and, as such, not part of an essential doctrine that should be strongly advocated to others.

It might have remained so if in 1996 I had not come across an article written by Rev. Paul King, comparing a contemporary religious movement with the teachings of Albert Benjamin Simpson.[2] Buried in King's footnotes was an almost casual affirmation that both G. Campbell Morgan and A.B. Simpson alike had believed that there were certain prerogatives connected with binding and loosing which were given to the Church.

That brief reference initiated discussions with Paul King. I found him to be a born researcher with doctrinal instincts similar to my own. Further research revealed that binding and loosing was present in both the Old and New Testaments, that early Jewish beliefs and Matthew's Gospel were indeed interrelated, that various Church Fathers expressed their views on the subject and that the Scriptures generally have a great deal to say about binding and loosing. I could not have been more surprised at where the research led.

We have chosen to write popularly but at the same time have set the material in an academic framework which assumes that others will proceed from here. Paul King's influence extends far beyond those places where the editorial "we" appears.

What has resulted may be the only full-length treatment of binding and loosing currently available. Categorically, it meshes with the ongoing interest in spiritual warfare. I am convinced that this material will immeasurably strengthen those who make use of the believer's spiritual weapons. But it goes beyond that. *Binding and Loosing* will add to, and perhaps subtract from, current missiological methods. It may also be added to the enlarging library on prayer.

One of the common ways that evangelicals approach this doctrine is from the on-ramp of church discipline. Others, perhaps the majority, associate binding and loosing with spiritual warfare. My focus—until well into the research of this book—had been from the "whatever" on-ramp of Matthew 18:18. I saw binding and loosing as a tool for any area of life and Christian ministry. (You should not then be surprised that one of the most dramatic illustrations in these pages has to do with loosing the flow of grass seed to a mill—definitely a "whatever.") It was only as I began to dig deeper into the material, especially Matthew 12 with synoptic input from Mark and Luke, that I came to realize that the binding and loosing theme could be and probably should be approached from the on-ramp of spiritual warfare. Of course, my wife had told me from the beginning that this would be a book on spiritual warfare!

Whatever your on-ramp to the subject of binding and loosing may be, I believe that in these pages you will find a great deal to stimulate your thinking. The truth is ample and large enough for all. My prayer is this:

> *Lord, let this book glorify You.*
> *Let all praise be ascribed to the Lord Jesus Christ.*
> *And, Lord Jesus, may there be many others who find their*
> *way to liberating understandings through these pages.*

Welcome to the journey!

K. Neill Foster
February 7, 1998

Endnotes

[1] K. Neill Foster, *Warfare Weapons* (Camp Hill, PA: Christian Publications, 1995).

[2] Paul King, "A.B. Simpson and the Modern Faith Movement," in *Alliance Academic Review*, ed. Elio Cuccaro (Camp Hill, PA: Christian Publications, 1996), 11.

The House That Wouldn't Sell

Eleven years is a long time to have a house up for sale, but that is how long Dr. Randy Corbin had been trying to sell a home he owned in Western Pennsylvania.

In the providence of God, I had invited him to read an early draft of this text. By his own admission, he read it slowly and often shared something from this text with his wife at the breakfast table. And, telling no one, he loosed the unsold house.

The following day, there was a call from the distant real estate agent, announcing that an offer was just received on the house. It was for the exact amount of the asking price.

Eventually, the offer became a sale. But still Randy remained silent. Only after the settlement did he tell his wife and me how God had intervened in their lives using the truths unfolded in these pages.

Part I

BINDING AND LOOSING: WHAT IT'S ALL ABOUT

". . . how can anyone enter a strong man's house and carry off his possessions unless he first ties up the strong man? Then he can rob his house." (Matthew 12:29)

"Simon Peter answered, 'You are the Christ, the Son of the living God.'

"Jesus replied, 'Blessed are you, Simon son of Jonah, for this was not revealed to you by man, but by my Father in heaven. And I tell you that you are Peter, and on this rock I will build my church, and the gates of Hades will not overcome it. I will give you the keys of the kingdom of heaven; whatever you bind on earth will be bound in heaven, and whatever you loose on earth will be loosed in heaven.' " (Matthew 16:16-19)

"I tell you the truth, whatever you bind on earth will be bound in heaven, and whatever you loose on earth will be loosed in heaven." (Matthew 18:18)

1

THE DOCTRINE
IN A NUTSHELL

I N ONE OF THE LAST SERMONS A.W. Tozer ever preached, I heard
him tell a story about a man getting on a bus. On his lapel
he was wearing a sign about the size of a dinner plate (a
slight exaggeration, no doubt) which identified him as a friend
of Jesus. As I recall, Dr. Tozer observed that "the Lord's treasures are indeed in earthen vessels," and that "some of those
vessels are a bit cracked!" He went on to admit that he had
gone out of his way to identify himself with that "cracked ves-
sel."

No doubt all of us will admit that there are people and movements which claim to be Christian with whom we would rather
not be too closely identified. While I am awarding the status of
"cracked" to no one, the practice of binding and loosing also
has some uncomfortable (at least for me) "friends." The friends
of this teaching do not, in my estimation, help the cause of the
biblical understanding or the usefulness of binding and loosing.

The "Friends"

For example, some Roman Catholics insist that Peter was the first pope and that binding and loosing, because of its Matthew chapter 18 context, is the prerogative of priests and bishops alone.

Other friends of binding and loosing are those who indiscriminately bind and loose anything and everything—even the church mouse! A woman recently told me that she had attended a church where "everything" was bound and loosed as a common practice. It had, as she said, "scared her a lot."[1] This kind of behavior, it seems to me, is a caricature of the biblical teaching. It does not adorn the doctrine of Christ. (See Titus 2:10.)

Yet other friends of binding and loosing are found in the "territorial spirits" movement. Some attempt to build an entire doctrine around references to the prince of Persia (Daniel 10:20) and the Ephesians 6 hierarchical format of the counter-kingdom. The result, in some cases, is a paradigm based on the animistic assumption that the counter-kingdom derivations and pronouncements of lying spirits can be relied upon to assist in spiritual mapping.[2]

Other friends of binding and loosing are some teachers of the so-called Faith Movement who associate binding and loosing with unbiblical ideas such as the suggestion that God has removed His order from the world and that it is now to be superimposed by Christians who have come to understand how to exert biblical authority.

Still others assure us that miracles have ceased, that the gifts of the Holy Spirit are not for today but for another dispensation. Although there is no biblical base for suggesting that binding and loosing is an expression of a spiritual gift, these friends would say that the supernatural events that often surround binding and loosing should not be expected today.

There are other friends as well who doubt that binding and loosing is anything more than instruction for church discipline as suggested by the Matthew 18 passage.

All of these, in one way or another, caricature binding and loosing. From them I wish to distance myself (we will return later to consider the various scenarios). With good will and charity, allow me to describe and define what, for want of a better term, I call the "evangelical doctrine of binding and loosing."

This doctrine is not an affirmation that Peter was the first pope and that binding and loosing is the prerogative of priests and bishops. Nor is this doctrine a supporting argument for what is commonly known today as the Faith Movement. Such matters as territorial spirits and prayer walks will also be considered in that they impinge significantly on the subject of binding and loosing. Bert Warden has called such new ideas in the kingdom, particularly the passion for territorial spirits, "a long leap" and speculative.[3]

Definition of the Doctrine

The doctrine of binding and loosing, in my view, has been built upon the Protestant Reformation and the priesthood of all believers. The authority of the believer, as a scriptural concept, is part of the completeness of every believer in Jesus Christ (Colossians 2:10). Consider yet again that the marvel, indeed the mystery, of "Christ in you, the hope of glory" (1:27) is expressed in binding and loosing. Jesus Christ, living in us, enables us to bind and loose as the expression of His power and authority. The impulse for binding and loosing comes from heaven, and we discover once we have bound or loosed that God has been there first. Our part, as we shall see, is to bind what has already been bound and to loose what has already been loosed.

This doctrine is rooted also in the sinless life of Jesus Christ. Binding and loosing is made possible by His atoning death and His ascension to the right hand of the Father. His present ministry of intercession for us includes the potential for binding and loosing. It is dependent upon His position over all authorities of any kind and as possessor of all authority in heaven and earth (Matthew 28:18). These concepts of binding and loosing affirm that indeed Jesus Christ rules.

This Jesus Christ is the One with whom the believer is seated (Ephesians 2:6). We are in Him and He is in us (John 14:20). Through Him we bind and loose. If the strong man must be bound so that his treasures may be plundered, we do it (Matthew 12:29). If we must admit that Peter upon his confession was authorized to bind and loose, so be it (16:16-19).

When Jesus later promised that where two or three were gathered in His name, He also was there in the midst, we do not object (18:20). Where Jesus said that if two were agreed upon anything (18:19), it would be done, we do not draw back. Nor do we retreat when the Savior immediately promises His disciples that whatever they bind would be bound, and whatever they loosed would be loosed (18:18). We understand this binding and loosing process to be irrevocably linked with heaven, dependent always on the sovereign will of God. And, most amazingly, it is carried out by believers who are willing to seek the glory of God and accept their completeness and authority in Him to bind and to loose.

Preposterous? Of course! But is it biblically solid? Does it submit itself to the glory of God? Is it Christologically correct? And is it true that every believer is complete in Him? Are all believers seated with Him who is our glorious inheritance, the focal authority of all authority of every kind? Clearly, yes!

And is binding and loosing different than asking and receiving in prayer? Again, the answer is yes. Believers' authority emphatically implies that the believers do the binding and loosing. You and I do it.

This matter of who really does the binding and loosing is a subject to which we will return. Right now, the question must simply be: Is asking in prayer something you and I do? The biblical record demands an affirmative answer.

> And I will do whatever you ask in my name, so that the
> Son may bring glory to the Father. You may ask me for
> anything in my name, and I will do it. (John 14:13-14)

Asking is something we as Christians do. So is binding and loosing.

In a church in Montana, long before spiritual warfare became a common theme among evangelicals, I was teaching spiritual warfare principles at 6:30 each evening, one hour before the service began. In one of those sessions we came to the subject of binding and loosing. Finally, I told the people, "If you hear all of this teaching and then continue to ask the Lord to bind and loose, you have not understood. You have missed the point. Binding and loosing is something *you* do."

One brother had a prayer rut. He always included in his prayer, "Oh Lord, bind the devil." I waited for the moment to arrive when he would pray. If ever any prayer was funny, his was. He garbled his words. He slid in and out of his rut. He never quite was able to pray, "Oh Lord, I bind." He simply could not embrace the concept that he, as a believer in Jesus Christ, was to do the binding!

If you sense that you are commissioned—even sometimes ordered—to bind and to loose on God's behalf, then you are in pursuit of the glory of God, you are sensing your completeness in Jesus Christ and you are exercising the authority of the believer.

The classic writer in these matters is J.A. MacMillan. His comments are dramatic.

So unreasonable to the natural mind seems the proposi-
tion of Jehovah to His people (Isaiah 45:11) that they
should "command" (KJV) Him concerning the work of
His hands, that various alternative readings of the passage have been made with the intent of toning down the
apparent extravagance of the divine offer. Men are slow
to believe that the Almighty really means exactly what
He says. They think it an incredible thing that He would
share with human hands the throttle of divine power.
Nor have they the spiritual understanding to compre-
hend the purpose of the Father to bring those who have
been redeemed with the precious blood of His dear Son
into living and practical cooperation with that Son in the
administration of His kingdom.[4]

Understandable? I hope so.

Staggering? Obviously.

But that is what this book is all about. And there is a very great
deal to tell. A comprehensive and thoroughly biblical understanding of binding and loosing is its objective.

Narrowing the Focus

One of the difficulties with writing a book is deciding how
wide or narrow its focus will be. In 1978 I was asked to chron-
icle the story of the Georgia dam break that decimated a college
campus, leaving thirty-nine people dead.[5] My editorial assistant
and I traveled to Toccoa Falls College, the school that had suffered so much. Once there, the question became: Where does
one start with such a project?

Dozens of people had stories to tell. Rosalyn Carter and other
dignitaries had been there to comfort and bring aid, and the families of the bereaved arrived to be at the sides of their grieving
loved ones.

The decision was finally made. We would include only the stories of people who had suffered the loss of a loved one. After ten days of interviewing and three days of furious writing, followed by three months of polishing, the book was done. The result was a dramatic account of death, disaster and dynamic faith that proved to have strong soul-winning power.

Similarly, the committee before which I defended my Ph.D. did the unthinkable—they tossed out hundreds of pages of my precious research! In the end, I recovered. On a warm California day I marched down the aisle with many others much younger than I. Evidently the decimated remnants of my work had been approved.

Now what about this book? How do we tackle a subject such as binding and loosing? How can we manage to get a handle on it in such a way that it will be a blessing to God's people and a productive addition to His kingdom?

The decision here is singular: to focus on the meaning and ministry of the biblical doctrine of binding and loosing. To do that we will research and explain the meanings of three principle Greek terms—*deo, luo* and *nikao*—as they appear in Scripture. We will, in the process, consider three passages in Matthew and a parallel passage in Luke. The Old Testament also will be consulted, and the New Testament cognates of the two main Greek words—*deo* and *luo*—will be listed.

We will then consider the biblical derivations of binding and loosing by:

- studying what the Old Testament says about binding and loosing

- deciphering the symbolism of binding and loosing in the New Testament

- determining what the New Testament says about believers' completeness and authority in Christ

- clarifying how to bind the strong man and spoil his house

- surveying binding and loosing from a missiological perspective

- comparing and contrasting binding and loosing in Matthew and Luke

- discovering how the disciples practiced binding and loosing

- gaining Jesus' perspective on binding and loosing as forbidding and allowing, and loosing as forgiveness

- explaining how to make the glory of God the chief end of the practice of binding and loosing

Deo/Luo *Language*

The Greek word *deo* means "to bind," "to bind together," "to bind to," "to wrap up," "to chain." The term is used variously to mean imprisonment, supernatural binding, declaring forbidden or permitted, imposing or removing an obligation, imposing and removing a ban.

The word *luo* is used for "the freeing of those in prison,[6] . . . the opening of things that are closed,[7] . . . the destruction of foundations and walls, . . . also of fetters."[8] In the New Testament it means "to loose," "release," "to free," "to dissolve something into its parts," i.e., "to break down or destroy," "to dismiss or set aside."[9] Notice particularly that loose—*luo*—"is rich in compounds which give nuances to the basic meaning."[10]

In the New Testament a person can be loosed from:

1. Sin (1 John 1:9)
2. Satan (Luke 13:12, 16; 1 John 3:8)
3. Bondage of the tongue (Mark 7:35)
4. Debt (Matthew 18:27)

5. Prison (Acts 22:30)
6. Sickness (Luke 13:12)

The two terms—*deo* and *luo*—are sometimes used in conjunction with each other, so that we may speak of the *deo/luo* construct. In addition, other words and phrases are also used to describe the *deo/luo* concept. The major one is *nikao* which Luke, in his synoptic parallel, substitutes in the place of Matthew's *deo*, further amplifying and enriching the study.

Perhaps now, after reading these few brief explanations, you understand the urgency to focus and to refuse to follow every rabbit trail. Join me as we trace the definition and practice of binding and loosing, first through the annals of history to the present day and then through the Scriptures.

Endnotes

[1] Conversation with author, Bradenton, FL, February 1997.

[2] Spiritual mapping has been defined as "creating a spiritual profile of a community based on careful research" (George Otis, Jr. as cited by Art Moore, "Spiritual Mapping Gains Credibility Among Leaders," *Christianity Today*, 12 January 1998, 57).

[3] Bert Warden, "In the Face of Spiritual Warfare," *Alliance Life*, 12 February 1997, 15. Additional comments on this matter are made by Robert J. Priest, Thomas Campbell and Bradford A. Mullen, "Missiological Syncretism," in *Spiritual Power and Missions*, ed. Edward Rommen (Pasadena, CA: William Carey Library, 1995), 39: "We are being asked to accept accounts [territorial spirits concepts, for example] of events as the epistemological basis for constructing new doctrines about unseen realities. . . . After all, Paul warns us not to accept old wives' tales or doctrines of demons, but to test doctrinal claims rigorously (1 Timothy 4:1, 7; 1 Thessalonians 5:21). Such testing is a biblical demand, not evidence of . . . unbelief." Their caution resonates with Warden.

Paul L. King, "The Restoration of the Doctrine of Binding and Loosing," in *Alliance Academic Review,* ed. Elio Cuccaro (Camp Hill, PA: Christian Publications, 1997). King does a careful analysis of the thought of those who erroneously have assumed that the binding and loosing teaching has been a twentieth-century phenomenon. He demonstrates that some current authors such as Hank Hanegraaff and John MacArthur advocate ideas in conflict with such evangelical stalwarts as G. Campbell Morgan, Watchman Nee, A.B. Simpson and the sometimes controversial Henry Ward Beecher.

[4] John A. MacMillan, *The Authority of the Believer* (Camp Hill, PA: Christian Publications, 1997), 55.

[5] K. Neill Foster with Eric Mills, *Dam Break in Georgia* (Camp Hill, PA: Horizon Books, 1978). This is the story of the Toccoa Falls College flood in 1977.

[6] Gerhard Kittel, ed., *Theological Dictionary of the New Testament (TDNT)*, trans. Geoffrey W. Bromiley (Grand Rapids, MI: Eerdmans, 1964), 2:60-61.

[7] Kittel, *TDNT*, 4:328. One of the meanings of *luo* is "the opening of things that are closed." Rev. O.H. Bublat's account as follows would not ordinarily be considered as loosing, except when we understand the various nuances of *luo*. "The principle of renunciation mentioned in Second Corinthians 4:2 is a powerful weapon of spiritual warfare which binds the enemy and looses the captive. It breaks the enemy's hold, even as the renunciation of an alien's former flag and country looses that country's claims on one who changes his national allegiance.

"Brian (a fictional name) was a brilliant Haight-Asbury hippie who had accepted Christ as Savior a few weeks prior to our meeting at an altar of prayer. When I asked how I could help him, he showed me his painfully clenched fists, cramped shut. He informed me that in ignorance he had attended a meeting where a chicken-blood sacrifice was offered. It was there that his hands had twisted into their present position.

"I carefully explained to him the legal principle of renunciation. He immediately grasped the idea and together we proceeded to make a complete renunciation of all things evil, even back to four generations.

"Instantly, his fists sprang open. The renunciation, made verbally, in the name of the Lord Jesus Christ, had broken the enemy's hold. Where ground was once given to Satan's kingdom, it had now been taken back and freedom reigned. What repentance alone could not do, and what it had not done over a two-week period, renunciation did in seconds."

[8] Ibid., 4:335-336.

[9] Ibid., 4:328.

[10] Ibid.

"Thank You for Loosing My Daughter"

We had met Jake and Laura* many years earlier. On this very special day we were in my office. The day was special because of the story they told. Jake, sitting in my study along with his wife, Laura, and another couple, was reaching back twenty-seven years to tell me things I had long forgotten.

The initial event took place at a Bible camp, a rugged campground for Native peoples. I had been there several times, always arriving tired and dirty after navigating more than 100 miles of twisting, turning bush road.

"You got there and told us you didn't know why you had come," Jake said, laughing at the obvious incredulity reflected on my face. As an itinerant evangelist, I normally went only where I was invited, only where I would be preaching! My forgotten foray into the wilderness appeared to have no human rationale.

In any case, according to Jake's rehearsal of events, we talked with his daughter in my car—just Jake, his daughter and me. That conversation was only a faint memory for me.

As Jake reconstructed the incident, he recalled that it had culminated in prayer and the loosing of his daughter from a lesbian relationship. The dominant partner was reportedly occultly subjected and had a cross tatooed on her forehead. She also had given Jake's daughter a cap with a cross embossed on the front of it. By faith, in words I no longer remember, we loosed her in the name of the Lord Jesus Christ from that lesbian liaison.

Then I further informed Jake, so he said, that there would be further things to deal with before she would come clear. That statement proved to be true.

Back home, Jake and Laura carried on the loosing. With their daughter's agreement, they burned garments that both girls had worn. They burned pictures of the two of them together. There was one picture that was especially cherished. It was "hard to get to the fire." Somehow I was not surprised at that.

This illicit bond had complicated relationships in the household. The other children were reacting to the presence of evil. Jake and Laura's preteen daughter particularly was becoming sensitive to the relationship.

"We got together in the bedroom and held hands in a circle," he continued. "My wife and I were there, and the three children. I loosed our family from the power of hate, repeatedly and vigorously in the name of the Lord Jesus Christ." Suddenly, finally, the power of darkness gave way.

At that point in the story, Jake's wife chimed in to tell us that there was a storage area above the bedroom closet with a door that opened outward and downward. By this time I began to anticipate how this story would end. Exit phenomena in the counter-kingdom do have similarities.

As they broke through in prayer and loosing, the door of the storage area flopped open and a rush of "evil" wind poured into the room, past the family, down the hall and out the front door.

Their family was free.

"Where is your daughter today?" I asked.

"She is married, has a family and is a Christian teacher," came the reply.

And the rest of Jake and Laura's family?

They too are walking with the Lord.

This account has been altered to maintain the privacy of this family.

Part II

Binding and Loosing:
The Historical Factors

"During the past 450 years and particularly in the last century and a half, Christianity has been more influential in the life of the human race than at any previous time."

—Kenneth Scott Latourette[1]

2

THE JEWISH CONCEPTS

Iɴ Iꜱʀᴀᴇʟ, ᴏɴ ᴛʜᴇ ᴇᴠᴇ of the high holy day of Yom Kippur, October 1995, Rabbi Avigdor Iskin, according to news reports at that time, stood outside Prime Minister Rabin's house and pronounced a curse on him.

The curse Iskin put on Rabin read in part, "And on him, Yitzhak, son of Rosa, known as Rabin, we have permission . . . to demand from angels of destruction that they take a sword to this wicked man . . . to kill him . . . for handing over the Land of Israel to our enemies."

This binding curse is purported to work within thirty days. On November 4, 1995, Yigal Amir assassinated Rabin. The imprecatory prayer had apparently been conducted with the required forum of ten people.[1]

We have already seen that binding and loosing is an expression of authority and as such predates the universe as we know it. Before the world was framed, God was the "I ᴀᴍ" (Exodus 3:14). Before the world was framed, Christ was "with God" (John 1:1), the Lamb "slain from the creation of the world" (Revelation 13:8). And before the world was framed and God said, "Let there be light" (Genesis 1:3), the "Spirit of God was hovering over the waters" (1:2).

This principle of authority which was "in the beginning" continues until today to exhibit God's nature, character and power. The Jewish culture of the Old Testament knew about authority. With society itself being hierarchical, authoritative governance was an integral part of every facet of Jewish life, including the religious.

> Judaism has traditionally held to the unity and eternal spirit of the one true God. God created everything and actively governs the universe.[2]

The basic principles of authority in the Old Testament are evident from the Garden of Eden—authority within the animal kingdom, human authority over animals, human authority within societal structures, etc. Abraham *commanded* his family after him (Genesis 18:19, KJV). Moses exhibited authority when he ordered Aaron to throw down his rod (Exodus 7:9). Later, when Moses struck the rock, he was again acting authoritatively (17:6). Elisha's mandate to the widow was, "Go around and ask all your neighbors for empty jars." The result was deliverance for her entire family (2 Kings 4:3-7). Nehemiah's admonition, "Come, let us rebuild the wall" (Nehemiah 2:17), was not an invitation. It was an order which elicited a ready response: "Let us start rebuilding" (2:18).

Authority was a pervasive concept in New Testament times as well. The culture into which Jesus was born was Jewish, but under the authority and control of Rome. The Jews understood the ramifications of authority only too well.

The centurion, a Roman, also understood authority. He *was* authority. But when he saw Jesus, a Jew, healing, he begged Him to speak the authoritative word in order that his servant could be healed (Matthew 8:8-9).

The Jewishness of Matthew's Gospel in which is found our

two key words for binding and loosing—*deo* and *luo*—is widely accepted. Its structure, its fabric, its vocabulary—all affirm a unique reflection of the Israeli mind.

The editors of one study Bible note:

> Written originally for the Jews, the Gospel of Matthew presents Christ as the Son of David and the Son of Abraham. Because He is portrayed as King, His genealogy is traced to King David; and the place of His birth, Bethlehem, the home of David, is emphasized. Seven times in this Gospel Christ is spoken of as "the son of David."[3]

How then does the binding/loosing (*deo/luo*) language fit into the Jewish context of Scripture?

Commentator Robert Mounce observes that binding and loosing were "technical terms used by rabbis indicating the authority to lay down binding rules or to declare exemption from them."[4] Similarly, the famous Jewish historian, Josephus, said of the Pharisees, "they exile and recall, loose and bind."[5] Both of these examples focus on legislative or community matters.

But binding and loosing for the Jewish leaders did not rest solely with such parameters. According to William Barclay,

> The Rabbis had a saying: "The keys of birth, of the rain, and of the resurrection of the dead belong to God." That is to say, only God has the power to create life, to send the rain, and to raise the dead to life again. The phrase always indicates a special power.[6]

If I understand Barclay correctly, even the managing of the supernatural and the controlling of spiritual forces were part of the Jewish concept of binding and loosing, a part, however, which belonged only to God and not to His earthly followers.

Craig Keener likewise observes that "many early Jewish sources report that Satan or demons were 'bound,' or imprisoned, after God subdued them."[7]

Though the apocryphal books are not Scripture, they enlighten us further as to the Jewish atmosphere into which Jesus Christ was born and for which Matthew later penned his Gospel. For instance, the apocryphal book of the Psalms of Solomon 5:4 says, "No man shall take prey from a mighty man, unless he has first conquered him." Jesus might have been alluding to this passage (based on Isaiah 49:24-25) when He spoke of binding the strong man in Matthew 12:29. And in the book of Tobit 8:1-3, an angel bound a demon. In that instance, the binding took place after the demon was compelled to leave.

According to Jewish theology, certain angels were assigned tasks of binding (1 Enoch 10:4-12).[8] Again, in the same passage, the angel Raphael is commanded to bind the fallen angel Azazel, and the angel Michael is commanded to bind the fallen angel Semjaza and his associates. In First Enoch 18:16 and 21:1-2 the heavenly powers are bound. (See also the Greek Apocalypse of Baruch and First Enoch 62:5ff; 69:27-28.)

One of the apocryphal passages has a quasi-New Testament ring to it. In the Testament of Levi 18:12, the Messiah binds Beliar (probably Satan): "And Beliar shall be bound by him, and he shall give power to children to tread upon the evil spirits." Again, the Testament of Levi makes reference to Isaiah 24:21-22:

> In that day the Lord will punish the powers in the heavens above and the kings on the earth below. They will be herded together like prisoners bound in a dungeon; they will be shut up in prison and be punished after many days.[9]

Here, the children of the Messiah have binding authority over the powers of heaven.

What information about binding and loosing may be gathered from this brief excursion into the apocryphal literature extant in the period into which Jesus Christ was born?

First, we see that the concept of binding particularly, with some mention of loosing with reference to the supernatural, was common to the Jewish world in which Jesus lived. We concur with Hiers,

> If we take seriously the substantial body of synoptic evidence which indicates that Jesus thought and acted in terms of the . . . thought world of some of his Jewish predecessors and contemporaries, we may reasonably infer that he would have used the expressions of "binding and loosing" in the sense most commonly found in the intertestamental writings. . . .[10]

In that world, not only God bound and loosed. The angels too were involved, as well as godly men. Christ's teaching on binding and loosing in His time and culture would be generally understood in much the way we are seeking to understand the concepts of that day today. Those understandings will prove valuable as we move forward.

Endnote—Part II

[1] Kenneth Scott Latourette, *A History of Christianity* (San Francisco: Harper and Row Publishers, 1975), xvi.

Endnotes

[1] "Man convicted in Rabin curse," *Philadelphia Inquirer* (29 May 1997).

[2] J.D. Douglas, ed. *Encyclopedia of Religious Knowledge* (Grand Rapids, MI: Baker Book House, 1991), 469.

[3] Notes, *Oxford NIV Scofield Study Bible* (New York: Oxford University Press, 1978), 969.

[4] Robert H. Mounce, *Matthew, A Good News Commentary* (San Francisco: Harper and Row, 1985), 163.

[5] Eduard Schweizer, *The Good News According to Matthew* (Atlanta: John Knox Press, 1975), 343.

[6] William Barclay, *The Gospel of Matthew,* The Daily Bible Study Series (Philadelphia: The Westminster Press,. 1975), 2:144.

[7] Craig S. Keener, *The IVP Bible Background Commentary: New Testament* (Downers Grove, IL: InterVarsity Press, 1993), 80.

[8] A.H. Charles, *The Apocrypha and Pseudopigrapha of the Old Testament* (London: Oxford University Press, 1913, 1964), 2:193-194, 200-201, 227-228, 235, 535.

[9] Ibid., 2:314-315.

[10] Richard H. Hiers, "Binding and Loosing, The Matthean Authorization," *Journal of Biblical Literature,* 1985, 104:2:249.

The Case of the Complimentary Tirade

Deloris Sunda

I had gone to a pretrial hearing with a lady from our church whose husband was endeavoring to take from her as much as he could get while filing for divorce. The wife had done everything possible to hold the marriage together, but her husband was determined to separate. She was being dragged into an ugly courtroom battle.

My friend and her lawyer were in one room while the estranged husband and his female lawyer were in another. Out in the hallway of the courthouse building, I sat on an old bench alternately reading and praying.

Shortly, the husband and his lawyer emerged into the hallway. Not knowing who I was, he sat down on my right, with the lawyer to his right. Although I was trying to concentrate on my book, I could not help but overhear his angry and agitated tirade against his wife.

Grieved in my spirit, I closed my eyes and prayed, *Lord Jesus, this man needs to think godly thoughts toward his wife. I cannot speak aloud to the evil spirits that are telling him to speak these lies. Would You, on this occasion, come and help me by binding the evil spirits that are causing him to lie about his wife?* I then asked the Lord to bind the evil spirits of anger, rage, distrust, malice and as many others as I could think of as their natures were revealed by the man's ongoing harangue.

Still occasionally turning a page in my book, I was amazed to suddenly hear the man tell the lawyer, "You know, my wife has always been a good mother to our children. I really cannot fault her for the way she has cared for them and our home." He continued thus with a number of truthful and complimentary statements.

At that, I could not resist turning my head and looking toward the lawyer. Her face was filled with astonishment. Her mouth dropped open as she stared at her client in disbelief.

That day it became very clear to me that yes, the powers can be bound.

3

THE EARLY
CHURCH FATHERS

I F THE NONSCRIPTURAL SOURCES have insight for the setting of the binding and loosing context, such as the Jewish references seem to have had, do not the Church Fathers likewise have something to say to us moderns?

The answer again is yes. Their experience (which by another name is history) *is* useful in discernment (Hebrews 5:14, NKJV). But, again, this is not to suggest that the writings of the Church Fathers carry the authority of Scripture. Not at all. But their witness should be received as advice and counsel from elders, as those who have walked the path before us. What they said, thought and wrote must be considered.

References to binding and loosing in the writings of the Church Fathers occur, but are infrequent, until we get to Augustine (A.D. 354-430) and Chrysostom (A.D. 349-407), who each make allusion to the Scriptures on binding and loosing. Although our study of these early Fathers will take a bit of concentration and maybe a degree of downright hard work for a few pages, it will form a crucial basis of understanding for the rest of our discussion by demonstrating both general patterns and a variety of interpretations regarding the concept of binding and loosing.

Irenaeus, who lived in the second half of the second century, in his writing entitled "Against Heresies," comments on Matthew 12:29.

> Through man himself, he [Satan] should, when conquered, be bound with the same chains with which he had bound man, in order that man, being set free, might return to his Lord, leaving to him [Satan] those bonds by which he himself had been fettered, that is, sin. For when Satan is bound, man is free.[1]

In other words, binding and loosing was a present reality for Irenaeus. His "bind" and "loose" vocabulary makes that clear.

Irenaeus also teaches that Satan was bound by Jesus in the keeping of the commandment (Law of God) through His temptation. In overcoming Satan, the strong man, Irenaeus believed that Jesus showed Himself to be the true, ultimate Strong Man.[2] Irenaeus is here concurring with the common view of Matthew 12 that the strong man must be bound by the Stronger before his goods can be carried off.

Methodius (A.D. 260-312) in his "Oration on the Psalms" writes, "Blessed is He that cometh in the name of the Lord . . . , to bind the strong man that is against us."[3] As is obvious from the verb tenses, Methodius does not view Jesus as merely having bound Satan in the past, but as presently binding him in the third century. If in the third century, I ask, why not in the twenty-first century?

Tertullian, also writing in the early third century concerning Matthew 16:19, comments that "the Church has the power of forgiving sins," but adds that he will not exercise that power if it would result in a person continuing to sin.[4] In other words, the power of forgiving must go hand in hand with the power of exercising discipline—as in the cases of Ananias, Sapphira and Elymas. Ananias and Sapphira were struck down and died, judged for their hypocrisy (Acts 5:1-11); Elymas was struck with blindness for his resistance to the gospel:

> But Elymas the sorcerer (for that is what his name means) opposed them [Barnabas and Paul] and tried to turn the proconsul from the faith. Then Saul, who was also called Paul, filled with the Holy Spirit, looked straight at Elymas and said, "You are a child of the devil and an enemy of everything that is right! You are full of all kinds of deceit and trickery. Will you never stop perverting the right ways of the Lord?" (Acts 13:8-11)

Tertullian indicates that the power of binding and loosing should be taken seriously and not exercised indiscriminately, for it is ultimately the prerogative of the Holy Spirit:

> "The Spirit of truth" has indeed the power of indulgently granting pardon to fornicators, but wills not to do it if it involve evil to the majority.[5]

Further, Tertullian says,

> Accordingly, "the Church," it is true, will forgive sins: but [it will be] the Church of the Spirit, by means of a spiritual man, not the Church which consists of a number of bishops. For the right and arbitrament is the Lord's, not the servant's; God's Himself, not the priests.[6]

In other words, Tertullian did not see binding and loosing as an ecclesiastical function. To him it was essentially a spiritual function. In that century, there was an aversion to the concept that an apostle alone might have the power of binding and loosing, suggesting instead a general, arbitrary, judicial or legislative decision-making authority. Tertullian rightly admonished that the binding and loosing action must be initiated not by man but by the Holy Spirit and in the will of God.

Tertullian also interpreted binding and loosing in a variety of ways, for he says that Peter "bound" Ananias with "the bond of death" and loosed or "absolved" the lame man (Acts 3) "from his defect of health."[7] The binding of Ananias was a supernatural act of discipline from God, and the healing of the lame man was a type of loosing from bondage. However, Tertullian viewed the legislative decisions of the Church concerning conduct as a type of binding and loosing as well.

Speaking of the decision of the Church Council in Jerusalem regarding what was permitted and forbidden for Gentiles, i.e., to abstain from "fornication and from blood," Tertullian wrote:

> Why do they indulgently relax so many bonds, except that they may wholly bind us in perpetuity to such as are more necessary? They loosed us from the more numerous, that we might be bound up to abstinence from the more noxious.[8]

Tertullian may seem complicated and perhaps something is lost in the translation, but, as is obvious from his vocabulary, he had firsthand knowledge of binding and loosing. He notes from Acts 15:28 that the binding and loosing was not a human decision; "It seemed good to the Holy Spirit."

To rehearse Tertullian's contribution to our understanding of binding and loosing, binding could mean retaining sins and exercising discipline by removing health or forbidding certain conduct. Loosing could mean forgiving sins, healing bodies or permitting certain conduct.[9]

Cyprian (A.D. 200-258), a pupil of Tertullian, continues his mentor's understanding of binding and loosing in reference to the keys of the kingdom passage in Matthew 16:19 where the disciples were given the power to bind and loose:

> Therefore the power of remitting sins was given to the apostles, and to the churches which they, sent by Christ, established, and to the bishops who succeeded them by vicarious ordination.[10]

Note that Cyprian also understood that while Peter was the first to receive the power of binding and loosing, Christ gave to all the apostles equal power.[11] He was moving toward the position advanced here that binding and loosing is the prerogative of all disciples; indeed, it is the privilege of all believers.

Augustine, of the fourth century, in his consideration of binding and loosing, notes that those who have been a spoil of Satan, now, through salvation, become the spoil of Christ, "but in a good sense, as those who are snatched from that strong one when he is bound by a stronger."[12] He interprets Revelation 20:3-4—the binding of Satan for a thousand years—in an amillennial sense as applying to the present-day Church:

> It is not to be supposed that this refers to the last judgment, but to the seats of the rulers and to the rulers themselves by whom the Church is now governed. And no better interpretation of judgment being given can be produced than that which we have in the word, "What

ye bind on earth shall be bound in heaven; and what ye
loose on earth shall be loosed in heaven."[13]

Augustine, as one of the most influential of the Church Fathers,
clearly connects the binding of Satan with the authority of binding
and loosing and, with foresight, notes that the Church has that
authority through those who govern. Augustine uses the present
tense in referring to Matthew 12:29, saying that "He who binds the
strong man, taketh away his goods, and maketh them His own
goods," indicating, along with Methodius, that Christ is still in
that day binding the strong man.[14]

In another section he declares, "Christ therefore hath bound
the devil with spiritual bonds, by overcoming death, and by as-
cending from Hell above the Heavens: He hath bound him by the
Sacrament of His incarnation."[15]

So Augustine views the binding of Satan by Christ as something which has been accomplished through Jesus' invasion of
Satan's territory on earth, and also (do not miss this), that there
are continuing acts of binding. Were Augustine alive today, I
think I would try to persuade him to endorse this book!

In a stance which today would be called strikingly evangelical,
Augustine also declares that Peter alone is not representative of
the Church in receiving the keys of the kingdom (Matthew
16:19).[16] In that statement, he sets himself against the traditional
Roman Catholic idea which would later emerge.

Chrysostom (A.D. 349-407), moving beyond Augustine in liter-
alness, uses the language of binding and loosing in a variety of
ways: the retaining and remitting of sin, overcoming demonic
forces, rebuking sin, loosing those bound in sin, disease, poverty
and affliction, and opening and closing heaven through prayer.
In his mind binding and loosing was an authority to be exercised
by priests and others not only in sermons but in what today we
call the authority of the believer.

For they who inhabit the earth and make their abode there are entrusted with the administration of things which are in Heaven, and have received an authority which God has not given to angels or archangels. For it has not been said to them, "Whatsoever ye shall bind on earth shall be bound in Heaven, and whatsoever ye shall loose on earth shall be loosed in Heaven." They who rule on earth have indeed authority to bind, but only the body: whereas this binding lays hold of the soul and penetrates the heavens; and what priests do here below God ratifies above, and the Master confirms the sentence of his servants.[17]

For Chrysostom, the authority of binding and loosing was a real spiritual action in which "this binding lays hold of the soul and penetrates the heavens."[18] Priests, he thought, had the authority to retain and remit sins, but it was a spiritual transaction, not perfunctory. Chrysostom sees the James 5:14-15 "prayer of faith" exhortation as an example of that authority.

For not only at the time of regeneration, but afterwards also, they have authority to forgive sin. "Is any sick among you?" It is said, "Let him call for the elders of the Church and let them pray over him, anointing him with oil in the name of the Lord. And the prayer of faith shall save the sick, and the Lord will raise him up; and if he have committed sins they shall be forgiven him."[19]

Such authority, though, Chrysostom emphasized, was not based on human interests, but on those of Christ, the Master:

Despise thine own concerns, and thou wilt receive those of God. This He Himself wills. Despise earth, and seize upon the kingdom of heaven. Dwell there, not here. Be formidable there, not here. If thou art formidable there, thou wilt be formidable not to men, but to demons, and even to the devil himself. . . . Such were the Apostles, despising a servile house and worldly wealth! And see how they commanded in the affairs of their Master. "Let one," they said, "be delivered from disease, another from the possession of devils: bind this man, and loose that. This was done by them on earth, but it was fulfilled as in Heaven."[20]

In this sermon, Chrysostom related binding and loosing to dealing with demons and disease. He also preached a sermon on loosing others while ourselves being bound, even as Paul loosed others while imprisoned:

Let us loose them that are bound by poverty, by affliction. There is no comparison between opening the doors of a prison, and releasing an enthralled soul. There is no comparison between loosing the bonds of prisoners and "setting at liberty them that are bruised."[21]

While some of these early Fathers apply ecclesiastical authority only to governing leaders, Chrysostom and Augustine before him seem to interpret it (as within these pages) as applying to all believers, or, in Reformation terminology, they seem to understand and even anticipate the emphasis upon the priesthood of all believers as it was to later emerge during the Reformation.

Chrysostom also points out the paradox of binding and loosing in Paul and Silas' imprisonment in the Philippian jail and their release through the earthquake as a result of praise:

Do you mark what happened? . . . There a girl was released from a spirit, and they cast them into prison, because they had liberated her from the spirit. . . . What is equal to this? He is put in bonds, and looses, being bound; looses a twofold bond: him that bound him, he looses by being bound. These are indeed works of (supernatural) grace.[22]

He relates this physical loosing to a heavenly loosing, referring to Matthew 16:19:

Let us think over that night, the stocks, and the hymns of praise. This let us do, and we shall open for ourselves—not a prison, but—heaven. If we pray, we shall be able even to open heaven. Elias both shut and opened heaven by prayer (James 5:17). There is a prison in heaven also. . . . Let us pray by night, and we shall loose these bonds.[23]

Chrysostom's sentiment is that this binding/ loosing paradox seems to be a recurrent theme in Scripture: Joseph was bound, and being released, releases others from bondage of famine, and he who was bound has authority to bind princes. Paul and Silas loosed, then they were bound, and being bound, they loosed the jailer.

Chrysostom goes on to use the language of binding to refer to the rebuking of sin by church leaders.[24] He emphasizes, however, that this is not an arbitrary or harsh exercise of authority:

A teacher who does not himself say these things as of authority, nor as one in the position of a ruler, but is that of a kindly guardian. For we do not say these things as wishing to exhibit our authority. . . . For we indeed wish to use this power for loosing.[25]

Chrysostom's view is that "it is not man who binds, but Christ who has given unto us this authority."[26] This concept is crucial to the larger understanding of the doctrine of binding and loosing.

Cyril, bishop of Alexandria from 412-444, in making reference to Matthew 18:19, speaks of launching "the weapon of their concord in prayer."[27] Though this is a brief reference in an apocryphal story, in the context he evidently viewed this snatch of Scripture (Matthew 18:18-20) as relating to warfare prayer against demonic spirits.

Cyril also refers to Peter bearing the keys of the kingdom of heaven when he healed Aeneas (Acts 9:33-34), raised Tabitha (Dorcas) from the dead (9:36-40), and saw heaven opened in a trance (10:9-16).[28] Most importantly, these references demonstrate that Cyril held a broad interpretation of the power of binding and loosing, most of which was supernatural in nature, an interpretation that is not in conflict with the ideas advanced here.

In fact, Augustine and Chrysostom particularly appear to be far ahead of some of us today who are coming late to the powerful realities of binding and loosing. We are privileged to have insight into their linguistically convoluted writings and context. Church history, although not Scripture, does serve to inform us of how those who have gone before believed and comprehended these truths.

Endnotes

[1] Irenaeus, "Against Heresies," *The Ante-Nicene Fathers (ANF)*, eds. Alexander Roberts and James Donaldson (Grand Rapids, MI: Eerdmans, 1978), 1:550.

[2] Ibid., 1:421 (see also 1:448, 456).

[3] Methodius, "Oration on the Psalms," *ANF*, 6:397.

[4] Tertullian, "On Modesty," *ANF*, 4:99.

[5] Ibid.

[6] Ibid., 4:100.

[7] Ibid., 4:99.

[8] Ibid., 4:86.

[9] Ibid.

[10] Cyprian, "The Epistles of Cyprian," *ANF*, 5:394.

[11] Ibid., 422.

[12] Augustine, "City of God," 20:30, *Nicene Fathers and Post-Nicene Fathers* (*NFPF*), ed. Philip Schaff (Grand Rapids, MI: Eerdmans, 1979), 1:2:449.

[13] Ibid., "City of God," 20:9, 1:2:430.

[14] Ibid., "On the Psalms—Psalm 48," Section 4, 1:8:165.

[15] Ibid., 1:8:290.

[16] Ibid., "Matthew 16:19," 1:8:537.

[17] Chrysostom, "On the Priesthood," *NFPF*, 1:9:47.

[18] Ibid., 1:9:47.

[19] Ibid., 1:9:48.

[20] Ibid., 1:13:516.

[21] Ibid., 1:13:91-92.

[22] Ibid., "Homily 36: Acts 16:25-26," 1:11:225.

[23] Ibid., 1:11:226.

[24] Ibid., 1:14:387-388.

[25] Ibid., 1:14:387.

[26] Ibid.

[27] Cyril, "Catechetical Lecture," *NFPF*, 2:7:38.

[28] Ibid., 2:7:130.

God Uses Even Broken-down Cars!

The pastor had led his church into adopting a New Testament form of government with a plurality of elders under the leadership of a pastor. At a business meeting called to confirm those nominated to be elders, a vocal group of four families managed to sow discord and disunity by insisting that one of their group be included in the eldership.

Rather than voting on the issue, it was decided to spend a month in prayer and discussion. But the stalemate persisted. The dissenting group promised to bring further disruption at the next business meeting.

Prior to that meeting, the pastor spent three days in prayer and fasting, binding the spirits of dissension and disunity. On the day of the meeting, none of the dissenters showed up. The selection process was completed peacefully.

Later, it was revealed that the reason none of the dissenters attended the meeting was that the cars (plural) of the entire group had broken down!

The congregation was amazed at the power and intervention of the Lord.

Loosing the Seed

Many years ago in the small town where we lived, there was a farmers' strike or, more properly, a blockade in which pickets took up positions to prevent delivery of seed to processing plants. Because our family owned such a plant, we were among those being picketed. Tempers flared. Violence threatened. The atmosphere in that once-peaceful town seemed charged with hate and fear.

Late one night, I came to a spiritual realization—the forces abroad in our town were evil. Out in our backyard, I lifted my hands toward the starry sky and said something like this: "Lord, in the name of Jesus Christ, I come against these forces and I break their power and bind them completely. And I loose the flow of seed into the plants."

The next day a judge notified the agitators that their strike was illegal and their goals illegitimate. An injunction was issued. That same day the seed began to flow.

A few days passed and we noticed that no deliveries were being made to another plant in a nearby community. I had forgotten to include that plant in the loosing! Following another prayer-and-loosing session, the seed began to flow there too.

One man had been particularly aggressive during the blockade. Reportedly, in the local bar he had threatened to burn down our plant. He also began to hassle my father for his faith in Christ, endangering him physically and asking him in front of a group of angry farmers, "Foster, how many churches have you built?"

At that juncture, my brother hit the man in the face. Though I did not witness the incident, I must confess I like that little detail of the story, though I am not sure I ought to be liking it! I was glad, nevertheless, that my brother had defended my father.

The man's rage knew no bounds—it only increased. At the local bar he repeated his threats about "burning Foster out."

Before he carried them out, however, he returned to his farm to bring in the rest of his harvest. Regrettably, shortly thereafter, an open worm gear on a harvesting machine caught the man's clothes and killed him.

The community was stunned. The believers in our church said nothing, though I think that to a person they felt that the man had been judged. When God's name was interjected into the battle, it no longer was a controversy between some farmers and a family company.

Ironically, the day the man was buried was the very day the large transports arrived in town to once again haul away the processed seed.

4

THE REFORMERS

THE REFORMERS MAY BE DEFINED as spiritual pioneers who lived, generally speaking, during the sixteenth century. They include Martin Luther, John Calvin, Huldrych Zwingli, Menno Simons—all known for their passion to return to the supremacy of Scripture and for leading large sectors of Christendom out of the Roman Catholic Church. This chapter thrusts us into the thoughts of these Reformers and their understanding of this emerging doctrine.

In this matter of binding and loosing, the Roman Church adopted an ecclesiastical view, i.e., only the Church (its priests and bishops) could exercise that power. Into the milieu of exaggerated superstition and belief in the demoniacal came the Reformers with their emphasis on the primacy of Scripture. This conviction, in time, would lead to their affirmation of the priesthood of all believers.

In discussing the Reformers, there is the temptation to impose current thought patterns and contemporary Christian belief and practice upon people who lived hundreds of years ago. Such impositions are generally unfair and detrimental to our understanding of their views. That is particularly true of the discussion of our theme of binding and loosing.

Almost unanimously, these men were most interested in establishing political freedom and liberating themselves from the excesses of superstition prevailing at that time in the Roman Catholic Church. In such a hierarchical, monarchical and predemocratic context, it is not surprising that binding and loosing was generally associated with ecclesiastical discipline or exorcism and, as such, was pushed to the periphery during those years of spiritual struggle.

However, when we discuss Menno Simons and Huldrych Zwingli, who represent the less formal, more pietistic facets of the Reformation, we notice that they are predictably more inclined toward binding and loosing as a believer's prerogative and less inclined to delegate such a privilege to the clerical structures of the Church and to the exercise of discipline.

Luther, on the other hand, though he believed in the reality of demonic forces, did not advocate direct exorcism:

> We cannot expel demons with certain ceremonies and words, as Jesus Christ, the prophets, and the apostles did. All we can do is in the name of Jesus Christ pray the Lord God, of His infinite mercy, to deliver the possessed persons. And if our prayer is offered up in full faith, we are assured by Christ Himself (John 16:23), that it will be efficacious, and overcome all the devil's resistance. I might mention many instances of this. But we cannot of ourselves expel the evil spirits, nor must we even attempt it.[1]

While Luther did believe that satanic forces could be overcome by prayer, faith and the preached Word,[2] his more passive understanding of the authority of the believer and indirect view of confronting spiritual forces weakened the potential for what today would be called the full exercise of the believer's authority. He seemed to be undecided about the role of exorcism, at one point eliminating the rite from his *Handbook of Baptism* (1523), but including it in his second edition (1526).[3]

However, Luther did upon occasion go against his general advice by advising the addressing of such forces directly. To one pastor who was experiencing supernatural disturbances with poltergeists actually hurling pots and pans, his counsel was both amusing and forthright:

> Let Satan play with the pots. Meanwhile, pray to God with your wife and children and say, "Be off, Satan! I'm lord in this house, not you. By divine authority I'm head of this household, and I have a call from heaven to be pastor of this church."[4]

John Calvin, too, believed in the reality of demonic activity, but forbade the ancient practice of exorcism at baptism, emphasizing instead the overcoming of demonic forces by prayer, faith and putting on the full armor of God.[5]

Menno Simons also opposed exorcism prior to baptism, but for a different reason—the Roman Church connection with infant baptism.[6] He embraced believer's baptism. Obviously, infants were incapable of belief.

The Reformers were uncomprehending, not realizing there was a theological baby in the bathwater. Professor Timothy Warner asserts,

> The elimination of the renunciation of the devil by baptismal candidates is another reflection of the Western worldview with its lack of a functional view of demons.[7]

Nevertheless, the Reformers did have some measure of success at curbing the power of satanic forces. In 1535 Luther commented,

> About ten years ago we had an experience of a very wicked demon, but we succeeded in subduing him by perseverance and by unceasing prayer and unquestioning faith. . . . By this means I have restrained many other similar spirits in different places, for the prayer of the Church prevails at last.[8]

Because of their persevering prayer and faith, God honored their prayers in spite of their apparent ignorance of the biblical teaching of believers' authority.

After the Reformation, some German Lutheran churches still retained the exorcism rite while others eliminated it. Still others made it optional.[9] One author, famous for his writing on spiritual warfare, comments, "Rationalism then did away with exorcism. From this time it disappeared from the liturgy."[10]

The common practice and belief in Reformed churches after the tradition of John Calvin and until the end of the nineteenth century, was to deny the use of direct spiritual authority in exorcism. The writer of the introduction to *Demon Possession and Allied Themes* by nineteenth-century Presbyterian missionary John Nevius makes this observation:

> Missionaries in China have all proceeded with great caution in this matter. Dr. Nevius and others have avoided any measures which might lead the people to suppose that they claim the power to cast out devils even in Jesus' name. Nor does it appear that any native minister has claimed any such power. The most that has been done has been to kneel down and pray to Jesus to relieve the sufferer, at the same time inviting all present to unite

in the prayer; and it seems a well established fact that in nearly or quite every instance, the person afflicted, speaking apparently in a different personality and with a different voice, has confessed the power of Jesus and has departed.[11]

Nevius recognized the power of the Word of God in deliverance and many times saw demons leave simply through the reading of the Bible:

A prayer offered by a Christian, foreign or native, or even proximity to a Christian place of worship, has driven away the demon, and restored the demoniac to a sound mind, praising God.[12]

The relatively low view of the believer's authority during the time of the Reformation may have been related to the amillennial interpretation of the binding of Satan in Revelation 20. Amillennialists believe this Scripture means that Satan, the strong man, was bound by Christ's life and death, and consequently is bound in this present age. So while there may be some limited satanic activity, there is no great need for the exercise of binding and loosing since, in the present day, according to amillennial theology, he has already been bound.[13] Still, in the Reformation period, Huldrych Zwingli was among the first to sense the recovery of the authority of the believer in binding and loosing when he questioned the "whatever you bind and loose" application of Matthew 16:19 and 18:18 to bishops only.[14]

Although he understood binding as church discipline as an expression of the keys of Peter, he believed the authority belonged to the Church, not to an individual such as the pope or bishops.[15] For Zwingli, to loose, therefore, is nothing less than to raise to sure hope the heart that is despairing of salvation; to bind is to abandon the obstinate heart.[16]

The binding and loosing keys, according to Zwingli, were "feeding," by which he meant preaching the gospel or teaching of the Word of God.[17] For him, when Jesus "explained to them what was said in all the Scriptures" by revelation after the resurrection (Luke 24:27), it was an example of loosing. Jesus was using the keys of loosing.[18]

Mark 4:34 supports that idea. When Jesus "explained all things to His disciples" (NKJV), the word *epiluo,* a compound of *luo* literally meaning "to loose upon," is used. Preaching and teaching equaled loosing.

Zwingli also believed in "counterfeit keys" which, in the disobedient, could loose or release evil and sin because of corrupted and indiscriminate absolution which did not result in repentance. Against that backdrop, he saw exploding evil in a festive and malignant scenario:

> . . . a carnival of every kind of crime so unrestrained and so widespread that no tongue, no pen, can describe what a quantity of evils of every kind have been let out by these Keys. You . . . allowed your strong box or wallet to be entered with these Keys.[19]

But for the obedient believer,

> God has bolted the door with the bolt of His word [binding], which no force, no skill, can break, so that however these Keys turn they cannot get into the consciences or the strong boxes of them that trust in God.[20]

Zwingli began to see that the authority of binding and loosing was something real, available to all believers. The emerging comprehension of the priesthood of all believers would inevitably lead to the full understanding of the authority of the believer.

All the Reformers, particularly Menno Simons and Zwingli, to a man had strong opinions on this matter of binding and loosing. They were reacting to the superstition and nonbiblical postures of the established Church, while at the same time reaching out for the plain truth of Scripture and seeking to affirm the priesthood of all believers. In affirming that priesthood, they were not far from understanding the authority of the believer and what is becoming an evangelical understanding of binding and loosing.

The unfolding of this doctrine in the last 150 years is the next leg of our journey.

Endnotes

[1] Frederick S. Leahy, *Satan Cast Out* (Edinburgh: The Banner of Truth Trust, 1975), 113.

[2] Ibid., 112.

[3] Kurt Koch, *Christian Counseling and Occultism* (Grand Rapids, MI: Kregel Publications, 1972), 277.

[4] Leahy, *Satan Cast Out,* 114.

[5] Timothy M. Warner, *Spiritual Warfare: Victory over the Powers of This Dark World* (Wheaton, IL: Crossway Books, 1991), 120-121.

[6] *The Complete Writings of Menno Simons* (Scottdale, PA: Herald Press, 1956), 252.

[7] Warner, *Spiritual Warfare,* 112.

[8] Ibid., 111.

[9] Koch, *Christian Counseling and Occultism,* 277.

[10] Ibid.

[11] John L. Nevius, *Demon Possession and Allied Themes* (Chicago: Fleming H. Revell, n.d.), v.

[12] Ibid., 7 (see also 76).

[13] Ibid., 111.

[14] Ibid., 27-28.

[15] Huldrych Zwingli, "Choice and Free Use of Foods," in *Twenty Centuries of Great Preaching*, eds. Clyde E. Fant, Jr. and William M. Pinson, Jr. (Waco, TX: Word, 1971), 2:119.

[16] W.P. Stephens, *The Theology of Huldrych Zwingli* (Oxford: Clarendon Press, 1986), 271.

[17] Huldrych Zwingli, *Commentary on True and False Religion,* eds. Samuel Macauley Jackson and Clarence Nevin Heller (Durham, NC: The Labyrinth Press, 1981), 378.

[18] Ibid., 378-80.

[19] Ibid., 175.

[20] Ibid., 175-176.

Heavenly Health Care

Stanley Tam

The director of a youth camp in New York state once invited me to speak to his young people. As we fellowshiped together, he shared an experience of that summer.

In town on business one day, he met the camp doctor on the street. He greeted the man, who looked at him but did not return the greeting. This so puzzled the camp director that he turned and retraced his steps to catch up with the doctor.

"Is something wrong?" he asked caringly.

"I realize I'm not your camp doctor anymore," the man said. "I thought I gave you good service at modest cost."

"But you're still our doctor," the director said. "We're as pleased as we ever were with your services."

"You have a new doctor," came the terse response.

"No, we don't."

"Now, look," the doctor contended, "my nurse checked our records yesterday. By this time last year, you sent me over sixty sick kids. This year you've sent only three."

"That's because we've had only three campers needing your attention," responded the director.

What had happened, this camp director explained to me, was that he had been in a Bible study in which the practice of rebuking and binding Satan was presented and discussed.

Some of the participants protested, saying this practice was done primarily by a certain theological group. Wisely, however, the teacher pointed out that a daily practice of rebuking Satan is for all Christians.

"We began the practice at camp this year," he told me. "Every morning, by faith, we rebuke and bind Satan and his demons. With our authority as God's children, we forbid evil forces to touch our campers. That, we are convinced, explains the summer health situation with our young people."[1]

Endnote

[1] Stanley Tam, *God's Woodshed* (Camp Hill, PA: Horizon Books, 1989), 53-54.

5

THE DOCTRINE RESTORED

THE CONCEPT OF BINDING AND LOOSING as a doctrine has gained new prominence in the last two centuries, particularly in the last 150 years. Its emergence has coincided with the modern missionary movement, understood by most students of these matters to have begun with William Carey (1761-1834). Thus, binding and loosing has come to reflect a stance of evangelical advance against the dark powers and a modern willingness to send Christian missionaries to the darkest corners of the world.

Although taken to be a peripheral doctrine by some, we cannot simply dismiss binding and loosing as a marginal teaching when such recognized leaders as Charles Spurgeon, A.B. Simpson, Andrew Murray, Jessie Penn-Lewis, Watchman Nee and several more contemporary authors all advocate binding and loosing. Even the dispensationalist Merrill Unger speaks of the loosing of believers from demonic forces.[1]

For those who may suggest that binding and loosing is only or primarily ecclesiastical and not direct confrontation with supernatural forces, then some accounting must be made of these great Christian leaders as well as ordinary believers who through the centuries have taught and practiced binding and loosing with blessed results. Surprisingly, perhaps, we find a pattern of development in the restoration of lost truth about the authority of the believer, particularly in its forbidding and allowing expressions.

During the Middle Ages, as we have seen, binding and loosing had become institutionalized, formalized and relegated to the authority of priests or bishops in legislative and judicial decisions, retaining or remitting sins. Sometimes it was used in the ritual of exorcism.[2]

Then, Martin Luther and the Reformation brought a restoration of belief in the priesthood of the believer, but the negating of the existing ecclesiastical structures meant a new start in comprehending and applying that priesthood. Luther's unfortunate abandonment of the religious order concept in Catholicism meant that the Roman Catholics alone seemed determined to press the missionary mandate. Until the days of William Carey and the Moravians, with a few pietistic exceptions, the missionary enterprise was essentially unrevived by the Protestant Church.

Still, as mentioned in the last chapter, in the Reformation period, Huldrych Zwingli exhibited a sense of recovery as touching the authority of the believer in binding and loosing when he questioned the application of Matthew 16:19 and 18:18 to bishops only.[3] Following that, the German Lutheran Pietist movement emphasized the restoration of the priesthood of the believer,[4] and the Wesleyan Revival, also influenced by Pietism and its descendants, the Moravians,[5] continued to bring about a greater awareness of the authority of the believer. In fact, Wesley himself engaged in exorcisms upon occasion as evil spirits manifested themselves.[6]

However, the authority of the believer and one of its most dramatic evidences—binding and loosing—was apparently not wholly understood until the nineteenth century. Possibly that renewed understanding emerged through the ministry and teaching of Johann Christoph Blumhardt[7] and Dorothea Trudel,[8] but certainly through the teaching of Blumhardt's son, Christoph.

Christoph Blumhardt followed in his father's footsteps more as a theologian working out doctrinally what his father had discovered and pioneered practically. In an 1897 sermon entitled "The Church of Jesus Christ," he appears to limit the authority of the believer to those who truly perceive its reality:

> It is a great mistake to think that every theologian, every pastor can loose and bind. . . . Only one who receives God's revelation can be a man who looses or releases. . . . The Living Church of Christ may be made up of poor, simple, little people; it will yet be able to loose and set free.[9]

With the restoration of teaching about believer's authority through the movement of the Spirit in the late nineteenth and early twentieth centuries, came a growing awareness of the nature and authority of binding and loosing. One of the earliest nineteenth-century teachings on binding and loosing as the authority of the believer came from the famous preacher, Henry Ward Beecher (1813-1887), preaching on Matthew 16:19. He calls believers' authority "the opening and shutting power of the Christian life," asserting that

> every praying man and every praying woman . . . has this power of the keys. . . . And every man that has that spirit has God's keys in his hands, and has authority to bind and loose—to bind lies and all iniquity, and to set loose all those that suffer oppression by reason of spiritual despotism.[10]

Andrew Murray was perhaps the next great preacher to affirm the concept of binding and loosing. In his book *With Christ in the School of Prayer*, published in 1885, Murray declared that "God rules the world by the prayers of His saints." And he prays,

> Grant especially, blessed Lord, that your Church may believe that it is by the power of united prayer that she can bind and loose in heaven, cast out Satan, save souls, remove mountains, and hasten the coming of the Kingdom.[11]

Charles Spurgeon soon followed, endorsing the practice of binding and loosing. Speaking in 1888 of the believer's privilege and authority in prayer, Spurgeon makes reference to the concept: "Thus are Elijahs trained to handle the keys of heaven, and lock or loose the clouds."[12]

The pivotal year for the recovery of the doctrine of binding and loosing appears to be 1897. F.B. Conybeare demonstrated in an article that Jesus' statements about binding and loosing were parallel to expressions and practices in Jewish culture and spiritual experience. He was followed in 1906 by other scholars such as Bousett who also recognized the connection between binding and loosing and demonology. In 1914, Dell followed,[13] and ultimately there was Oesterreich with his monumental work in 1921.[14]

Now, let us retreat once again to 1897.

Long before the Welsh revival, at a China Inland Mission Conference in that year, Jessie Penn-Lewis was teaching on the authority of the believer, providing the doctrinal structure necessary for the understanding of binding and loosing from Ephesians 1:

> The Cross is the gate into this heavenly sphere, so that if the Holy Spirit reveals to us that when we are sub-

merged into the death of Christ, we are loosed from the
claims of sin, the flesh, and the devil, He will as certainly impart to us the life of the Risen Lord. He will
lift us in real experience into our place in Him, seated
with Him in the heavens far above all principalities and
powers . . . far above the powers of darkness.[15]

Further she says,

> The soul hidden with Christ in God has authority over
> all the power of the enemy, for he shares in the victory
> of Christ. In Him he has power to tread on serpents
> and scorpions, and power to deliver and loose others
> from the bonds of the evil one.[16]

We are beginning to see a gradual but definite and fuller development in the Church's interpretation of the binding and loosing
Scriptures.

During the same time period, A.B. Simpson, founder of The
Christian and Missionary Alliance, began teaching the believers'
position in Christ according to Ephesians 1:

> He "raised us up with Christ and seated us" (2:6) with
> Him in the heavenlies. This is much more than resur-
> rection. It is ascension. It is taking the place of accom-
> plished victory and conceded right, and sitting down in
> an attitude of completed repose, from henceforth ex-
> pecting with Him until all our enemies be made our
> footstool. . . . It is throne life. It is dwelling with Christ
> on high, your head in the heavens even while your feet
> still walk the paths of the lower world of sense and
> time. This is our high privilege.[17]

Whether Simpson was influenced by Penn-Lewis or Blumhardt we cannot be sure, but apparently they all came to the same basic comprehensions, either through the Holy Spirit independent of one another or perhaps through consultation. At any rate, by 1903 Simpson was also recognizing that a broad principle of binding and loosing was given to the Church:

> He has given authority to His servants to remove from this fellowship everything in opposition with its holy character. He has invested this discipline with the most sacred and binding authority, and He tells us in this passage [Matthew 18:18-20] that what we bind on earth, He will bind in heaven, and what we loose on earth He will loose in heaven.[18]

In Simpson's view, this did not infer mere discipline or excommunication, for

> such an act on the part of the Church of God [as in First Corinthians 5:5] will be followed by the Lord's effectual dealing in all such cases. . . . God's hand will deal with the offender through temporal judgment.[19]

Simpson likens this power of binding to Paul's handing over to Satan the incestuous man from the Corinthian church. He also understood the authority of loosing to include loosing or freeing ourselves from fear, the power of evil habits and sickness.[20]

It would appear that as a result of the 1904-1906 revival in Wales, in America and around the world, there emerged a fuller understanding of the implications of binding and loosing in evangelicalism. In their 1912 book, *War on the Saints*, Jessie Penn-Lewis and Evan Roberts wrote,

> The Church of Christ will reach its high water mark
> when it is able to deal with demon possession; when it
> knows how to "bind the strong man" by prayer; "com-
> mand" the spirits of evil in the name of Christ, and de-
> liver men and women from their power.[21]

Penn-Lewis also wrote an article containing teaching on binding the strong man entitled, "How to Pray for Missionaries."

> In Matthew 12:29 the Lord said, first bind the strong
> man, and then "spoil his goods." How can you "bind"
> the strong man if you will not recognize his existence
> and face the fact that he is the hidden cause of evil?
> The Church must learn this "binding" power of prayer
> for it is written, "Whatsoever ye shall bind on earth
> shall be bound in heaven" (Matthew 18:18, KJV). And
> what can this "binding" mean except restraining the
> working of the enemy by appealing to the conquering
> power of Him who was "manifested that he might de-
> stroy the works of the devil"?
> Here is an illustration of what I mean. Once in the
> north of England, on a great market square, crowds of
> people were listening to the communists and atheists
> speaking. Some of their best speakers were there try-
> ing to stir up the people, and attacking the Christian
> workers of the town and their work. A minister who
> knew something of this prayer warfare called his
> Christian people together on the Sunday afternoon
> and showed them from the Scripture how Satan was
> at the back of this attack on the market square, and
> that the thing to be done was to "bind" the adversary.
> The Spirit of God made it so clear that about one hun-
> dred Christians took Christ at His word, and aloud,

with united hearts and voices, they said, "In the name of Jesus Christ we bind the strong man from stirring up these people and from attacking God's work." They sang a hymn of victory and committed themselves in faith to a position of absolute reliance upon God to fulfill His Word. The next day a division arose among the atheists; their leader disappeared from the town, and a week later he was arraigned before the police court and sentenced for other matters in his life. Then the authorities intervened, and stopped the whole campaign on the market square, and the devil's attack was brought to nought.[22]

In the 1921 book, *The Secrets of Victory*, Carrie Judd Montgomery wrote an entire chapter on binding and loosing, calling it a "recent understanding."[23]

Robert A. Jaffray, pioneer missionary to China and Indonesia in the early part of the twentieth century, put into action in his meetings the practice of binding demonic forces.[24] Likewise, in 1929, the famed biblical expositor, G. Campbell Morgan, also taught a wider application of the principle of binding and loosing.[25]

In 1932, Christian and Missionary Alliance missionary John A. MacMillan compiled the seminal book on believers' authority from his series of articles based on Ephesians 1.[26] In effect, he did the foundational theology at that time for the ever more widely understood practice of binding and loosing. The ninth edition of the unabridged version of Jessie Penn-Lewis and Evan Roberts' 1912 book *War on the Saints* makes reference to MacMillan's articles in the *Alliance Weekly*.[27] Perhaps MacMillan was influenced by his mentor Robert Jaffray and the teachings of Penn-Lewis and Roberts.

In 1934, Chinese spiritual leader Watchman Nee, influenced

by Penn-Lewis, Simpson and Andrew Murray, also taught authoritative prayer and the power of binding and loosing.[28] So we see that by the early twentieth century the teaching on binding and loosing as the believer's authority proliferated among evangelical leaders.

By 1960, modern fundamental evangelicals like Dick Hillis, writing for Moody Press, were recognizing that "prayer is not enough," admitting:

> We learned further that it is not enough to pray or sing, though I believe Satan hates both prayer and song. We must resist the devil and command that he depart.[29]

In 1965, Theodore Epp, founder of the Back to the Bible Broadcast, wrote a book entitled *Praying with Authority* in which he said,

> If Satan has blinded and bound men and women, how can we ever see souls saved? This is where you and I enter the picture. Spoiling the goods of the strong man has to do with liberating those whom Satan has blinded and is keeping bound.[30]

Contrary to the claims of some contemporary leaders like Hank Hanegraaff,[31] the concept of binding and loosing is not exclusively the interpretation of the modern Faith Movement and charismatic teaching. Dutch scholar H. Van der Loos, for example, in his 1965 book asks, "Why should not men in their turn be able to bind . . . ?"[32] In 1973, Kurt Koch advocated the practice,[33] soon followed by Merrill Unger who wrote with understanding about renunciatory practices as well as loosing.[34]

Then in 1981 New Testament scholar and Gordon-Conwell Seminary professor J. Ramsay Michaels asserted,

The work of binding and loosing—binding the strong man and loosing his captives—the work that dominated Jesus' ministry and filled his vision, will be the work of his disciples during the period of his absence.[35]

Similarly, Bill Gothard, while not advocating the rebuke of Satan directly, did affirm in 1982 that we can and should bind Satan:

Before we attempt to reclaim a loved one who has come under Satan's power, we must first bind Satan. Otherwise, he works through that loved one to create a reaction toward every attempt at restoration.[36]

Such references abound and there is little point in endlessly multiplying the endnotes. However, Mark Bubeck, who is a respected Bible teacher in the area of binding and loosing, has a comment on Matthew 12:29 which helps us conclude here:

As believers, united with Christ in His authority, we are able to so war against Satan that we can bind him, tie him up and rob or take away what he wants to claim as his own. . . . We are to see ourselves as invincible soldiers of Christ who can advance against this "strong man" Satan, invade his domain, and take away from him those people and spiritual fortifications he claims.[37]

In summary, binding and loosing as an expression of our completeness in Jesus Christ and the authority of the believer is a valid and vital doctrine. Birthed in the New Testament, promulgated in various forms by the Church Fathers, lost for the main part during the superstition of the Middle Ages and the Reformation reactions, the teaching of binding and loosing has reemerged as a result of the holiness revival of the late nineteenth century and the writings of noncharismatic evangelicals in the early twentieth century. These truths belong to no one sector of the Church. Rather, they are indispensable weapons in spiritual warfare, evidence that when the enemy comes in like a flood, a standard will be raised against him.

Endnotes

[1] Merrill F. Unger, *What Demons Can Do to Saints* (Chicago: Moody Press, 1977), 180. What is little known about Unger is that he had a Foursquare Pentecostal background before he became the well-known dispensationalist that he was. When I published my second book (*The Third View of Tongues* [Camp Hill, PA: Horizon Books, 1975]), I received a very personal and thoughtful letter from Dr. Unger in which he discussed his theological roots.

[2] Theodoret, "Letters of the Blessed Theodoret, Bishop of Cyrus," CLXX, *Nicene Fathers and Post-Nicene Fathers (NFPF)*, ed. Philip Schaff (Grand Rapids, MI: Eerdmans, 1979), 2:3:343; Gregory, "Epistles of St. Gregory the Great," Epistle XL, *NFPF*, 2:12:228-229; Leo, "Sermons of Leo the Great," Sermon 3:3, *NFPF*, 2:12:117; Pope Callistus, "The Epistles of Pope Callistus," 2:6, *The Ante-Nicene Fathers (ANF)*, eds. Alexander Roberts and James Donaldson (Grand Rapids, MI: Eerdmans, 1978), 8:617; Zephyrinus, "The Epistles of Zephyrinus," The First Epistle, *ANF*, 8:609; Pope Urban I, "The Epistle of Pope Urban I," *ANF*, 8:620.

[3] Huldrych Zwingli, "Choice and Free Use of Foods," in *Twenty Centuries of Great Preaching*, eds. Clyde E. Fant, Jr. and William M. Pinson, Jr. (Waco, TX: Word, 1971), 2:119.

[4] C. John Weborg, "Reborn in Order to Renew," *Christian History*, 5:2:29, 35.

[5] Robert G. Tuttle, Jr., *John Wesley: His Life and Theology* (Grand Rapids, MI: Zondervan, 1978), 220-221.

[6] *The Journal of John Wesley* (Chicago: Moody Press, n.d.), 81-83.

[7] R. LeJeune, *Christoph Blumhardt: His Life and Message* (Rifton, NY: The Plough Publishing House, 1963), 20, 165.

[8] A.J. Gordon, "The Ministry of Healing," in *Healing: The Three Great Classics on Divine Healing*, ed. Jonathan L. Graf (Camp Hill, PA: Christian Publications, 1992), 215, 221-223.

[9] R. LeJeune, *Christoph Blumhardt,* 165.

[10] Henry Ward Beecher, *The Biblical Illustrator: St. Matthew*, ed. Joseph S. Excell (New York: Rudolph and Co., n.d.), 345-346.

[11] Andrew Murray, *With Christ in the School of Prayer* (Springdale, PA: Whitaker House, 1885, 1981), 117.

[12] Charles Haddon Spurgeon, *Faith's Checkbook* (Chicago: Moody Press, n.d.), 28. Reference might also be made to D.L. Moody as cited by Mrs. Charles Cowman, *Springs in the Valley* (Minneapolis, MN: Worldwide Publications, 1968), 63; E.M. Bounds, *The Preacher and Prayer* (Grand Rapids, MI: Zondervan, 1950), 100; and Jessie Penn-Lewis, *Prayer and Evangelism* (Dorset, England: Overcomer Literature Trust, n.d.), 5-6.

[13] Joseph A. Burgess, *A History of the Exegesis of Matthew 16:17-19 from 1781 to 1955* (Ann Arbor, MI: Edwards Bros., Inc., 1965), 105.

[14] T.K. Oesterreich, *Possession, Demonaical and Other* (New Hyde Park, NY: University Books, 1966), 170.

[15] Jessie Penn-Lewis, *The Warfare with Satan* (Fort Washington, PA: Christian Literature Crusade, 1963), 63.

[16] Ibid., 65.

[17] A.B. Simpson, *Christ in the Bible Commentary* (Camp Hill, PA: Christian Publications, 1992), 5:413-414.

[18] Ibid., 4:96.

[19] Ibid.

[20] Ibid., 3:491.

[21] Jessie Penn-Lewis and Evan Roberts, *War on the Saints* (New York: Thomas Lowe, 1912, 1963), i.

[22] Jessie Penn-Lewis, "How to Pray for Missionaries," *The Alliance Weekly*, 12 June 1937, 74.

[23] Carrie Judd Montgomery, *The Secrets of Victory* (Oakland, CA: Triumphs of Faith, 1921), 67-74. Montgomery was an influential evangelist in Buffalo, NY, long associated with The Christian and Missionary Alliance. (See Robert L. Niklaus, John S. Sawin and Samuel J. Stoesz, *All for Jesus* [Camp Hill, PA: Christian Publications, 1986], 269-270.)

[24] John A. MacMillan, *Encounter with Darkness* (Camp Hill, PA: Christian Publications, 1980), 56-57.

[25] G. Campbell Morgan, *The Gospel According to Matthew* (Old Tappan, NJ: Fleming H. Revell, 1929), 233.

[26] John A. MacMillan, *The Authority of the Believer* (Camp Hill, PA: Christian Publications, 1997).

[27] Penn-Lewis and Roberts, introduction to *War on the Saints,* n.p.

[28] Watchman Nee, *God's Plan and the Overcomers* (New York: Christian Fellowship Publishers, 1977), 72-77.

[29] Dick Hillis, "Prayer Was Not Enough: China," *Demon Experiences in Many Lands* (Chicago: Moody Press, 1960), 39.

[30] Theodore Epp, *Praying with Authority* (Lincoln, NE: Back to the Bible Broadcast, 1965), 98, as cited by Neil T. Anderson in *The Bondage Breaker* (Eugene, OR: Harvest House Publishers, 1993), 87. My perspective is unique in the case of Theodore Epp in that Rev. Clifton McElheran, at that time a missionary of the Sudan Interior Mission, had, in 1963, become part of a deliverance team where I was also involved. McElheran's contacts included Theodore Epp and, in fact, McElheran was thoroughly debriefed by Epp prior to and perhaps during the writing of *Praying with Authority.* There is no doubt that McElheran practiced binding and loosing as the following Nigeria testimonial makes clear.

> The quiet of early morning was pierced by wailing which came from within a compound where we were lodging. News had come to a young girl that her Christian fiancé, several villages away, had been poisoned to death. As we and the two evangelists made our way to the village to offer condolences, we passed a spirit hut. Displayed on its roof were the clothes of [another] young Christian who had been poisoned the week before as a warning to others should they follow Christ.
>
> When we arrived at the village, we saw a large crowd milling about awaiting the burial ceremony. Since the grave was being dug in the bush contrary to their custom, the evangelists sensed they were going to bury [the man] as an outcast. Offering to give him a Christian burial only stirred up a big commotion. We called the evangelists aside and together we knelt down and called upon God. As we in Jesus' name

bound the strong man in this situation, a hush fell over that whole crowd. The father came forward and handed over his son's body. Amidst singing, reading the Word, and preaching, the body was committed to the ground in a suitable place (Clifton McElheran, *Let the Oppressed Go Free* [Calgary, AB: self-published, n.d.], 22).

Further, according to McElheran (in conversation on August 15, 1997), Epp was involved with him in the deliverance of a person from an institution, and on at least one other occasion, Epp on his own had practiced loosing with dramatic results.

[31] Hank Hanegraaff, *Christianity in Crisis* (Eugene, OR: Harvest House, 1993), 257-258; John MacArthur, Jr., *Our Sufficiency Is in Christ* (Dallas: Word Publishing, 1991), 213ff.

[32] H. Van der Loos, cited by Richard H. Hiers, "Binding and Loosing, the Matthean Authorizations," *Journal of Biblical Literature,* 1985, 104:2:238.

[33] Kurt Koch, *Demonology, Past and Present* (Grand Rapids, MI: Kregel Publications, 1973), 154.

[34] Merrill Unger, *What Demons Can Do*, 179-180.

[35] J. Ramsay Michaels, *Servant and Son: Jesus in Parable and Gospel* (Atlanta: John Knox Press, 1981), 301.

[36] Bill Gothard, *Rebuilder's Guide* (Oak Brook, IL: Institute in Basic Youth Conflicts, 1982), 119 (see also 114-121).

[37] Mark I. Bubeck, *Overcoming the Adversary* (Chicago: Moody Press, 1984), 113 (see also 20, 37).

Crying Wind

Rosalind Rinker

Author Rosalind Rinker tells a fascinating story about Crying Wind, a young woman who had responded to Rinker's radio ministry. Here is Rinker's account in her own words.

I was delighted beyond measure when Crying Wind wrote her first book, *Crying Wind*, and then her second, *My Searching Heart*. Her struggle from one culture—Navajo—to another—Christian, her worship of the wind, her tenacity to keep going and the final publishing of her story of how Jesus found her have brought many of Native American heritage to Christ as well as many Caucasians.

Then the blow fell! Crying Wind was blacklisted as having misrepresented her story. Her books were pulled from the market.

Her letters to me were full of unspeakable pain. She was desperate beyond all comfort. Did Christians do things like this? Why should she live any longer? Didn't God care, either? Why did this happen?

Finally I got the whole story of what actually did happen. [Someone she wrote about] in her second book was goaded by some well-meaning friend to ask for a large portion of her royalties. She explained why she couldn't give him that. He was not only offended, but he was angry and left muttering that he'd fix her. He did. He went to the publisher and said that Crying Wind had told them a pack of lies. Without a thorough investigation, the publishers acted, destroying the books.

So now what?

I took it to our Friday morning prayer group and together we claimed the binding of Satan who was oppressing this child of God and claimed that Christ's victory would loose her and vindicate her.

One day the Lord spoke to me so plainly that I had to act. Why didn't I do something about it? Why didn't I help her find another publisher? I called my long-time friend Bob Hawkins and told him the story.

He said, "Ros, find a bigger publisher than I am. I've only been in this a few years."

I tried telephoning directly to the two publishers who print my books and was told to send copies of her book.

More than a month passed with no word from anywhere. We kept praying and kept reminding the Lord of His promise, and that those two books be unbound and loosed to give blessing and salvation.

This is a story that has long needed to be told, and I'm glad I can tell it in the context of answered prayer.

One day the telephone rang. Bob Hawkins wanted Crying Wind's telephone number. He wanted to publish her books! What had happened? He had attended a conference of some kind and had met a person who was knowledgeable concerning the true story about her books. Bob suggested that the books *Crying Wind* and *My Searching Heart* be called biographical novels.

In less than a month the presses were running and 60,000 books had been sold. All praise and thanks be to the Lord Jesus.[1]

Endnote

[1] Rosalind Rinker, *How to Get the Most Out of Your Prayer Life* (Eugene, OR: Harvest House, 1981), 135-138, condensed.

As a publisher, I was independently aware of these same events and also tried to get Crying Wind's books. Bob Hawkins beat me to it.

Part III

BINDING AND LOOSING: THE THEOLOGICAL FACTORS

Theology is the queen of the sciences. Apart from her gracious rule, unhappy doctrine, grievous error and damnable heresies all arise. Under her sovereign care, truth confronts, flourishes and finally prevails!

"Fair and regal lady, rest comfortably with us, we pray."

6

BINDING AND LOOSING
IN THE OLD TESTAMENT

"HOW MANY OF YOU SING IN BED?" That was my question as I tested some of this material in a prework devotional period at our office. Throughout the rest of the day I conducted an informal survey among the nearly forty employees. I discovered that there are indeed Christians who sing in bed—not all, but some.

What has this to do with binding and loosing, you may ask. The basis of my question was the Old Testament verse, "Let the saints rejoice in this honor and sing for joy on their beds" (Psalm 149:5). Three verses later, we discover that one of the things the singing saints do is "bind their kings with fetters, their nobles with shackles of iron" (149:8).

It is extremely important to know that the teaching of binding and loosing finds its roots in the Old Testament. In the overall view and construction of biblical theology, anything that lacks antecedents in the Old Testament is more difficult to embrace and less likely to figure as a significant doctrine in the New Testament. For that reason, this chapter is pivotal. Thankfully, in symbolic ways as well as in clear declarations, both binding and loosing find their roots in the Old Testament.

Binding and Loosing in the Pentateuch

One of the most poignant accounts of binding and loosing in the Old Testament, or in all of Scripture for that matter, is the story of Abraham preparing to offer Isaac on a stone altar (Genesis 22).

The drama was intense. A journey to Mount Moriah for the purpose of offering a sacrifice to God was being undertaken without taking the animal to be sacrificed. Perhaps during the journey Isaac himself wondered if he would be the offering. The possibility of such tension and intrigue lies latent within this account.

After Abraham announced his belief in the resurrection, he specifically told his servants, "*We* will worship and then *we* will come back to you" (22:5, emphasis mine). If Isaac were going to die, God, according to Abraham's expression of faith, would raise him up. His plan and purpose was to put to death Isaac, his authentic firstborn son, in obedience to God. The Bible clearly says that Abraham went so far as to bind Isaac (22:9) and place him on the altar.

Being familiar with the story, we all know that, when in the providence of God a ram was caught in the thicket, Isaac was loosed. Although the text does not explicitly say that, it must logically be assumed.

The analogy of this passage with New Testament binding and loosing is helpful. Abraham does the binding, and he obviously does the loosing. But God supplies the ram. The miraculous intervention and power comes from God. Clearly, the patriarch Abraham was acting out only what had already been settled in heaven. Binding and loosing is, in the Old Testament, as in the New Testament (Matthew 18:18-19), irrevocably connected with heaven.

That there is no overt evil in this illustration, unless it was Abraham's intent to murder his son, should make clear that binding and loosing need not always refer to evil. Why should it? The loosing of the colt in Mark 11:2-7 has no evil connotation at all. The "whatever" of Matthew 16:19 and 18:18 need not be locked into conflict with evil.

Binding and Loosing in the Psalms

Psalm 105 has attracted a lot of attention as one of the great binding and loosing passages in the Old Testament. In the narrative, Yahweh is sending Joseph to be bound and later loosed—all in divine providence.

> He sent a man before them—
>   Joseph, sold as a slave.
> They bruised his feet with shackles,
>   his neck was put in irons,
> till what he foretold came to pass,
>   till the word of the LORD proved him true.
> The king sent and released him,
>   the ruler of peoples set him free.
> He made him master of his household,
>   ruler over all he possessed,
> to instruct his princes as he pleased
>   and teach his elders wisdom.
>   (105:17-22)

This passage, it is thought, shows that Joseph was bound, then he was loosed and received power to bind. In Psalm 105:22, Joseph binds princes, an apparent reference to Genesis 41 where the original incidents are chronicled.

That passage can be claimed with confidence to be part of the background to the commission of Peter [to bind and loose]. . . . Psalm 105:22 construes it . . . to bind (*le 'esor*) his princes according to his spirit (i.e., at his pleasure).[1]

And there's more.

Spurgeon seems fascinated with the reversals of fortunes in Joseph's life and like others, connects Psalm 105:22 to binding.

This verse signifies to exercise control over the greatest men in the kingdom, which power was conferred on Joseph by Pharoah. . . . The capability of binding is to be regarded as an evidence of authority; a power of compelling obedience; or, in default of inflicting punishment.[2]

Spurgeon persists in his interpretation: "He who was bound obtains authority to bind. He is no longer kept in prison, but keeps the prisons."[3]

A.F. Kirkpatrick makes a similar comment,

Joseph, who so lately was "bound in prison," is invested with authority to imprison even princes, and in virtue of his wisdom is made the director of Pharaoh's counsellors.[4]

Matthew Henry likewise relates Joseph and this passage of Scripture to the spiritual authority of binding and loosing.[5] The recurrent theme: Joseph was bound and, being released, releases others from bondage to famine. He who was once bound now has authority to bind princes.

Let us move to the focus on binding and loosing in the Psalms. In Psalm 149, praise in the mouths of the saints is equated with a double-edged sword in their hands.

Let the saints be joyful in glory: let them sing aloud
upon their beds.
Let the high praises of God be in their mouth, and a
twoedged sword in their hand;
To execute vengeance upon the heathen, and punishments
upon the people;
To bind their kings with chains, and their nobles with
fetters of iron;
To execute upon them the judgment written: this
honour have all his saints. Praise ye the LORD.
(149:5-9, KJV)

A church in Oakland, California discovered the offensive
power of praise and how by it the "kings and nobles" can be
bound.

> Shiloh Christian Fellowship had always been known
> as a worshiping church, and the members believed
> earnestly in the power of worship to bind the enemy.
> They did not realize how much the word had gotten
> around about their worship until one day they re-
> ceived an invitation from the Oakland Police Depart-
> ment. Would they be willing to go to Pleitner Avenue
> and see what could be done for the area? Pleitner Ave-
> nue at the time was infested with drug lords, pimps
> and prostitutes, a rough, dangerous part of Oakland.
>
> After they got over their surprise at the invitation,
> they said they would be glad to go. As they prayed,
> they devised a plan. Working with police they marked
> off an area of the street to have a block party. They
> planned to give away clothes, cook hot dogs, worship
> God according to Psalm 149 and then preach an evan-
> gelistic message. The church went back for three Sat-

urdays in a row. . . . The police told the media about the parties and reported the results in the newspaper. According to the police reports, seventy percent of the drug lords moved out of the Pleitner Avenue area after the parties.[6]

Praise, then, is a weapon, like the Word of God (Hebrews 4:12) or similar to the Word of God. Moreover, people are capable by their praise of inflicting vengeance on the nations, punishment on the peoples, binding the kings with fetters, shackling their nobles with iron, carrying out the sentence written against them (Psalm 149:7-9).

This is a shift in thinking from Psalm 2, where the king subdues the enemies, to this psalm where the saints do battle. Commenting on these verses, Kirkpatrick points out, "In Psalm 2 the Messianic king, here [Psalm 149] the Messianic people, subjugates the nations."[7]

Derek Kidner in his commentary applies verses 6-9 of the 149th Psalm to "the church militant," saying, "Our equivalent of binding kings with chains (verse 8) is to 'take every thought captive to obey Christ' (2 Corinthians 10:5)."[8]

The psalmist adds, "This [binding of kings] is the glory of all his saints." Another version puts it this way, "This honour have all his saints" (Psalm 149:9, KJV). This passage strongly suggests the authority of the believer—*all* the Lord's saints are granted the honor of binding.

The Old Testament was given with a specific intent to prefigure and foreshadow that which is to come (Romans 15:4). Properly, then, we may expect to find analogy and symbolism relating to binding and loosing—which we have done—along with such direct teaching as is offered in Psalm 149.

Loosing in Isaiah

Fasting, which is the subject of Isaiah 58:6, alluded to in the previous chapter, is yet another clear reference to loosing in the Old Testament. Fasting looses the chains of injustice, unties heavy burdens, breaks every yoke and lets the oppressed go free. But Isaiah also makes it clear that God is not pleased with showy, noisy, argumentive fasts laced with false humility (58:3-5). Fasting, like praise, does loose prisoners. Later in this book we will launch into an extended examination of fasting as the delightful discipline.[9]

The fact that there are references to binding and loosing in the Psalms and Isaiah should not escape our attention. These two books, above all others in the Old Testament, are spiritual warfare texts. Through fasting, "[c]hained prisoners will be set free [loosed]. They will not die in prison. They will not go without food" (Isaiah 51:14, GWV).

Even so brief a survey as this clarifies the fact that binding and loosing is a concept present and active in the Old Testament. Were that not so, our overall argument about binding and loosing as a pervasive biblical doctrine would be considerably weakened.

Conversely, with binding and loosing prevalent under the Old Covenant, we can predict its appearance even more clearly in the symbolism of the New Covenant—joyfully so.

Endnotes

[1] Wilhelm Gesenius, *Gesenius' Hebrew and Chaldee Lexicon* (Grand Rapids, MI: Eerdmans, 1949, 1974), 68.

[2] C.H. Spurgeon, *Treasury of David* (Grand Rapids, MI: Baker Book House, 1978), 5:62. Spurgeon is favorably citing George Phillips, 1846.

[3] Ibid.

[4] A.F. Kirkpatrick, *The Book of Psalms* (Cambridge: University Press, 1957), 620.

[5] Matthew Henry, *Commentary on the Whole Bible* (New York: Fleming H. Revell Co., n.d.), 5:233.

[6] Cindy Jacobs, *Possessing the Gates of the Enemy* (Grand Rapids, MI: Chosen Books, 1994), 176.

[7] Kirkpatrick, *The Book of Psalms*, 831.

[8] Derek Kidner, *Psalms 73-150,* Tyndale Old Testament Commentaries (London: InterVarsity Press, 1975), 490.

[9] K. Neill Foster, "Fasting: The Delightful Discipline" (Camp Hill, PA: Christian Publications, 1995).

The Bar That Never Opened

Sometime in the 1950s a revival was taking place in Southern Alabama. Many were coming to Christ and the pastor in charge was consumed with the ongoing moving of the Holy Spirit. One day, he noticed a building being constructed across the border in Florida. When he learned that it was intended to be a bar, a sense of outrage began to fill his soul. Surely this was a direct attack of Satan on the work the Holy Spirit was doing just over the border.

So intense did the threat of the bar seem that the pastor finally felt he had to take some action. Together with his wife and a young man who worked with them, they got into a pickup and drove onto the Florida property. There, in the cab of the pickup, they prayed something like this: "Dear Lord Jesus Christ, we recognize this bar as a threat to the working of the Holy Spirit. In the name of the Lord Jesus Christ, we forbid it ever to open."

The construction continued and, as I recall, the furniture and equipment were installed. But the bar did not open.

In 1996, I was speaking at an informal session for elders and their wives in a church in Stow, Ohio. In relating this incident, I mentioned that as far as I knew, the bar had never opened, but admitted that I lacked information from more recent times.

A hand shot up and one of the elders asked to speak.

"I know the details of this incident," he said. "That bar never did open." I was thrilled—and amazed.

7

BINDING AND LOOSING
SYMBOLICALLY IN
THE NEW TESTAMENT

SYMBOLISM IS OFTEN A NEARLY EXACT SHADOW! In fact, sometimes the shadow seems more informative than the reality. Scripture affords a great deal of insight from events which are both narrative and symbolic. Illustrations abound. For instance, Jesus Himself stated that the communion bread and wine were symbols of His body and His blood. Then, of course, in the Old Testament, there were the rainbow, the pillar of cloud and the pillar of fire. But nowhere is biblical symbolism more dramatic than in the matter of binding and loosing. We will look at four examples.

"Unwind Him!"

The resurrection and unwinding of Lazarus (John 11) is one of the most striking miracles performed by Jesus. Lazarus, brother of Mary and Martha, had died. Although summoned earlier by the sisters, Jesus delayed His coming until after Lazarus was dead. Finally arriving at the grave site, He shouted, "Lazarus, come out!" (11:43). Lazarus had already been dead four days. He should have been—and perhaps was—by then a stench-exuding corpse. Nevertheless, in response to Jesus' call, Lazarus shuffled forth resuscitated by the energy of resurrection power miraculously supplied by the Son of God.

But Lazarus was still bound in his grave clothes. Instead of doing it Himself, Jesus ordered the disciples to "loose him, and let him go" (11:44, KJV). The loosing, apparently, was the obligation of those who followed the Master. The miraculous power of raising the dead was supplied by Jesus, but the unwinding, the freeing, the loosing, was done by others. As we mentioned earlier, loosing is something the believer does. Like in the story of the filling of the water pots, "You do it!" is what Jesus says.

Jesus did not *not* unwind Lazarus because He could not. His supernatural power was unquestionably sufficient to have snapped those bonds. If He could reverse the process of decay, overcome the stench of a rotting corpse and raise a dead body from the grave, the bonds were hardly a problem. Still, loosing became the prerogative of the disciples.

Similarly today, loosing is the prerogative of disciples—those who are willing to step forward and unbind Lazarus. It was Spurgeon's observation that there are indeed many like Lazarus all about us in the kingdom of God. Receptors already of divine life, they await the unbinding ministry of those who love and care for them.[1]

Augustine also connected the loosing of Lazarus from his bonds with the authority of binding and loosing given to the disciples:

> Consider this very case of Lazarus: He comes forth, but with his bands. He was alive already through confession, but he did not yet walk free, entangled as he was

in his bands. What then doeth the church to which it was said, "Whatsoever ye shall loose, shall be loosed"; but what the Lord said forthwith to His disciples, "Loose him, and let him go?"[2]

Again Augustine says,

At the voice of the Lord's cry, the bands of necessity were burst asunder. The powers of hell trembled, and Lazarus is restored alive. . . . He came forth from the tomb alive, but he could not walk. And the Lord said to the disciples: "Loose him, and let him go." "He" raised him from death, "they" loosed him from the bonds. . . . This office hath He given to the disciples to whom He said, "Whatsoever ye shall bind on earth, shall be bound in heaven also." . . . He knows how by His cry to burst asunder the burdens of earth, He knows how to restore life within by Himself, and to deliver him to the disciples to be loosed.[3]

Jesus Needs a Colt

Another incident in the New Testament with powerful symbolic value relates to the colt upon which Jesus would ride into Jerusalem. The animal and its mother were needed by our Lord (Matthew 21:2-7; Mark 11:2-7; Luke 19:30-35).

In these accounts, the supernatural is again supplied by Jesus. Where the disciples were to go, what they would expect to find and what they were to say to the owners of the animals were all arranged by divine providence. Yet, after the disciples arrived, and after permission to take the animals was secured, there remained one more thing to do—the colt had to be loosed.

Once again, the analogy is clear. Our Lord tends to that which humans can never attempt. But, in an economy of the miraculous, He restrains Himself—the disciples are to do the loosing. So they untie the animals and take the colt to Jesus.

In the same way, there are many who have been brought into a confluence of divine providence who need to be loosed and taken to Jesus. If this incident tells us anything about binding and loosing, it is that our Lord supplies the miraculous while expecting His disciples to handle the mundane. Jesus frames the miracle. The disciples—including you and me—add the final touches.

After using the *deo/luo* language in three previous instances (Matthew 12, 16, 18) in this story, Matthew records the same terminology in the same story a fourth time (21:2-7). This time *deo/luo* connotes humans loosing something that has been bound so that Omnipotence can make use of it. This usage is not accidental. It is intended to be part of Matthew's theological agenda. Note the following:

1. This incident brings together believing participation and divine power.

2. This act of loosing implies the exercise of believers' authority.

3. The loosing is not indiscriminate nor frivolous, but for the purpose of Jesus' will—"The Lord needs them" (Matthew 21:3).

One Happy Woman!

A third symbolic incident involves the woman who is bent over with a crippling spirit (Luke 13:10-13):

On a Sabbath Jesus was teaching in one of the synagogues, and a woman was there who had been crippled by a spirit for eighteen years. She was bent over and could not straighten up at all. When Jesus saw her, he called her forward and said to her, "Woman, you are set free from your infirmity." Then he put his hands on her, and immediately she straightened up and praised God.

We know that this woman was a woman of faith, a daughter of Abraham. Ought she to have been loosed? Jesus apparently thought so—He was emphatic in the affirmative. Satan had kept the woman bound for eighteen years, but Jesus spoke the words of liberation. She was instantly healed, instantly loosed and set free to worship and praise God.

This story is significant in that it demonstrates loosing having to do with sickness. The implication is that loosing is an appropriate procedure to connect with praying for the sick. Further, it demonstrates that the authority of the believer intersects with divine healing, to say nothing of its latent connection to binding and loosing.

In the story also, Jesus uses the metaphor of loosing an ox or donkey from a stall to lead him to water to justify the loosing of this woman on the Sabbath. Jesus speaks the word, proclaiming the woman free. According to Neil Anderson, loosing does not necessarily mean speaking to the demon directly, but making faith declarations which he calls "announcing."[4]

Further regarding this woman, Simpson notes, "This does not at all imply that she was a bad woman or under the control of the wicked one in her spirit and life."[5] He points out that Jesus said the woman ought to be freed:

There is no greater word in Christian ethics than "ought." It is the word of conscience, of law, of everlasting right. It is a cable that binds both God and man. When God says "ought," there is no appeal, no compromise, no alternative, nothing but absolutely to obey.[6]

It is interesting to note that the Greek word for "ought" is *dei*, a cognate of *deo*, meaning "necessary" or "binding." It is almost as if Jesus is saying we are bound to release those who are bound, regardless of the circumstances.

Are there those today who are similarly bound?

Of course! Beyond doubt!

Can these bondages be demonic sicknesses and infirmities? Certainly!

For that reason, we must always be ready to pray for the sick, ready to loose them in Jesus' name from the bondage of Satan. Binding and loosing, it appears, may properly attend to anything, including cases of sickness and/or demonization. Liberty can and does come through Jesus Christ, the Son of God. He is the source of divine and supernatural power. But those who are complete in Him (Colossians 2:10) have their duties as well.

A Certain Jail

The last symbolic lesson focuses on a certain jail in Philippi in which Paul and Silas found themselves. Probably the first miracle is that they sang all night—providing an impromptu concert for other prisoners (Acts 16:23-34).

Then an earthquake strikes and the place is shaken. The prisoners are loosed. This time there seems to be no economy of the miraculous. One of the marvels of this incident is that the loosed prisoners do not at once break forth in insurrection. No, they are controlled (even bound) by Paul who announces to the terrified jailer, "Don't harm yourself! We are all here!" (16:28).

The loosing is triggered by praise. God looks after all of the loosing—there is nothing for the loosed to do but listen to Paul and marvel at the works and glory of God.

What do these four symbolic illustrations say to us? I believe they say that God at all times retains His divine right to loose and to bind. They also say that sometimes there is a division of labor—God's and ours. And, as always, heaven is irrevocably linked to earth in the matter.

Endnotes

[1] Charles Haddon Spurgeon, "Unbinding Lazarus," in *C.H. Spurgeon's Sermons on the Miracles* (Grand Rapids, MI: Zondervan, 1958), 231-244.

[2] Augustine, "Sermons on New Testament Lessons," 17:2-3 *Nicene Fathers and Post-Nicene Fathers (NFPF)*, ed. Philip Schaff (Grand Rapids, MI: Eerdmans, 1979), 6:311.

[3] Ibid., 6:415.

[4] Neil T. Anderson, *Setting Your Church Free* (Ventura, CA: Regal Books, 1994), 271-272.

[5] A.B. Simpson, *Christ in the Bible Commentary* (Camp Hill, PA: Christian Publications, 1992), 4:335.

[6] A.B. Simpson, *The Gospel of Healing* (Camp Hill, PA: Christian Publications, 1994), 119-120.

"If God Fills Me Any Fuller . . ."

A few years ago I was invited to preach a campaign in a Montana town. The young pastor had been laboring faithfully for some time, but one man, a backslider whom we shall call Harry, had rejected his friendship.

"I'll never go back into that church again," he vowed.

The pastor understood binding and loosing. He persistently loosed Harry from his backsliding. He was so sure that Harry was going to return to his spiritual moorings that he had taken a 3"x5" card and written a date plus, "Today I loosed Harry."

All week we prayed and loosed. We even went to visit Harry several times. But each time he was watching a football game. We were after the man's soul, but we couldn't get the TV off!

Finally, we came to the last day of the special meetings, a Sunday. The man did not come to the morning service. So, after lunch I phoned him.

"Will you come to the service tonight?" I asked.

"I will," came the firm reply. Later, as he milked the cows, he told his wife he was going to church. "But if those two preachers get on my back," he added, "I'll just bolt out of there."

The time for the evening service arrived, and the man strode into church. He listened to the gospel as if he had never heard it before. When the invitation was given he was the first to respond. Others followed until the front pew of the church was filled with inquirers. We prayed with each one.

As I approached Harry, all I felt in my heart to say was simply, "Brother, in Jesus' name, I loose you. I loose you."

Immediately he said, "I take it. I take it." Yet, when I looked into his eyes there seemed to be a lack of assurance even though his words were positive. We said goodnight and went our separate ways. But I was uneasy. I knew Harry needed more help.

The next morning, the pastor and I went to his home once more. The news was fabulous.

"When I got home last night," he said, "I put on my pajamas and went into the living room to pray. As I knelt down by that stool, all of a sudden the Lord set me free. If God fills me any fuller it will blow a hole in my chest!"

The man had been loosed—he was free!

8

THE BELIEVER'S
COMPLETENESS IN CHRIST

THE DOCTRINE OF THE BELIEVER'S COMPLETENESS in Jesus Christ has received new prominence in recent years through the ministry of Neil Anderson. Among his writings which have encouraged believers to celebrate their position in Christ is his groundbreaking book, *The Bondage Breaker*.[1] He expresses his beliefs in powerful statements like this:

> A true knowledge of God and our identity in Christ is the greatest determinant of our mental health. A false concept of God and the misplaced deification of Satan are the greatest contributors to mental illness.[2]

He also strongly urges believers to reinforce their identity in Christ through affirmative statements such as the following:

I am the salt of the earth (Matthew 5:13).
I am the light of the world (Matthew 5:14).
I am part of the true vine, a channel of Christ's life (John 15:1, 5).

I am Christ's friend (John 15:15).

I am chosen and appointed by Christ to bear His fruit (John 15:16).

I am a slave of righteousness (Romans 6:18).

I am enslaved to God (Romans 6:22).

I am a son of God; God is spiritually my Father (Romans 8:14-15; Galatians 3:26; 4:6).

I am a joint heir with Christ, sharing His inheritance with Him (Romans 8:17).

I am a temple—a dwelling place—of God. His Spirit and His life dwell in me (1 Corinthians 3:16; 6:19).

I am united to the Lord and am one spirit with Him (1 Corinthians 6:17).

I am a member of Christ's body (1 Corinthians 12:27; Ephesians 5:30).

I am a new creation (2 Corinthians 5:17).

I am reconciled to God and am a minister of reconciliation (2 Corinthians 5:18-19).

I am a son of God and one in Christ (Galatians 3:26, 28).

I am an heir of God since I am a son of God (Galatians 4:6-7).

I am a saint (Ephesians 1:1; 1 Corinthians 1:2; Philippians 1:1; Colossians 1:2).

I am God's workmanship—His handiwork—born anew in Christ to do His work (Ephesians 2:10).

I am a fellow citizen with the rest of God's family (Ephesians 2:19).

I am a prisoner of Christ (Ephesians 3:1; 4:1).

I am righteous and holy (Ephesians 4:24).

I am a citizen of heaven, seated in heaven right now (Philippians 3:20; Ephesians 2:6).

I am hidden with Christ in God (Colossians 3:3).

I am an expression of the life of Christ because He is my life (Colossians 3:4).

I am chosen of God, holy and dearly beloved (Colossians 3:12; 1 Thessalonians 1:4).

I am a son of light and not of darkness (1 Thessalonians 5:5).

I am a holy partaker of a heavenly calling (Hebrews 3:1).

I am a partaker of Christ; I share in His life (Hebrews 3:14).

I am one of God's living stones, being built up in Christ as a spiritual house (1 Peter 2:5).

I am a member of a chosen race, a royal priesthood, a holy nation, a people of God's own possession (1 Peter 2:9-10).

I am an alien and a stranger in this world in which I temporarily live (1 Peter 2:11).

I am an enemy of the devil (1 Peter 5:8).

I am a child of God and I will resemble Christ when He returns (1 John 3:1-2).

I am born of God, and the evil one—the devil—cannot touch me (1 John 5:18).

I am *not* the great "I AM" (Exodus 3:14; John 8:24, 28, 58), but by the grace of God I am what I am (1 Corinthians 15:10).[3]

Complete in Christ

Anderson, of course, would be the first to direct us to the main Scripture passages on completeness in Christ, Colossians 1 and 2. These marvelous chapters are the biblical setting for the Magna Carta of Christian completeness.

> For in Christ all the fullness of the Deity lives in bodily form, and you have been given fullness [completeness] in Christ, who is the head over every power and authority. In him you were also circumcised, in the putting off of the sinful nature, not with a circumcision done by the hands of men but with the

circumcision done by Christ, having been buried with him in baptism and raised with him through your faith in the power of God, who raised him from the dead.

When you were dead in your sins and in the uncircumcision of your sinful nature, God made you alive with Christ. He forgave us all our sins, having canceled the written code, with its regulations, that was against us and that stood opposed to us; he took it away, nailing it to the cross. And having disarmed the powers and authorities, he made a public spectacle of them, triumphing over them by the cross. (Colossians 2:9-15)

Prior to this text, there is the well-known phrase in 1:27, "Christ in you, the hope of glory." It was upon this verse that Albert Benjamin Simpson focused with unusual and fervent intent. He saw the indwelling Christ as the witness of his salvation, as the empowerment he needed for sanctification and holiness and as the inherent faith of the Son of God when he prayed for the sick. For Simpson, being indwelt by Jesus Christ was no small matter. For him, completeness in Christ meant holy habitation, a constant and personal communion with the Lord Jesus Christ. A.W. Tozer adds this detail:

> When A.B. Simpson was an old man and about to give up his pulpit in New York, an old gentleman who had been an usher for 20 years in Simpson's church said, "Well, Brother Simpson has had only one sermon in 20 years. Wherever Brother Simpson began, he always ended up in this: 'Christ in you, the hope of glory.' "[4]

Simpson's hymn says it so very well.

This is my wonderful story—
Christ to my heart has come;
Jesus, the King of glory,
Finds in my heart a home.

Christ in me, Christ in me,
Christ in me—Oh, wonderful story;
Christ in me, Christ in me,
Christ in me, the hope of glory.[5]

When A.W. Tozer lent his considerable descriptive powers to a depiction of "Christ in you, the hope of glory," he put it this way:

This is God's supreme and final gift. Not the pearly gates, not the golden streets, not heaven, not even the forgiveness of sin, although these are God's gifts too, such as a king might give to his queen—a dozen gifts, and then the supreme, final gift worthy of royalty. So not a dozen, nor two dozen or a thousand, but countless hundreds of thousands of gifts God lays before His happy people, and then He bestows this supreme gift. He makes us the repository of the nature and Person of the Lord Jesus.[6]

The main biblical passage on Christian completeness is launched by this glorious antecedent—"Christ in you, the hope of glory" (1:27). This incomprehensible reality is the biblical foundation upon which Christian completeness rests.

A Twofold Admonition

Following the glorious antecedent, there emerges a twofold admonition: "So then, just as you received Christ Jesus as Lord, continue to live in him" (2:6), followed by verse 8:

See to it that no one takes you captive through hollow and deceptive philosophy, which depends on human tradition and the basic principles of this world rather than on Christ.

Most believers remember something about their conversion to Christ, often down to the minutest details of the event. Counting on that sacred memory, Paul urges the Colossians to walk in the same way that they received Christ—continue to live in Him. Or, put another way, inasmuch as Christ the hope of glory is in you, walk in Him just as you received Him.

The latter part of the twofold admonition is clear as well. The admonition to "see to it" or "beware" indicates lurking danger and great peril. That peril resides in those who will try to deceive, trap and take people captive with philosophy and vanities. Does Athens have anything to say to the man or woman in whom Jesus Christ dwells in His fullness? Paul's answer was an emphatic no, even though his own education was eminently advanced. Since Christ—the hope of glory for all mankind—is in us, the philosophies and machinations of this world order are empty indeed.

The Fourfold Explanation

Paul presses on with a fourfold warning:

1. You Colossians do not need philosophy, for in Christ dwells all the fullness of the Godhead bodily.
2. You are complete in Christ—what incomprehensible fullness!
3. Because Christ in you is indeed the hope of glory, you are—yes, you are—complete in Christ.
4. And, to top it all off, Jesus Christ is the Head of every power and authority. The philosophies and vanities of the

world are at best puny spirits from the netherworld. And even if they are not, but are instead the powers over the powers over the powers, no matter. Jesus Christ is above them all.

Colossians! Brothers! Sisters! Celebrate your marvelous completeness in Jesus Christ!

In brief, the explanation is this:

1. In Christ all the fullness and completeness of the godhead lives bodily (2:9).
2. You are complete in Him (2:10).
3. Christ is the Head of every power and authority (2:10).
4. God made you alive in Jesus Christ (2:13).

To paraphrase Paul in today's idiom, "These things being so—Christ in you being the hope of glory—your completeness, dear Colossians, is assured by the headship of Jesus Christ over all the powers, Christ's power already being exhibited in you by His divine presence, and further to be exhibited, if necessary, in resurrection power. Celebrate, celebrate your completeness in Him! Hallelujah for Christian completeness!"

The Marvelous Instrument

"This marvelous cross, this bloody instrument by which we have been forgiven," Paul might have continued, "by which the writs against us have been forever canceled—this rugged wood by which Jesus Christ publicly showed His power over all principalities and powers—is the instrument by which we are complete in Christ. If there were no victorious cross, there would be no holy completeness. No cross—no Christ in us, the hope of glory. Indeed, we know so well that the preaching of the cross is foolish to those who do not believe, but for those of us who are saved, it is the power of God" (see 1 Corinthians 1:18).

Can we do any less than embrace the cross?

> There's room at the cross for you;
> There's room at the cross for you.
> Though millions have come,
> There's still room for one—
> Yes, there's room at the cross for you.[7]

Why is this theme of completeness in Jesus Christ essential to a biblical view of binding and loosing? How does it relate to the concept of binding the strong man?

Many commentators believe that only Jesus Christ can bind the strong man. In fact, that indeed was the teaching of Christ. Anderson's contribution here cannot be ignored. He has reasserted the completeness of the believer in Christ in such a powerful way that many thousands have found freedom through the reading, study and application of his books.

"The only identity equation that works in God's kingdom is: You plus Christ equals wholeness and meaning," he asserts.[8] Despite his claim that he is not an exorcist, Anderson advocates a form of deliverance which he terms a "truth encounter,"[9] in which he encourages people to make declarations of truth by "renouncing" and "announcing" in terms of binding and loosing.[10] Renouncing, we should add, was a part of the exorcism process of the early Church Fathers. Anderson may actually be doing a work of pre-exorcism or prophylactic exorcism without realizing it or desiring to call it such. One thing, however, is clear: His teaching on completeness in Jesus Christ removes many of the crutches on which demonization stands.

A Transfer of Jesus' Nature

Likewise, the emphasis of Paul on the indwelling Christ (Colossians 1:27) implies not only a transfer of Jesus' nature into the life of the believer but infusion of His completeness and authority as well. If Christ dwells within, can that person be less than complete? Hardly. To suggest otherwise is to erode the very person of Jesus Christ.

Then there is the matter of Peter. He receives authority to bind and loose (Matthew 16:19). What is the theological basis for his doing so? Is it his special status in Church history or is it his special status in Jesus Christ in whom he believed and in whom he lived? The answer is self-evident, especially when we consider that later the disciples at large also received the power to bind and loose (18:18).

And upon what basis might we assume that the disciples of Jesus Christ bound and loosed? Did they too have special status in time and space? Or was it likewise because they were indwelt by Jesus Christ and empowered by the Holy Spirit?

The Colossians were told that they were "complete in him" (2:10, KJV). Paul again used the concept which implies fullness and maturity, declaring that the prayers of Epaphras had as their object the completeness and full assurance of the Colossians (4:12).

Peter, in his first letter, likewise celebrates the position of believers. "You also, like living stones, are being built into a spiritual house to be a holy priesthood, offering spiritual sacrifices acceptable to God through Jesus Christ" (1 Peter 2:5). And later, Peter reminds his readers that they are a chosen people, a royal priesthood, a holy nation, a people belonging to God, [able to] declare the praises of him who called [them] out of darkness into his wonderful light (2:9, author's paraphrase).

Those who are complete in Jesus Christ are variously described as "mature," "enjoying Christ's fullness," "living stones," "part of a spiritual house," "members of royalty" and receiving "a holy priesthood."

All of this takes us back to the verse so celebrated by A.B. Simpson: "Christ in you, the hope of glory" (Colossians 1:27). Jesus made it clear during His years of ministry that, "[o]n that day you will realize that I am in my Father, and you are in me, and I am in you" (John 14:20). The awareness of the believer's completeness in Jesus Christ is a great affirmation and encouragement to all who have ever struggled to escape bondage and addiction.

But there is another side to this marvelous coin: Those who are complete in Jesus Christ and in whom He dwells may speak with authority and act upon the authority He imparts. This foundational awareness of our faith gives us a platform for exercising the authority of Christ. This follows an earlier biblical pattern: Jesus first established His relationship with His disciples, then He sent them with His authority (Luke 10). The same principle and pattern applies to us. We too, having through His blood and His cross gained a relationship with Him, are the possessors of that same authority. The authority to bind and to loose is simply an expression of Christ's indwelling, our completeness in Him and His outworking through us.

You have just read two of the most pivotal paragraphs in this book. I am not just pouring out inconsequential prose. When Christ's indwelling is adequately understood, binding and loosing readily becomes more comprehensible. When Christ dwells in me, the concept that I bind and I loose is not so preposterous after all.

Endnotes

[1] Neil T. Anderson, *The Bondage Breaker* (Eugene, OR: Harvest House Publishers, 1993).

[2] Taken from: *Winning the Spiritual Warfare* by Neil Anderson, Copyright © 1991 by Harvest House Publishers, Eugene, Oregon, 22. Used by permission.

[3] Taken from: *Victory over the Darkness,* pp. 45-47, by Neil T. Anderson, copyright 1990, Regal Books, Ventura, CA 93003. Used by permission.

[4] A.W. Tozer, "God's Greatest Gift to Man" (Camp Hill, PA: Christian Publications, 1995), 3-4.

[5] Albert B. Simpson, "Christ in Me," in *Hymns of the Christian Life* (Camp Hill, PA: Christian Publications, 1978), 166.

[6] Tozer, "God's Greatest Gift," 12.

[7] Ira R. Stanphill, "Room at the Cross for You," in *Amazing Grace* (Grand Rapids, MI: Kregel Publications, 1990), 181.

[8] Anderson, *Victory over the Darkness,* 21.

[9] Neil T. Anderson, *Helping Others Find Freedom in Christ* (Ventura, CA: Regal Books, 1995), 16.

[10] Neil T. Anderson, *Setting Your Church Free* (Ventura, CA: Regal Books, 1994), 271-272.

Bill Finds Freedom

Neil T. Anderson

A man named Bill came to my office one Sunday afternoon. I barely knew him, and I didn't have much time to chat. But I was concerned about Bill, so I began, "I'm glad you're here, Bill. May I ask you a personal question?" Bill nodded. "Have you ever trusted in Christ to be your Lord and your Savior?"

"No."

"Would you like to?"

"I don't know, Neil," Bill answered with a slightly troubled expression.

I brought out a salvation tract and read it through with him. "Do you understand this, Bill?"

"Yes."

"I'll pray a simple prayer of commitment, and you repeat it after me, phrase by phrase, okay?"

"Okay."

"Lord Jesus, I need you," I began.

Bill began to respond. "Lor-r-r. . ." Then he locked up completely. I realized that I had invaded the territory of the strong man, Satan, and he didn't want to let go of Bill.

"Bill, there's a battle going on for you," I said. "I'm going to read some Scripture and pray out loud for you. I'm going to bind the enemy and stand against him. As soon as you can, you just tell Jesus what you believe." His eyes told me that the battle within him was raging.

I started reading Scripture and praying aloud every prayer I could think of to bind Satan and set Bill free. After several minutes of prayer and Scripture, Bill suddenly groaned, "Lord Jesus, I need you." Then he slumped back in his chair like he had just gone ten rounds with the world heavyweight champion. He looked at me with tear-filled eyes and said, "I'm free." I had never used the word "freedom" with him; that was his expression. But he was free and he knew it.[1]

Endnote

[1] Taken from: *The Bondage Breaker, Youth Edition* by Neil Anderson and Dave Park, Copyright © 1993 by Harvest House Publishers, Eugene, Oregon, 91-92. Used by permission.

9

THE AUTHORITY
OF THE BELIEVER

FOUNDATIONAL TO THE UNDERSTANDING of the subject of binding and loosing is the concept of the authority of the believer. Believers' authority could be called the "powerless power" because the one exercising it has no power in or of him- or herself. This authority of the Christian believer is delegated, not inherent authority. It emanates from an outside source. It is vested authority from Omnipotence Himself, intended to flow through each and every believer.

No one has better explained the characteristics of this authority than J.A. MacMillan, missionary and college professor.

> Authority is not prayer, though the worker who prays can alone exercise authority. Moses cried unto the Lord at the Red Sea (Exodus 14:15ff), beseeching Him to work on behalf of His people, only to receive the strong reproof: "Wherefore criest thou unto me? speak unto the children of Israel, that they go forward" [KJV]. And as he lifted his face in amazed protest because the way ahead

was blocked by impassable waves, Jehovah spoke again: "Lift thou up thy rod, and stretch out thine hand over the sea *and divide it*" (14:16, emphasis added). . . . God delights to delegate His power to men when He can find believing and obedient servants to accept and exercise it.[1]

Levels of Authority—The Animal Kingdom

In the scriptural view of the world, authority levels are always evident. Creation itself demonstrates authority. The lion is the king of the beasts and everything else turns aside for him (Proverbs 30:30). That means that if a lion meets a dog on a path, the dog will turn aside—as would a cow, an elephant or an ostrich. Authority (and perhaps survival) makes it so.

If a cow meets a horse on the path, again one must turn aside. It will be the cow—unless she is angry! Why? Because of the authority structures inherent in the animal world. (Now we know why cowboys ride horses!) If perchance a cat meets a dog on the trail, the cat will turn aside—unless of course the dog is very small or the cat is angry! And there is no question about what would happen if a cat should meet a mouse on the trail. Either self-preservation or hunger would surely prevail!

Even among animals of the same kind there are levels of authority. When I was a boy we had a cow named Nancy. She was sloe-eyed, deceptively low-slung and indisputably the boss (or should I say belle?) of the barnyard. When new cows joined the herd, she battled them into submission. When dogs threatened her calf (or any other cow's calf), she charged off to do battle. She was the only cow I ever saw who, at least to my boyish understanding, had a personality and a conscience. It was a sad, sad day when Nancy went to market.

But I learned some memorable lessons about authority from

Nancy. Perhaps you will, too. I am persuaded that if we can see God's authority structure function in nature, we will find ourselves able to understand and experience the authority of the Christian believer.

Authority over Animals

Genesis 1:26 and Psalm 8:4-8 relate the fact that mankind has been given dominion or authority over the animal world.

> Then God said, "Let us make man in our image, in our likeness, and let them rule over the fish of the sea and the birds of the air, over the livestock, over all the earth, and over all the creatures that move along the ground." (Genesis 1:26)

> What is man that you are mindful of him,
>   the son of man that you care for him?
> You made him a little lower than the heavenly beings
>   and crowned him with glory and honor.
> You made him ruler over the works of your hands;
>   you put everything under his feet:
> all flocks and herds,
>   and the beasts of the field,
> the birds of the air,
>   and the fish of the sea,
>   all that swim the paths of the seas.
>   (Psalm 8:4-8)

A child may walk into a herd of cattle and though he or she weighs no more than forty pounds and the animals are an average of 600 pounds each, the herd will divide to give way before that tiny human being.

The farmer in the middle of a field has authority over a charging bull. But if the farmer is not prepared to exert that authority, he had better climb the nearest tree!

A woman is confronted with a mouse in her living room. Although she has authority over the mini-creature, I'm not sure she will be willing to get down off the furniture to exert it!

Why does man wield such power? How does man wield such power? The answer? We have God-delegated authority over animals. There are, of course, exceptions because the world is sin-contaminated. The exceptions only prove the rule.

Missionary David Thompson tells a marvelous story from the life of pioneer missionary Don Fairley of Gabon, Africa. Always gifted with animals, Fairley worked at a zoo in Santa Barbara prior to going to the mission field. One day in 1925, an earthquake hit. We pick up the story from there.

"Don was working with his animals when the first shocks hit. Seconds later, the chauffeur for the Fleischmann estate appeared at the entrance to the zoo and yelled for everybody to get away as quickly as possible before any of the animals got loose. The atmosphere of the compound became one of terror.

"Don's first thought was for the animals under his care. He felt a sense of responsibility for them and, despite the chauffeur's pleas, was not willing to leave. Seconds later, the limousine roared off down the road with all the workers of the estate and the zoo inside. Only Don remained.

"He grabbed a shotgun from his office and ran to examine the cages. A black panther was hanging upside down from the roof of his cage, snarling. But the door was secure. The leopard in a nearby cage was leaping back and forth in panic, but the cage had not been seriously damaged. The monkeys were screaming. In the bird cages, dozens of them had banged themselves on the screens and were lying on the ground stunned or dead.

"Suddenly, Don heard his elephant Culver trumpeting from the stockade behind him. He picked up his small hooked stick and ran toward the enclosure. The stockade gate was still closed, but the elephant had escaped onto the road leading toward the highway. His ears spread wide in rage, his eyes red with panic, the frantic animal was pulling up five- and six-inch California oaks by their roots one after another, swinging them over his back and throwing them to the side of the road.

"When he saw Don out of the corner of his eye, he stopped and wheeled. As the elephant lumbered toward him, Don stood perfectly still. The huge animal did not hesitate, but, as though it were in battle, rushed at the lone man in front of him. There was no place for Don to run or hide.

"'In Jesus' name, shut your mouth!' Don cried in as loud a voice as he could. At the sound of his voice, the elephant stopped abruptly just ten feet from Don. The animal lowered its trunk, dropped its ears and began making the familiar squeaks of companionship elephants make to others in the herd. It drew its breath, wrapped its trunk around Don, lifted him up into the air and, turning him upside down, lowered him gently to the ground. Still trembling with fright, Don caressed Culver's trunk and talked to him gently until the animal gradually calmed down. Then, with his stick over Culver's ear, Don guided him around and around the lot, eventually leading him back into the broken stockade."[2]

Don Fairley was able to exert his authority over Culver because God, as part of His creation plan, has established that humans have authority over the animal kingdom. That night, Don Fairley slept with his arm over the elephant.

Authority over One Another

Now, we move to another level—one person exerting authority

over another person. The centurion who talked with Jesus understood this.

> "Lord, I do not deserve to have you come under my roof. But just say the word, and my servant will be healed. For I myself am a man under authority, with soldiers under me. I tell this one, 'Go,' and he goes; and that one, 'Come,' and he comes. I say to my servant, 'Do this,' and he does it." (Matthew 8:8-9)

The Scriptures go on to say that Jesus was "astonished" and healed the man's servant "at that very hour."

The mayor of the city, the chairman of the board, the president of the company, the husband of the home—all have positions of authority. An army wouldn't be an army without a command structure. Without such basic authority structures, there would be anarchy and chaos.

If we can understand the function of human authority, we will easily grasp the principles of believers' authority. Read on.

Authority over Spiritual Forces

Above the levels where human authority exists, there is a spiritual realm occupied by spiritual forces. There are spirit beings who, through the fall of man in Eden, have gained a place where they are able to dominate people.

> As for you, you were dead in your transgressions and sins, in which you used to live when you followed the ways of this world and of the ruler of the kingdom of the air, the spirit who is now at work in those who are disobedient. (Ephesians 2:1-2)

I doubt that evil spirits could gain dominance over persons who have never sinned. Unfortunately, we are all sinners and thus vulnerable to their insidious control.

Jesus confronted a spirit which had bound a woman for eighteen years.

> On a Sabbath Jesus was teaching in one of the synagogues, and a woman was there who had been crippled by a spirit for eighteen years. . . . When Jesus saw her, he called her forward and said to her, "Woman, you are set free from your infirmity." (Luke 13:10-12)

Satanic power had somehow gained control over this woman for eighteen long years. Although I am not suggesting she was necessarily victimized because of her own sin, Adam's sin certainly was an antecedent to her bondage.

Paul confronted a spirit of divination which had taken control of a young girl. Acts 16:18 tells us that that spirit too was dislodged in Jesus' name:

> Paul became so troubled that he turned around and said to the spirit, "In the name of Jesus Christ I command you to come out of her!" At that moment the spirit left her.

These demonic spirits, we must note, are themselves under authority. Satan is the head of a vast hierarchy of principalities, powers, rulers and forces of spiritual wickedness in high places.

> For our struggle is not against flesh and blood, but against the rulers, against the authorities, against the powers of this dark world and against the spiritual forces of evil in the heavenly realms. (Ephesians 6:12)

How many levels there are in this dark system we do not know. But the Bible does speak of the prince of Persia and the prince of Greece (Daniel 10:13-20), indicating that there may be satanic underlings who have specific authority over geographical areas of the world. We do know that Satan is not omnipotent, omniscient nor omnipresent. Because he has to travel around his worldwide kingdom of darkness, his projects and activities must necessarily be carried out by subordinates.

In the last paragraph I introduced two additional authority levels which exist upon the testimony of Scripture and those who have been involved in deliverance ministries. Studying the names and ranks of demons is an investigation which, though somewhat enlightening and intriguing, tends to bring an unhealthy focus on Satan who is properly and significantly called the prince of this world. For that reason, we will not pause here.

The Believer's Authority

The next level of authority—in addition to animal, human and demonic levels, including Satan of course—may surprise you. It is that of the believer. A more visual illustration of what we have been saying about authority structures can be found on the following page.

The powerful fact is that at the moment a person believes in Jesus Christ he or she changes position (represented by the arrow). Whether the believer feels it or not, he or she *is* above the enemy. If there is one page Satan would like to tear out of the Bible, it is the one on which these words were written to early believers:

> And God raised us up with Christ and seated us with him in the heavenly realms in Christ Jesus. (Ephesians 2:6)

The Authority of the Believer

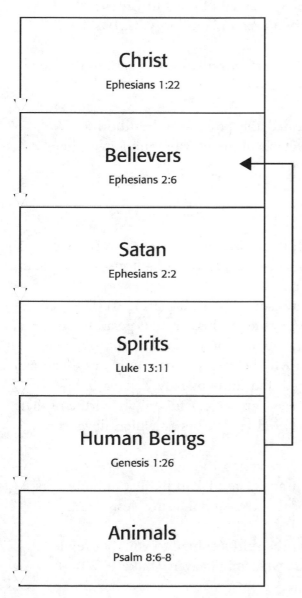

Christ

Ephesians 1:22

Believers

Ephesians 2:6

Satan

Ephesians 2:2

Spirits

Luke 13:11

Human Beings

Genesis 1:26

Animals

Psalm 8:6-8

When a person believes in Jesus Christ, by that act, identification with Jesus Christ in the heavenlies takes place. The believer thus gains in Christ an ascendancy over the powers.

Figure I

Colossians further describes the believer's position:

> . . . and you have been given fullness in Christ, who is
> the head over every power and authority. (2:10)

We must not forget the further revelation of Paul to the Colossians:

> And having disarmed the powers and authorities, he
> made a public spectacle of them, triumphing over them
> by the cross. (2:15)

Game Over

Jesus Christ, through the power of His death and resurrection, asserted and now maintains this position of authority. For Satan, it is already "game over."

Now the delightful, awesome, even staggering truth is that the Christian believer, by virtue of his or her position in Jesus Christ, shares the Savior's total dominance and mastery over Satan. That is the reason why believers are the only ones who can confront the demonized and authentically deliver them.[3] And, may I repeat, such believers are successful only by virtue of their position in Jesus Christ and His authority which flows through them.

The tendency upon discovering the immense power in believers' authority is to be unduly fascinated by it. Certainly it is an awesome thing and, for that reason, I am sure, Jesus said,

> Do not rejoice that the spirits submit to you, but rejoice
> that your names are written in heaven. (Luke 10:20)

Witch Hunting

It needs also to be said that exorcism should never, never become an end in itself. Contemporary Church history is strewn with the wreckage of good ministries which have been deflected into witch hunting and other hurtful emphases. The person who sets up a deliverance center and invites everyone to come with their demon problems will get far more than he or she bargained for. Deliverance does not lead the ministry, it emerges in the midst of ministry (Acts 16:16ff). A ministry which attaches any more than a peripheral interest to deliverance is a ministry threatened with disaster.

Other Avenues of Authority

There are other avenues of Christian authority similar to those in Mark 16. I have met Christian brothers who are greatly blessed in praying for the sick. Invariably they understand that Christ's authority over disease, as explained in Matthew 10:1, has been extended to them.

> He called his twelve disciples to him and gave them authority to drive out evil spirits and to heal every disease and sickness.

In addition, it is clear from Scripture that the ministry of leading new believers into the fullness of the Holy Spirit is one of authority. Simon the sorcerer may have had bad motives, but he did recognize that Peter and John had a ministry of authority (Acts 8:19). Through the apostolic ministry of authority, the Samaritan believers were filled with the Holy Spirit (8:17).

Other Examples

As I observed earlier (and the repetition is essential), there are some biblical illustrations which lend additional insight here. Jesus ordered His disciples to go and loose the colt for His triumphal entry into Jerusalem (Mark 11:1-6). Christ's supernatural power was no doubt sufficient to bring that colt spontaneously to His side or even to create a colt for the job. Instead, He sent His disciples to do the loosing. Jesus did only what was necessary! He described the colt and its location, but He left something for the disciples to do. And they did it.

Similarly, Jesus raised Lazarus from the dead even after the process of decay had set in. But though He unleashed His resurrection power into Lazarus' corpse (John 11:39-44), the disciples loosed him at Jesus' command.

Spurgeon believed, and I concur, that there are many like Lazarus in the Church today.[4] They are alive, but still hampered by grave clothes. They need to be loosed! Loosing them is a disciple's ministry.

Jesus also loosed a woman from a spirit of infirmity which had gripped her for eighteen years (Luke 13:10-16). Paul and Silas were in prison, but through praise their bonds were loosed (Acts 16:26). Isaiah, too, apparently sensed the necessity of loosing by declaring the loosing power of fasting (Isaiah 58:6).

A Warning

If binding and loosing is a ministry which at least in part is directed at the counter-kingdom, if it is a ministry directed against Satan—and it sometimes is—then I must give a warning: Caution needs to be exercised. As Dr. Tozer once observed, "The devil knows more judo than you've ever heard of."[5] We must remember that in disputing about Moses' body, even Michael the archangel did not dare bring a railing accusation against Satan (Jude 9). Any believer who is so foolish as to think he or she can taunt Satan will certainly get trouble—and lots of it. On the other hand, no believer sensing his or her absolute authority in Jesus Christ should ever fear the enemy.

All this teaching is based on a basic theological fact: Jesus Christ is far above all principalities and powers. We are complete in Him and seated with Him in heavenly places (Ephesians 1:20-22; 2:6). Each and every one of the tremendous spiritual weapons Paul describes begins and ends in Jesus Christ (2 Corinthians 10:3-6).

To live and experience Jesus Christ means, among other things, to exercise His power, to allow it to flow through us. Some will draw back in fear. They do not believe it can really be true that such authority is committed to believers. Like rookie policemen, complete with uniforms, boots, badges and training, they stand quaking at the curb. They are sure that if they stride out into the traffic and hold up their hands, nothing will happen.

Let me assure you that because of Jesus Christ the traffic *will* halt. If you call a halt to the forces of darkness they will, they must obey. Isn't it time we stepped off the curb and into the flow of life's traffic, out where the needs are? I think so.

Yield yourself completely to the Holy Spirit's control. Believe. Act. What happens will be awesome indeed!

Endnotes

[1] John A. MacMillan, *The Authority of the Believer* (Camp Hill, PA: Christian Publications, 1997), 62.

[2] David C. Thompson, *Beyond the Mist* (Camp Hill, PA: Christian Publications, 1998), 67-69. Other illustrations of human authority over animals are

found in William Linder, Jr., *Andrew Murray* (Minneapolis, MN: Bethany House Publishers, 1996), 41-42; and A.B. Simpson, *Christ in the Bible Commentary* (Camp Hill, PA: Christian Publications, 1992), 4:163.

[3] At issue here is the validity of the exorcisms that are produced in most if not all the religions of the world. My view is that they are not authentic deliverances, since the victims remain in Satan's control.

[4] Charles Haddon Spurgeon, "Unbinding Lazarus," in *C.H. Spurgeon's Sermons on the Miracles* (Grand Rapids, MI: Zondervan, 1958), 231-244.

[5] A.W. Tozer as cited by K. Neill Foster, *Warfare Weapons* (Camp Hill, PA: Christian Publications, 1995), 123.

The Case of the "Unplugged" Pastors

Name withheld

One day three pastors with whom we had been working in Africa came to our home. No sooner had we invited them in than they proceeded to lambaste us with all kinds of accusations. We were quite taken aback, not only because of the nature of the accusations (all untrue), but also because of the spirit in which they were made. We could not imagine what had provoked such an attack.

My wife left the room for a moment to check something on the stove. While there, she called upon the Lord and then, recognizing the spiritual dimension of this otherwise unwarranted attack, she bound Satan. The moment she walked back into the living room and sat down, the pastor who was speaking (rather vehemently) abruptly stopped talking, as if he had been "unplugged." It was shocking and unexpected, much like the experience of being in a roomful of people chitchatting and suddenly, by coincidence, everyone stops talking at once. After a moment of silence, one of the other pastors said, "Let's pray and go home."

To me, what is so striking about this incident is, first of all, the immediate and dramatic effect of the binding, and secondly, the unfortunate fact that the spirit or spirits that had to be bound were operating through Christian workers.

Part IV

Binding and Loosing: The Exegetical Factors

There are special places in the Scriptures that, when pressed (or even dissected), exude unique richness. This is wonderfully true in the binding, loosing, overcoming and forgiving passages.

Like a rose when crushed, the biblical text, when examined in this way, extends its own enduring fragrance.

10

THE MISSIOLOGICAL PERSPECTIVE

I N THE LAST CHAPTER WE LEARNED that above the levels of human authority there is a spiritual realm occupied by a hierarchy of spirit beings who through the fall of man in Eden have gained a place of ascendancy over people.

We also learned a powerful fact and wonderful secret: When someone believes in Jesus Christ, that person takes his or her place with Him in the heavenlies far above those rulers of darkness. Believers, because of the life of Christ within them, have authority over Satan and his emissaries!

In Matthew 12, a blind, mute and demon-possessed man was brought to Jesus. He "healed him," verse 22 says, "so that he could both talk and see." Immediately, the Pharisees accused Jesus of driving out the demons by Beelzebub. Jesus responded by telling them that a kingdom, a city or a household divided against itself cannot survive. "If I drive out demons by Beelzebub," He continues, "by whom do your people drive them out?" (12:27). What follows is a logical question: "How can anyone enter a strong man's house and carry off his possessions unless he first ties up the strong man?" (12:29). In other words, if Christ— or His followers—wish to rob Satan's kingdom of those under his control, does not the strong man (Satan) have to first be bound?

The answer is yes. But what does that have to say to us about evangelism—the missionary perspective? What does that have to say about witnessing to our neighbor? What does that have to say to the pastor who preaches every Sunday from the pulpit? What does that have to say to parents who wish to lead their children to Christ? What does that have to say to the missionary who is seeking to win those who have never heard the gospel? What are the implications of this binding and loosing of the strong man in our day? To find the answers to those questions, we begin by checking out the "strong man" passages in Mark and Luke.

> No one can enter a strong man's house and carry off his possessions unless he first ties up the strong man. Then he can rob his house. (Mark 3:27)

In Luke 11, Jesus emphasizes the Stronger Man:

> When a strong man, fully armed, guards his own house, his possessions are safe. But when someone stronger attacks and overpowers him, he takes away the armor in which the man trusted and divides up the spoils. (Luke 11:21-22)

In all three contexts (Matthew, Mark and Luke), Jesus is defending Himself against the accusation that He is functioning under the inspiration of Satan. Every kingdom divided against itself will fall, He asserts. However, Jesus seems to imply that when you bind Satan, the strong man, as He, the Stronger Man, is doing, it is then only a matter of course to spoil the enemy's house.

Is the Strong Man Really Bound?

Did Jesus really bind the strong man? Was He the first to bind the strong man? The commentators suggest that He did indeed, particularly in His hour of temptation. One says it most succinctly: "Satan is already bound though not so as to be rendered completely impotent."[1] Another asks,

> When was the strong man bound? . . . Maybe there is no answer to that question, but if there is, it is that Satan was bound during Jesus' temptations in the wilderness. . . . When Jesus faced the Tempter in the wilderness and conquered him, something happened. For the first time Satan found someone whom not all his wiles could seduce, and whom not all his attacks could conquer. From that time the power of Satan has never been quite the same. He is no longer the all-conquering power of darkness; he is the defeated power of sin. The defenses are breached; the enemy is not yet conquered; but his power can never be the same again and Jesus can help others win the victory He himself won.[2]

If Satan indeed was bound, how did he get loose? And is he still going about as a roaring lion in this age (1 Peter 5:8)? Certainly he is loose and roaring about. This brings us to a very important observation on the whole subject of binding Satan: Even the binding done by our Lord was situational and local, an interim binding of the strong man in a specific context of conflict and battle.

Moreover, the book of Revelation announces an eschatological binding of Satan (20:2), which suggests by its finality, as the commentators seem to agree, that even the binding which surrounded Jesus' temptation and victory in the desert was a binding only in the context in which it took place.

The complete defeat of Satan took place at the cross. Before His crucifixion Jesus told His disciples that the prince of this world would be driven out (John 12:31). Later, when He was about to ascend to heaven, He comforted the disciples with the news that the prince of this world "now stands condemned" (16:11). At the cross. That's where Satan was defeated.

Still, we all recognize that the counter-kingdom continues to exhibit its power in the interim until the time when Satan will be bound for a thousand years (Revelation 20:2). As a prince whose time is short, Satan pursues his doomed cause relentlessly and malevolently. One way of understanding Satan's situation is to think of a football game. There is a point at which the game is over, but there is still time on the clock. Satan still has some time on the clock, but it's short. In this day, the day of the Church, as the battle is joined, the binding and loosing of the strong man continues in anticipation of a coming day.

Jesus Defends His Ministry

Let's return for a moment to the Matthew 12 passage where the Pharisees are accusing Jesus of driving out demons with the power of Satan. Having already bound Satan in the wilderness, Jesus is now explaining the process and defending His ministry of deliverance. His defense, an apologetic, was necessary.

> Apologetics is the reasoned defense of the Christian religion. . . . It is also the defense and justification of the Christian worldview, the Christian faith, the Christian God, the Christian servant (and all that is of Christ and God) against the attacks, slanders, counterfeits, and deceptions of all the forces, powers and persons arrayed against them.[3]

Notice further that Jesus explains that a kingdom cannot be divided against itself. Curiously, no one in that crowd of Pharisees was disputing that anything was happening, as might be argued today. All concerned in that back-and-forth battle were agreed that demons were indeed being driven out. Apparently, the exit phenomena were totally convincing.

> But what is important for us is that this charge of Christ's being in league with Satan proves that there was something extraordinary to explain. If there had not been mighty works too remarkable to ignore and too notorious to deny, His enemies would never have taken refuge in so extravagant an hypothesis. . . . We have evidence, unintentionally given in support of the miracles wrought by Christ.[4]

Notice also that according to the context, the strong man represents Satan. God is omnipotent, the devil is not. He is, however, powerful. His power is great, but limited. He is potent, but not omnipotent. He may correctly be called the "strong man."

Notice too that the strong man has goods, even a house, which may be plundered. He has treasures, and clearly those treasures may be spoiled. Moreover, before the strong man's goods can be spoiled, he must first be bound so that his house can be entered.

One gets the perception of a dwelling with a single door. There, at the door, blocking all access, is the owner of the house—a massive, hulking, ferocious specimen. Behind him are the treasures of his household, guarded threateningly by this awesome and foreboding strong man.

If we pay attention to Luke's record, we realize further that the strong man comes "fully armed" (Luke 11:21-22). Some attention needs to be given to the armory of Satan. With what does the leader of the counter-kingdom protect his treasures? When the strong man is attacked is he overpowered? And is his armor in which he trusts taken away? Are there incidents of evangelistic and missiological nature in which the Church first binds the strong man and strips him of his armor? Could those times and places be connected with the great evangelistic ingatherings of history, the people movements from around the world where entire populations have rushed into the kingdom of God?

The answer is undoubtedly yes.

D.A. Carson, a well-known evangelical scholar, insists that the reference to possessions preserves the metaphor of the house and has no relation to demonic possession except metaphorically.[5] Are treasures in the strong man's house the souls of men? These teachings of Jesus Christ have direct bearing upon evangelistic endeavors and the missionary enterprise, as illustrated by the following incidents.

Holy Burglary

Timothy Warner relates the story of pioneer missionary John Paton which demonstrates the power of binding the strong man in order to spoil his goods.

Three of the most potent sorcerers in the New Hebrides Islands threatened to kill Paton through the power of an evil spirit named Nahak. Paton responded, "They have said they can kill me by Nahak, but I challenge them to do it if they can, without arrow or spear, club or musket, for I deny that they have any power against me . . . by their sorcery."[6] Warner explains what happened:

> When after a week these three demonized men were unable to do any harm to Paton—when they tried to resort to spears, God froze their arms in the air so they could not throw them—you may be sure that the peo-

ple "heard" the gospel with a clarity with which they did not hear it simply coming from the mouth of the missionary.[7]

A similar incident took place in Gabon associated with the ministry of Don Fairley, mentioned earlier. A widow in an isolated village had become a believer in Jesus Christ. The persecution was intense, and her life was taken. Consequently, the opponents of her message were encouraged to believe that the new teaching would not prevail.

However, a young evangelist named Theophile Mouckagni became greatly emboldened by the martyrdom of the elderly woman. Believers multiplied and matters came to a crisis one evening.

"The long-awaited confrontation finally began one night around midnight when a large group of *ngangas* [witch doctors] entered the village with flaming torches, magic ebony sticks with heads carved on them and a tightly woven box containing the skull of a powerful Bwitist ancestor. [Bwiti was one of the most powerful gods in that region.] The *ngangas* placed these objects on the ground around the little house where Theophile and [his wife] Pembe lived. As people in neighboring houses watched, the *ngangas* buried other objects in the ground to seal the Christians off from their source of power. Others carried wood and built a huge bonfire directly in front of Theophile's house.

"Far into the night they danced around the fire and around the house, chanting curses of death, sterility and madness upon the occupants. As the pounding of the drums increased, the *ngangas* whirled and leaped until the people watching in awe from cracked doorways no longer believed them to be merely human.

"At the peak of the frenzy, the men lit pitch torches and, holding them high, danced around the house. Theophile, Pembe and about ten Christians inside the house alternately prayed and sang. The men outside moved closer and closer to the house with their torches, finally bringing them down to the thatch roof. But for some reason, and despite many attempts, the *ngangas* could not get the flames to touch the straw.

"The *ngangas* abruptly broke from their dance around the house and returned to the fire to drink more *iboga* juice [a powerful drug]. Again they rushed at the house with their torches, but though they tried repeatedly, they simply could not cause their torches to make contact with the tinder-dry palm roofing. As the hours passed, the torches and the bonfire burned lower and the dancing weakened. The first streaks of dawn lightened the sky and the drums and chanting wavered, then stopped. The exhausted priests of Bwiti, with their smoking torches, slunk into the forest to regroup.

"When the *ngangas* had gone, Theophile and his little band stepped out of the house into the morning light and surveyed the scene. The people of the village also stepped out of their houses to see what had happened. They watched in amazement as Theophile and the other Christians pulled up the sacred poles and dug up the objects their tormentors had buried in the ground. Piling everything on the embers, the Christians unceremoniously reduced the *ngangas'* precious objects to ashes."

"Do Not Come"

"That morning Theophile wrote a letter and sent it by runner to the mission station at Bongolo.

> Dear brothers in Jesus,
> Our enemies have told the people that we are trusting in the white man to save us from them. They say that we have come to upset and to bring shame upon our

leaders and upon our people and that we can only stand because of the power of the white man. They accuse us of speaking publicly about sacred matters that should be kept secret and have denounced us to the people. Last night they tried to kill us, but God would not let them touch us. I have told them that God is living and present with us, that His Spirit is upon us and that we are not alone. We know that we are not alone, *so do not come* [emphasis added], do not approach us, but pray that here on this ground the people will know the truth that the Holy Spirit of Jesus is present and that the Son of God has power and authority.

"The missionaries and Christians in Bongolo were deeply disturbed by Theophile's letter, but they recognized that he had cut to the heart of the matter: Victory would only be total if God demonstrated His power over Bwiti using African believers. That day and night the Christians and missionaries at Bongolo fasted and prayed for the tiny church of Ivouta.

"The day was quiet and Theophile, Pembe and the other Christians with them slept. That evening the Christians again gathered in Theophile and Pembe's house to pray and sing. They knew that the *ngangas* would come again.

"Near midnight the priests of Bwiti returned carrying torches and spears. Once again they placed sacred objects and carved sticks around the house and built a bonfire. Fortified with *iboga*, they danced to the drums around the bonfire. When they were ready, they each took up a long, steel-tipped spear, encircled the house and on a signal, plunged their spears toward the flimsy walls. To their utter amazement, their spears never touched the bark walls. Instead, they were deflected as though an invisible shield stood between themselves and the house. They tried repeatedly, but they could not touch the house. Suddenly fearful, they withdrew to the forest in confusion. When the sun came up the next morning, the *ngangas* had scattered like so many fruit bats."[8]

Some may call this a power encounter. I agree. It is a power encounter in which our Lord's binding power prevailed, publicly and dramatically.

Currently in Gabon, two or three generations after the awful battles and the life-and-death struggles in the apostolic ministry of Don Fairley, a great harvest has come. I have been in many of the mission fields of the world, but never have I seen men and women rushing pell-mell into the kingdom as is happening in modern Gabon.

True Treasures Seized

In the case of all evangelistic endeavors, the true treasures are human souls. Indeed, "What good is it for a man to gain the whole world, yet forfeit his soul?" (Mark 8:36). The immense wealth of human souls under the control and domination of the strong man *can* be spoiled. The rescue takes place when the strong man Satan is bound. Then his house may be plundered. The intent is clearly missiological.

Jessie Penn-Lewis' article in *The Alliance Weekly*, "How to Pray for Missionaries," is one of the clearest statements relating Matthew's principle of binding and loosing to missions.

Here is an excerpt, her argument for an aggressive stance in missionary warfare.

> From the very beginning of His ministry, our Lord Jesus went forward with a steady, aggressive warfare against the powers of darkness. He also gave to His disciples the same authority, and in every place where

they went, they had two main things to do: i.e., to preach and to cast out demons (Mark 3:14, 15).

The Lord refused to deal with flesh and blood or with the secular powers of His time although He thereby disappointed many who would have accepted Him as the Messiah had He done so. His one objective, from the time of His baptism in Jordan to the hour of His finished work on Calvary, was the conquest of the prince of this world so that He might redeem his captives and put him to an open shame (Colossians 2:14, 15). For this purpose He came into the world (Luke 4:18; John 10:1-18); and on the eve of the Cross He was able to say, "Now shall the prince of this world be cast out" (John 12:31).[9]

Penn-Lewis had earlier addressed the authority of the believer in spiritual warfare in a missiological context at an 1897 China Inland Mission conference.[10]

Foundational Missiology

Not surprisingly, binding and loosing became a foundational understanding for the missionary outreach of The Christian and Missionary Alliance dating back to 1937. It is rooted even earlier in the actual missionary experiences of men like J.A. MacMillan and Robert A. Jaffray.[11]

In 1921, Carrie Judd Montgomery wrote,

Years ago we did not know how to loose people that were bound by the Devil. . . . Often our prayers cannot be answered until we are able to speak with authority and loose the one whom Satan has bound. . . . The Lord shows us in Matthew 12:29 that we "must first bind the strong man" before we can "spoil his goods." I can never begin to tell you what this power has meant in our ministry the last few years.[12]

Binding Is First

Similarly, missionaries intent upon reaching unreached people groups and resistant populations need to pay attention to this Scripture. The proper interpretation seems to be that first the strong man must be bound, then the unreached peoples and resistant populations can be sprung free from the deception and control of Satan.

Using the analogy of military strategy, other Christian leaders counsel binding the strong man before launching into a spiritual warfare offensive:

> A wise leader should first attempt to knock out his enemy's command headquarters and air support. If these elements can be disabled, then enemy ground troops can be crippled and scattered at will.[13]

Biblical scholar William Hendricksen recognizes this missiological purpose in Matthew:

> The devil is being, and is progressively going to be, deprived of his "furniture," that is, of the souls and bodies of men, and this not only through healings but also through a mighty missionary program, reaching first the Jews but later on the nations in general (John 12:31, 32; Romans 1:16). . . . Note how also in Luke 10:17, 18 the "fall of Satan as lightning from heaven" is recorded in connection with the return and report of the seventy missionaries.[14]

G. Campbell Morgan also understands Matthew's intent, holding the belief that the treasures, the "furniture" in the strong man's house, are indeed lost people:

> God's children who have entered into His victory by the Cross, also know something of what it is to bind the strong one. His Cross is the force that sets us free to spoil the house of the strong one, and rescue other souls.[15]

There are reasons, I think, that the Holy Spirit has placed this pivotal passage in all three of the synoptic Gospels. Each in its own way reinforces the missiological and evangelistic intent in binding the strong man and loosing the evangelistic impulse. All too often attempts are made to brush by the strong man to get to the work of the Lord. No Christian workers are more vulnerable to this error than the materialistic, secularistic, technological and spiritually insensitive missionaries from the Western world. If this study of the relationship of binding and loosing to evangelism and missions draws any conclusion at all, it is that such "brushing by" procedure is a grave, grave error in kingdom work—and that binding the strong man is a "first" work.

Endnotes

[1] R.V.G. Tasker, *The Gospel According to Matthew: An Introduction and Commentary* (Grand Rapids, MI: Eerdmans, 1961), 128.

[2] William Barclay, *The Gospel of Matthew,* The Daily Bible Study Series (Philadelphia: The Westminster Press, 1975), 2:36-37.

[3] Elio Cuccaro as cited by K. Neill Foster, "Apologetics and the Deliverance Ministry" (paper presented to the annual meeting of the Evangelical Theological Society, Philadelphia, November 1995), 1.

[4] Alfred Plummer, *An Exegetical Commentary on the Gospel of St. Matthew* (Grand Rapids, MI: Baker Book House, 1982), 176.

[5] D.A. Carson, *Matthew,* The Expositor's Bible Commentary (Grand Rapids, MI: Zondervan, 1984), 290.

[6] Timothy M. Warner, *Spiritual Warfare* (Wheaton, IL: Crossway Books, 1991), 128.

[7] Ibid., 129.

[8] David C. Thompson, *Beyond the Mist* (Camp Hill, PA: Christian Publications, 1998), 158-162.

[9] Jessie Penn-Lewis, "How to Pray for Missionaries," *The Alliance Weekly*, 12 June 1937, 73-74.

[10] Penn-Lewis, *The Warfare with Satan* (Fort Washington, PA: Christian Literature Crusade, 1963), 63, 65.

[11] J.A. MacMillan, *The Authority of the Believer* (Camp Hill, PA: Christian Publications, 1997).

[12] Carrie Judd Montgomery, *Triumphs of Faith* (Oakland, CA: Triumphs of Faith, 1921), 68.

[13] Jim Croft, "Waging War in the Heavenlies," *New Wine*, March 1977, 7.

[14] William Hendricksen, *New Testament Contemporary Exposition of the Gospel According to Matthew* (Grand Rapids, MI: Baker Book House, 1973), 527.

[15] G. Campbell Morgan, *The Gospel According to Matthew* (Old Tappan, NJ: Fleming H. Revell, 1929), 130.

Binding Satan among the Dafing

During the writing of this book, Wyman and Carma Nelson, missionaries to Burkina Faso, stopped by my office for a visit. In the process of the conversation, I mentioned that I was writing a book about binding and loosing. Wyman's face lit up, and it soon became evident that I had yet another dramatic incident to include in this text.

About 1992 an evangelistic trip was planned to the town of Yé (YEH), a center of the Dafing tribe of Burkina Faso. For years, perhaps as many as forty, attempts had been made to establish a church in this town. But it had not happened.

This evangelistic campaign, however, would be different. It was reinforced by five pastors, plus American visitors from Pennsylvania. The first day in Yé, the group spent their time in prayer. That night the gospel was preached with seemingly little effect and much inattentiveness. The next day, there was more prayer.

Concurrently with the prayer focus, a man from the community began to banter with one of the pastors to whom he was related. The harangue went something like this: "I am stronger than you. The spirit we have is stronger than the spirit you have." The missionaries and other pastors in the team were mostly unaware of this sidebar activity, that is, until missionary Steve Clouser prayed. His prayer concluded with the words, "We now bind Satan in this tribe and in this town, in the name of Jesus Christ."

At that instant, the man who earlier had been harassing and who now was sitting passively within earshot of the prayer meetings was suddenly struck from behind. Mrs. Nelson likened it to a person being hit with a baseball bat on the back of the neck. The man was flung out of his chair and landed spread-eagled on the ground. Groggily, he finally got to his feet and wandered away. Only later did the pastor who was related to the man fill in the details.

"Do you know who this man is who was harassing me?" he asked the prayer group. "He's the most powerful witch doctor in this area. He's the man to whom everyone goes when sacrifices are to be offered."

That night and in the days that followed, the Dafing began to believe in Jesus Christ. There is a church in that town today. And one godly leader has sensed the change. "The light has come to the Dafing," he says.

Indeed, it has—through the public binding of the strong man in a missiological context.

11

THE SYNOPTIC PERSPECTIVE

THE SYNOPTIC GOSPELS OF MATTHEW, Mark and Luke are by definition the perspectives of three men who were witnesses to the events surrounding the life and death of Jesus. Through comparing and contrasting these accounts, we will now proceed to further augment our understanding of binding and loosing.

As we have already observed, Matthew was the one chosen by the Holy Spirit to uniquely address Jesus' words and teaching about binding and loosing. But each of the other Gospels is valuable both for what it says and what it doesn't say. For instance, nothing is said about loosing in Matthew 12, nor in Mark 3, nor in Luke 11, but there are references to binding. Matthew is unique in that there are no parallel passages in Mark or Luke for the binding *and* loosing passages of Matthew 16 and 18. Chapter 12 of Matthew deals only with binding.

Similarly, the synoptic references to the binding of the strong man as described by Jesus do not address loosing. The loosing of the colt is described later in Matthew 21 and Luke describes the loosing ministry of Jesus in healing in chapter 13. If you are thoroughly confused by now, the point I am making is that in the synoptic parallels relating to the strong man, there is no mention of loosing. Only binding.

Some conclusions might be drawn about this balance in Scripture:

- All the synoptics associate binding (or overcoming) with the defeat of the strong man, who, by general though not total agreement of the commentators, is Satan.

- The focus in Matthew 16 is on Peter, the keys, the Church, the kingdom, binding and, of course, loosing.

- Matthew chapter 18 deals with church discipline, binding and loosing and the "whatever" which relates binding and loosing to various objectives.

Mark's Account

Since Mark is commonly believed to have written before both Matthew and Luke, his comments will be considered first, then contrasted with Matthew's text.

> In fact, no one can enter a strong man's house and carry off his possessions unless he first ties up the strong man. Then he can rob his house. (Mark 3:27)

> Or again, how can anyone enter a strong man's house and carry off his possessions unless he first ties up the strong man? Then he can rob his house. (Matthew 12:29)

Although Mark makes an affirmation of fact, and whereas Matthew poses a question, the similarities between these two verses are impressive. 1) The strong man has a house which can be entered. 2) There are possessions which can be carried off. 3) Binding comes first, followed by the carrying off of possessions. 4) Both passages assume that the house can indeed be spoiled and that the possessions formerly belonging to the strong man can be carried off. 5) Beelzebub, the "prince of demons" i.e., Satan, is mentioned in both.

Mark is silent concerning casting out demons by the Holy Spirit, whereas Matthew mentions it. Another issue Matthew picks up is the admission by Jesus that the sons of Abraham were driving out demons. Mark is silent on that matter.

Mark's tendency toward truncation means in this case that not a great deal is divulged about the actual binding of the strong man. Matthew's additions to the body of information by their detail indicate the presence of an authentic eyewitness—himself. If Mark, having written earlier, is one of Matthew's sources, Mark apparently is not the only source. Then, of course we have the inspiration of the Holy Spirit (2 Timothy 3:16).

Luke's Account

When we move to Luke, the textual mine is much richer. Probably the most significant change is that Luke distances himself from Matthew's usage of *deo* and *luo* (binding and loosing), and embraces *nikao,* a word which has the English translation of "overcome," or "overpower."[1] Nike™, which means "winner," is a modern trade name that helps us understand the meanings of *nikao.*

> When a strong man, fully armed, guards his own house, his possessions are safe. But when someone stronger attacks and overpowers [*nikao*] him, he takes away the armor in which the man trusted and divides up the spoils. (Luke 11:21-22)

Luke observes that the strong man is fully armed. This is the first hint that, just as Christian believers have weapons for their spiritual warfare (2 Corinthians 10:3-6), the strong man also is armed. What kind of armament does the strong man (Satan) have? How does he wield his weapons? What are his military devices? Scripture makes it clear that God's servants are not intended to be ignorant of Satan's devices (2:11).

The *nikao* element of binding and loosing introduces an issue of considerable interest. Exactly how aggressive should the believer be in overcoming and overpowering? There are many who advise Christians to adopt the more passive "standing" stance when confronted with spiritual warfare. There are, however, some strong biblical reasons for the advocacy of an aggressive stance in confrontations with the powers. Luke's *nikao* talk is one of those textual sites where an aggressive posture seems to be clearly taught, even insisted upon.

Unfortunately, many today are unaware of Satan's most oft-used devices.

Ten Favorite Weapons of Satan

A few paragraphs here on the armor of the strong man are permissible.

1. Unbelief. Doubt of God's Word, as exhibited in the Garden of Eden, is elemental to Satan. Unbelief, the most damning of all sins, is a preferred weapon of the dark prince (Genesis 3:1; Revelation 21:8).

2. Fear. Although not all fear is inappropriate, fear is an emotion that often emanates from Satan. The fearful and the unbelieving will one day be cast into hell, the Scriptures say (Revelation 21:8). But fearing God is the essence of godliness and there are, in addition, natural fears God has planted in the human heart to preserve our physical lives. Nevertheless, fear—terrorizing fear—is a chief instrument of Satan (2 Timothy 1:7). (The resurgence of fear-producing horror films, TV programs, literature and even jewelry is a pervasive indication of the enemy's strategy being played out in society.)

3. Idolatry. Idolatry (the worship of physical objects as God) seems wrapped within the human heart, reinforced by proud Satan himself. As one of the devil's chief instruments, it is everywhere denounced in Scripture (Exodus 20:4-5; Galatians 5:19-20; Colossians 3:5). First Samuel 15:23, interestingly enough, links arrogance with idolatry.

4. Sexual Promiscuity. Closely attached to idolatry is sexual promiscuity. Adultery and fornication are principal weapons in the enemy's arsenal. Homosexuality and lesbianism follow close behind. My observation is that almost all of Satan's prisoners are orchestrated by the pounding drums of sex and fear (Galatians 5:19; Romans 1:26-27).

5. Witchcraft and Rebellion. These two weapons of the enemy are linked in the Bible (1 Samuel 15:23). None are more susceptible to these particular wiles of Satan than the young as they begin to assert their independence. As accounts of murder and mayhem continue to play across news channel screens, it cannot be denied that witchcraft has penetrated the youth of our nation and beyond. Rebellion is not just inevitable youthful behavior. Rebellion, like witchcraft, is a wide on-ramp to the broad way.

6. Drugs. Likewise, drugs (*pharmakeia*) of all kinds are described as sorceries, witchcraft or magic arts in the New Testament, as in the Greek texts of Galatians 5:19 and Revelation

9:21; 18:23, and today, as never before, they slaughter millions. Facilitated by passivity of mind and will, these are demonic thresholds over which evil spirits happily jostle. Alcohol and nicotine too may be as deadly as heroin and crack.

7. **Lying.** Satan is a practiced liar (John 8:44; Revelation 21:8). Whether he is aiding and abetting the seduction of a virgin or bent on the destruction of a mature pastor or missionary, his whispered lies pave the way.

8. **Deception.** Satan is a deceiver (2 John 7) from the very beginning. His skill in deluding mature Christians is legendary. But he also deceives the very young in the faith, deflecting them away from the simplicity that is in Jesus Christ (Romans 16:18), the cross and the purity and integrity of the plain gospel.

9. **Power.** As Satan offered Jesus Christ the kingdoms of this world, he is still making seductive offers of power and pleasure. The wine of worldliness and the love of the world's systems and philosophies, though they failed with Jesus, seduce millions (Matthew 4:8; 1 John 2:15).

10. **Murder.** Finally, and this is not an exhaustive list to be sure, Satan is a murderer and destroyer from the beginning (John 8:44). Spiritual warfare has body counts that are real. Make no mistake: Satan is bent on taking men and women to hell as quickly as he is able. The ongoing murder of unborn babies is as lethal as the results of murderous fits of rage.

Since I have elsewhere devoted book-length attention to the believer's warfare weapons we can utilize against these wiles of Satan, I include only a list here: The Word, prevailing prayer, praise, the blood, fasting, the name of Jesus Christ, testimony, faith, unity, believer's authority, spiritual gifts, surrender, suffering and love. All of these weapons focus on the person of Jesus Christ. The superweapon—love—is the ocean upon which all must float.[2]

After that brief diversion into Satan's powerful, even deadly, terrain, we return to Luke's account. Luke introduces the Stronger One—clearly the Lord Jesus Christ. In Matthew and Mark's account, the identification of the strong man's conqueror is not so clear. Also, in Luke's account, the strong man is overcome, overpowered, conquered. The use of *nikao* by Luke carries with it the meanings of "conquer, overcome, prevail, get the victory."[3] Further, this is the word preferred by John in his epistles and in addressing the seven churches of Revelation. Luke also uses another word, *eperchomai*, which is used predominantly to signify the stronger coming upon the weaker.[4] Luke serves us best in clearly identifying the strong man and the Stronger Man.

Nikao *Talk*

The observation that *nikao* is part of the synoptic information about binding and loosing is very important.

> But when someone stronger attacks and overpowers him
> [the strong man], he takes away the armor in which the
> man trusted and divides up the spoils. (Luke 11:22)

The synoptic lesson should be grasped: *Binding and loosing equals overcoming, and overcoming equals binding and loosing.*

As much as I have sought to keep my focus narrowly on binding and loosing, this is one place where a detour is required. Every time *nikao* or its various cognates are used in Scripture, we must properly look for teaching on binding and loosing and the possibility of aggressive spiritual warfare. That is the powerful implication of Luke's record.

In Jesus' final words to His disciples, we find Him saying, "But take heart! I have overcome [*nikao*] the world" (John 16:33). John's teaching is identical to that of Luke—more *nikao* talk: "For everyone born of God overcomes [*nikao*] the world. This is the victory that has overcome [*nikao*] the world, even our faith" (1 John 5:4).

Thank God, the world is susceptible—and vulnerable—to being overcome! The way to deal with the world system is the *nikao* way, the Jesus way, the faith way. Abstaining from fleshly pursuits and separating from worldly pleasures are not enough. The world's presence and power must be overthrown in the life of each believer.

The New International Version of Luke 11:22 introduces the idea of "someone stronger." Another version, speaking of the Stronger Man, puts it this way, "But a stronger man than he [the strong man] may attack him and defeat him" (GWV). This nuance, clear in Luke, but unclear in Matthew, suggests that *aggressive spiritual warfare against the strong man is a biblical prerogative.* Such an offensive warfare posture is very different from that which many believe should include only the defensive "standing" posture of Ephesians chapter 6.

A writer well-known for his insight in warfare matters, describes an encounter with a Christian evangelist in Germany where such a stance against mediumistic healing was taken.

"One of the most notorious healers the Western world has known in this century spoke once in a town in Western Germany. Together with some praying friends, I decided to attend one of his meetings. As we sat there during the service, we began to pray. 'Lord Jesus, if this man is working for You, then bless his ministry and use him. If, however, he is opposing your work, then hinder [bind] his ministry tonight.'

"That evening the man was completely unable to work. In the

end he declared to those present, 'I can't do anything tonight, there are some counter-forces at work in the meeting tonight.'

"How could the ministry of a man of God be hindered by the prayers of his fellow Christians? Such prayers should only serve to bless his ministry.

"The earlier history of the evangelist I have just mentioned, however, is only too well-known to me. He comes from a markedly mediumistic background which has resulted in the fact that his ministry has been accompanied by a whole array of spiritistic phenomena."[5]

Stripping Away the Armor

Luke also speaks of stripping away the armor of the strong man (Luke 11:22). The question then becomes: Of what does the armor of the strong man consist? And how is it stripped away? Notice also that although the strong man trusted in that armor, it was nevertheless taken away. Luke vastly enlarges the whole concept of binding and loosing by introducing two new ideas: 1) Binding and loosing cannot be equated only with overcoming, but the fully armed strong man can be overcome. 2) His until-now undiscovered armor can also be stripped off and taken away. Luke forcibly introduces the concept of aggressive spiritual warfare.

What, then, has this synoptic overview contributed to our growing understanding of binding and loosing? Because of Luke's usage of the "overcomer" *nikao* language, the concept of *aggressive* spiritual warfare has been presented. In future chapters we will come to understand more of the ramifications this has for you and me today.

Endnotes

[1] James Strong, *The Comprehensive Concordance of the Bible* (Iowa Falls, IA: World Bible Publishers, n.d.), s.v. *"nikao,"* Greek #3528.

[2] K. Neill Foster, *Warfare Weapons* (Camp Hill, PA: Christian Publications, 1995), v-vi.

[3] Gerhard Kittel, ed., *Theological Dictionary of the New Testament*, trans. Geoffrey W. Bromiley (Grand Rapids, MI: Eerdmans, 1964), 2:681.

[4] C. Peter Wagner, *Confronting the Powers* (Ventura, CA: Regal books, 1996), 144-145.

[5] Kurt Koch, *Christian Counseling and Occultism* (Grand Rapids, MI: Kregel Publications, 1972), 18. As Koch hints, binding and loosing is effective in the whole area of charismatic manifestations. Welcoming all that is of the Holy Spirit of Almighty God and forbidding every expression that is not an expression of the Holy Spirit of Almighty God is a stance I take when confronted with utterances and manifestations. The reactions are often explosive, I must warn you. We are not to despise prophecy, but to prove everything in order to isolate and seize the good (1 Thessalonians 5:20-21). In such situations, I am careful to use the full name of the Lord Jesus Christ since the manifestation milieu is frequently dominated by alternate Jesus spirits who, of course, have no relationship to Jesus Christ, but were instead defeated at His cross.

Good-bye to the Fortune-teller

Joseph Broz III

One day on our way to the local supermarket we noticed that a palm reader/fortune-teller had set up business on the main street in town. Previous experience with fortune-tellers had taught me that 1) some use imagination and human abilities to make their predictions; 2) some are under the influence and power of Satan and his demons. I had seen how the advice sought and given by a palm reader had resulted in the breakup of Christian marriages through adultery and divorce. The Word of God instructs us clearly:

> There shall not be found among you anyone who makes his son or his daughter pass through the fire, or one who practices witchcraft, or a soothsayer, or one who interprets omens, or a sorcerer, or one who conjures spells, or a medium, or a spiritist, or one who calls up the dead. For all who do these things are an abomination to the LORD, and because of these abominations the LORD your God drives them out from before you (Deuteronomy 18:10-12, NKJV).

In the car I began to ask the Lord to show me what to do as His representative in the community. It was prayer meeting night. I shared with the Lord's people my concern about the fortune-teller's presence. I reminded the people that the Lord Jesus Christ had given us authority over the works of darkness and as Christians we represented the one true and living God. We could take up the authority the Lord had placed in our hands and the Lord our God would drive out the wicked influence of the fortune-teller's power and business.

We agreed to command in the strong name of Jesus that all evil spirits would cease to speak through this palm reader and leave our community and go to the abyss. We also desired to see the fortune-teller acknowledge that the Lord Jesus Christ was Victor.

Various Christians during prayer pronounced out loud words of rebuke against these evil spirits, binding them in the name of the Lord Jesus Christ, requesting the Lord God to give us the victory. During the next week or so, my two young sons prayed nightly that the Lord would send away the evil spirits and the palm reader from our neighborhood. Their school bus passed her office twice a day, at which times they also prayed.

Two weeks passed. One morning, while walking by the fortune-teller's house, I noticed a moving van being loaded. I asked the helpers what they were doing. "We are moving. The spirit guides will not talk to us here because of that church over there," one replied. They were pointing at our church! Our church is surrounded by no less than four other churches, but they singled us out.

I exclaimed out loud, "Thanks be to the Lord Jesus Christ who gives us the victory!" One of my sons said, "Dad, those evil spirits don't like prayer because Jesus made them leave."

And leave they did!

12

THE PETER PERSPECTIVE

I N PREVIOUS CHAPTERS I DISCUSSED at some length what I am calling missiological/evangelistic binding and loosing based on Matthew 12 and the synoptic passages in Mark and Luke.

Now we come to the binding and loosing passage connected with Peter in Matthew 16:18-19. Jesus is speaking:

> I tell you that you are Peter, and on this rock I will build my church, and the gates of Hades will not overcome it. I will give you the keys of the kingdom of heaven; whatever you bind on earth will be bound in heaven, and whatever you loose on earth will be loosed in heaven.

As we observed in the last chapter, Jesus had earlier asked a question of the disciples: "How can anyone enter a strong man's house and carry off his possessions unless he first ties up the strong man? Then he can rob his house" (12:29). The lines are drawn; the inference is clear: For effective spiritual warfare, for victory over the enemy, we must first bind the strong man. Then we can spoil his house.

Peter was one of the first who was given the authority to bind the strong man's house. He had just made a dramatic confession: "You are the Christ, the Son of the living God" (16:16). It was at once a confession of Jesus' messiahship and divinity. Jesus' response was to expand Peter's authority, commensurate, as it were, with his understanding. To paraphrase, "Peter, you are like a rock, all right, and the Father in heaven has shown you this."

Following that note of congratulation, Jesus explains that Peter will build the Church, that hell will not prevail and that He is giving the keys of the kingdom to Peter. "Whatever you bind on earth will be bound in heaven, and whatever you loose on earth will be loosed in heaven" (Matthew 16:19).

The Keys of the Kingdom

The keys seem to be an allusion to an Old Testament verse in which the Lord God prophesied that Eliakim would replace Shebna, the steward of the Davidic royal household: "I will place on his [Eliakim's] shoulder the key to the house of David; what he opens no one can shut, and what he shuts no one can open" (Isaiah 22:22). Prophetically, Eliakim's shoulder could be the shoulder of Jesus Christ.

Barclay again has an insightful comment. "So then what Jesus is saying to Peter is that in the days to come, he will be the steward of the kingdom."[1] In the third chapter of Revelation, Jesus is seen holding the keys to the house of David. But here in Matthew 16, He grants those keys to Peter and the Church.

Leon Morris writes, "It [a key] is an obvious symbol for admitting people through a door, but it was also used for exercising authority (the steward rather than the porter)."[2]

Watchman Nee identifies the keys as preaching and baptizing.[3]

Spurgeon understood the purpose of the keys to be threefold, for preaching, discipline and admission:

Peter used those keys at Pentecost, when he let three thousand into the church; in Jerusalem, when he shut out Ananias and Sapphira; and at the house of Cornelius, when he admitted the Gentiles.[4]

Neil Anderson describes the binding and loosing process as using the key of knowledge to set people free, but also expands it to include the idea of dealing with demonic powers.[5]

Similarly, the nineteenth-century preacher, Henry Ward Beecher, refers to the keys as

the opening and shutting power of the Christian life, [asserting that] every praying man and every praying woman . . . has this power of the keys. . . . And every man that has that spirit has God's keys in his hands, and has authority to bind and loose—to bind lies and all iniquity, and to set loose all those that suffer oppression by reason of spiritual despotism.[6]

If the keys are symbols of authority, then Beecher seems closest to the reality of the text (Acts 2:14-41). With authority Peter told the crippled man at the gate of the temple to walk. And he rose, walking and leaping (3:1-10). Peter was also the first to exhibit the skills of mass evangelism as he spoke to the crowds after Pentecost, opening the door to the kingdom of God in a massive evangelistic appeal.

Neither must we miss Peter's role in introducing Church discipline to the fledgling body of Christ (Acts 5:1-10). Ananias and Sapphira were the first to be judged by the Church, Peter being the human instrument.

And yet again, when faced with the duplicity of Simon the sorcerer in the book of Acts, Peter rains down judgment on Satan's emissary and he confronts Simon the pretender in dramatic fashion—again the use of the keys (8:9-25). Then Peter and John journey to Samaria to make sure the new converts also receive the Holy Spirit. Being an agent in the empowering of new believers is also, in my mind, another use of the keys by Peter (8:15-16).

Finally, the vision of the sheet (11:1-18) and Peter's acceptance of its message effectively opened up the till-then Jewish Church to the intent of the Holy Spirit to bring in the Gentiles. This Peter-experience profoundly affected Church history and is perhaps the most significant use of the keys.

By way of review, consider these possible uses of the keys by Peter:

1. Evangelism—3,000 believe.
2. Healing—"Silver and gold have I none!"
3. Church discipline—Ananias and Sapphira struck dead.
4. Confrontation with Simon—dealing with the powers.
5. Holy Spirit comes—falling upon new believers.
6. Gentiles welcomed into the kingdom—the story still unfolding.

To elaborate further, Peter apparently believed that he would do the same kind of works his Master had done. He believed that he could, with authority, preach the gospel. He had no doubt that Jesus Christ who was in him was greater than the dark prince who was empowering Simon the sorcerer. In each of these instances, Peter was using the keys of the kingdom and exhibiting the authority of the believer.

The Gates—What Are They?

What are the gates of Hades referred to in Matthew 16:18? Several commentators have useful analyses. William Barclay gives three possibilities: (1) the forces of evil as a fortress against the Church; (2) the government of hell opposing the Church; (3) Jesus, through His resurrection, bursting the gates of death.[7] The second one is Barclay's best interpretation, I believe. The gates of the city were where rulers and elders met to give counsel and issue decisions. "Gates" was a Jewish idiom for the place of government. "So then the phrase would mean: The powers, the government of Hades will never prevail against the Church."[8] That we believe to be true.

John Calvin had a similar interpretation: "By the word gates (*pulai*) is unquestionably meant every kind of power and of weapons of war."[9]

Matthew Henry sees spiritual warfare in this passage:

> The gates of hell are the powers and policies of the devil's kingdom, the dragon's head and horns, by which he makes war with the Lamb; all that comes out of hell-gates, as being hatched and contrived there.[10]

Neil Anderson quotes R.E. Nixon, connecting these verses with Matthew 12:29:

> The gates suggest the picture of a fortress or prison which lock in the dead and lock out their rescuers. This would imply that the Church is on the offensive, and its Master will plunder the domain of Satan.[11]

The best, and I think the correct, view is the one advanced by Greek professor and missionary to Brazil, Mark A. Downing:

> When we read Matthew 16:18, do we see an offensive or defensive Church? All too frequently the twentieth-century Church has seen itself on the defensive in this passage. But this is based on a series of faulty assumptions, misinterpretations and just plain poor reading.

Our first mistake is in our understanding of the word "church." The word translated Church in this verse is *ekklesia*. Although it is the common word for Church in the New Testament, it is only used twice in the Gospels—here in Matthew 16:18 and two chapters later in Matthew 18:17. When we read that Christ will build His Church, our twentieth-century frame of reference immediately begins to think, "I will build my church building." It is not difficult in our minds to add doors to that building, and from there we are apt to put gates on as well. As a result, we read the verse, all the while visualizing Satan attacking the gates of a church building.

But if we back up and understand that the word for Church means "assembly," we can begin to understand Christ's meaning in this verse. Jesus is talking about a body of believers, an assembly of His followers. Understanding that prevents us from putting doors or gates on His Church (His body, capital C), and therefore keeps us from misreading the following phrase: "the gates of Hades," not the gates of the Church.

The Greek lexicon helps us to further discover that the word *katiskusousin*—translated "overcome," "prevail against," "to have strength against" or "overpower"—has other possibilities as well. The word can also mean "withstand" and "to be strong to another's detriment." In other words, Jesus is describing the Church as an offensive assembly. It is marching out as a conquering army attacking the gates of hell. Moreover, these gates are not going to hold up against the onslaught. The Church will carry out its mandate of releasing those held in captivity inside Satan's fortress.[12]

Protestant Commentary

The concept of binding and loosing has drawn some rather perceptive Protestant commentary in contrast to the Roman Catholic interpretation of this passage. Considerable attention has been paid to the actual words used and the presence of neuter forms which take the application away from persons and toward objects.

"Whatever you bind" certainly cannot be limited only to persons. Whatever is whatever, even an unsold piece of real estate or a picketed mill.

Lenski says similarly, "This neuter, then, does not refer to persons but to the acts of persons."[13] I will not go as far as he does since my view is that "whatever" might indeed include persons, Satan, of course, being a person. Another negative is that the context of Church discipline in Matthew 18 involves relationships between people. Nevertheless, Lenski's argument is persuasive.

Hendricksen asserts,

> The very wording—note "whatever," not "whoever"—shows that the passage refers to things, in this case beliefs and actions, not directly to people.[14]

The Periphrastic Future Perfect Tense

In the next chapter I provide a lengthy explanation of a Greek verb tense complicatedly called the periphrastic future perfect tense. This form appears in both chapters 16 and 18 of Matthew. The implications must not be missed: All true binding and loosing begins in heaven, relates to the glory of God and issues from the hands and heart of a sovereign Lord.

Though criticisms have been leveled against extremism on

binding and loosing teachings, some leaders in the charismatic and faith movements teach that God must bind in heaven what we have bound on earth. Derek Prince, however, recognizes this periphrastic future perfect distinction in the Greek:

> You can only bind on earth what has already been bound in heaven. But it still places the responsibility upon us because, until we pray, the binding is not effective. It requires earth's action to make heaven's decree effective.[15]

The use of the future perfect tense in both passages indicates that the binding in heaven precedes the binding on earth. The New American Standard Bible translates it this way:

> Whatever you shall bind on earth shall have been bound in heaven, and whatever you shall loose on earth shall have been loosed in heaven. (16:19; 18:18)

Biblical scholar Leon Morris explains it this way:

> Jesus is not giving the church the right to make decisions that will then become binding for God. . . . He is saying that as the church is responsive to the guidance of God it will come to the decisions that have already been made in heaven.[16]

In the theology of the Reformer, Zwingli, "our binding on earth comes from, and is a sign of, the binding in heaven."[17]
Watchman Nee also understood this concept:

> Now perfect faith comes out of perfect knowledge of God's will. And thus we command what God has al-

ready commanded; we decide on that which God has already decided.[18]

Andrew Murray Speaks Out

Binding and loosing has for generations characterized the teaching of classic evangelical leaders. Andrew Murray: "God has made the execution of His will dependent on the will of man. His promises will be fulfilled as much as our faith allows."[19]

A German writer expresses a similar idea:

> Loosing a person is essentially a charismatic task. Before a counselor can take this step he must ascertain what God's will is. The counselor who looses a person too quickly can come under heavy attack from Satan.[20]

In Reformation times, Menno Simons voiced a like sentiment:

> These keys are given to no one but those who are anointed by the Holy Ghost. . . . These keys must not be made use of, except in the name of Him who left them in our care and by His power, that is, with the Spirit and Word. . . . Therefore we may well take heed lest we loose by our reckless self-will or boldness those whom He Himself has bound in heaven, or bind those whom He Himself has loosed in heaven.[21]

More recent scholarship expresses it this way, "Everything decided by the 'lower court' is confirmed by the 'superior court.'"[22]

Similarly, McCandlish Phillips sees a synergistic relationship between binding and loosing in heaven and on earth:

The limitation of Satan's power on earth is based on a joining together of the will of God and the will of man. . . . When the sovereignty of God is linked to the obedience of man, the will of God is put into effect, and when that happens Satan is checked.[23]

For too long we have busied ourselves explaining why Peter did not have special authority. (The Greek tenses make very clear that he personally received authority to bind and loose.) Much of this has been in reaction to the interpretation the Roman Catholics have given to this passage, making Peter the first pope and leader of the Church. Personally, I have never been satisfied with the traditional Protestant interpretations of the passage.

The grammatical-historical rule of interpretation for the Scriptures is, in its essence, this: If the literal sense makes common sense, seek no other sense. Specifically, if the grammatical-historical hermeneutic is applied here, what we discover is that Peter is personally promised something alluded to in Matthew 12 and, as we shall see later, something that was extended to the rest of the disciples in Matthew 18. Why should we feel theologically threatened if we admit that Peter actually was given authority to bind and loose, to forbid and allow? That in no way is a declaration that Peter was a pope nor that he was the supreme ruler of the Church.

The Holy Linkage

A very significant idea is presented by the translators of the Amplified New Testament: There is a holy linkage between heaven and earth, and there is the potential of binding on earth what is already bound in heaven once that divine impulse is received by the servant of the Lord. Note the inference here:

I will give you the keys of the kingdom of heaven, and

whatever you bind—that is, declare to be improper and unlawful—on earth must be already bound in heaven; and whatever you loose on earth—declare lawful— must be what is already loosed in heaven. (Matthew 16:19, Amplified)

The rationale is legitimized by a footnote in the Williams' Translation which explains that the perfect past participle implies "things in a state of having been already forbidden [or permitted]."[24]

Moreover, though the keys of the kingdom were given first to Peter, they were never keys of indiscriminate power and authority. Anticipated in Matthew 12, they are to be given to Peter (note the future tense which may refer to Peter's evangelistic endeavors after Pentecost) and they are to be shared with the disciples, as we shall see when we get to Matthew 18.

"Whatever"

We introduce that wondrous word "whatever" at this point. It appears in Matthew 16 and 18, but not in Matthew 12. I do not disagree that binding and loosing may indeed refer primarily to the strong man and the gates of hell. But the binding and loosing of Matthew 16, coordinated as it is with heaven, is for "whatever." It becomes a brother to the numerous "whatevers" of prayer found in Scripture, such as, "If you believe, you will receive *whatever* you ask for in prayer" (Matthew 21:22, emphasis mine).

One last observation: in chapter 16, the promise becomes very personal. Peter is told, "whatever *you* bind" and "whatever *you* loose" (my emphasis on the personal pronoun). "Peter, *you* are going to have to do this. Binding and loosing will be a part of *your* ministry."

In Matthew 12 Jesus uses an unspecified "anyone" who might

bind the strong man. Most commentators believe He is referring to Himself. But He does not limit the binding of the strong man to what He alone might do. That "whosoever" becomes a "you" in the encounter with Peter in Matthew 21:22, "If you believe, you will receive whatever you ask for in prayer. . . ." That means you.

By way of summary:

- Peter was given power to bind and loose.

- He exhibited it in his evangelistic and apostolic endeavors. Jesus made very clear that the gates of hell would never stand against the Church.

- He extended binding and loosing beyond evangelistic endeavors, beyond spiritual warfare contexts to the immense possibilities of the divine "whatevers."

- The Greek nuances make clear that forbidding and allowing is not random nor capricious, but issues instead from the heart of God.

In Tune with Hell

The conversation in Matthew 16 cannot be abandoned without reference to the dramatic change in our Lord's communication with Peter. One moment, Peter has the impulse of the Father. He senses the messiahship of Jesus and utters the grand pronouncement, "You are the Christ, the Son of the living God" (16:16). But the next moment (could he be attempting to use the newly bestowed keys?), Peter is in tune with hell, not heaven: " 'Never, Lord!' he said. 'This shall never happen to you!' " (16:22).

From one who has clearly been in tune with heaven are coming, incredibly, words straight from the father of lies, the devil himself. Now, instead of calling Peter a rock, Jesus calls him a *scandalon*—a stumbling block, a different kind of rock—and in

Peter's words Jesus recognizes a new form of temptation to kingship without the suffering of the cross.[25] That is why, in verse 23, Christ addresses Peter as Satan. In that moment, He saw him as a stumbling block of personified evil.

This yo-yo effect, when considered in the context of binding and loosing, evokes some powerful teaching. Satan can and does get into the thoughts of the Lord's elect. If Peter, an apostle, surrounded by the rest of the twelve and in the physical presence of the Savior Himself, can be invaded by ideas from the counter-kingdom, how much more so ourselves.

There's more.

Later, when Ananias and Sapphira acted out impulses implanted by Satan, Peter announced the judgment of God (Acts 5:3-10). His own compulsiveness had earlier elicited a similar though less drastic rebuke from the Master. Indeed, Peter would well remember that just after he had begun to follow Jesus, there had been the incident of the demonized man in the synagogue (Mark 1:21-25). Jesus had, in contemporary terms, told the evil spirit to shut up and get out of the man! And he had rebuked Satan in Peter in a very direct way.

Paul makes clear that the audience of preaching includes the powers (Ephesians 3:10; Colossians 1:23). My point here is that Satan does get into the minds and hearts of God's people, and he does attend church. Satanic working in Christian meetings should be assumed. Demonization? Not necessarily. But the presence of the enemy? Definitely.

The Energizer™ Bunny

Not all children of disobedience are outside the gathered Church. The Energizer™ bunny, so famous in TV advertising, describes very well the activity of the devil among the children of disobedience. In fact, the description of the "spirit who is now at work" uses the Greek verb *energao* (Ephesians 2:2). So this ungodly "energizer" comes to church? Yes, that is exactly what I am saying.

A number of the incidents related in this book take place in Christian contexts. Board meetings. Camp meetings. Worship services. Evangelistic services. All are vulnerable. None are immune. Guarding the flock of God includes binding and loosing in these contexts. Indeed, spiritual leaders should not be trembling at the possibility of stormy gatherings and perverse results when God's people get together. They need not be biting their tongues in situations where the serpent's head is emerging. Rather, God's glory can be affirmed and maintained in such instances through binding and loosing by the spiritually perceptive.

Bind and loose in the name of Jesus Christ! You will discover that the Head of the Church is very interested in what happens in such contexts. You will discover, too, that silent binding and loosing is very effective indeed. The difference in the spiritual climate can be profound.

Yes, Peter was overtaken by the enemy. Sometimes we too are likewise influenced. But there are divine remedies and godly solutions—including binding and loosing.

Endnotes

[1] William Barclay, *The Gospel of Matthew,* The Daily Bible Study Series (Philadephia: The Westminster Press, 1975), 2:145.

[2] Leon Morris, *The Gospel According to Matthew* (Grand Rapids, MI: Eerdmans, 1992), 425.

[3] Watchman Nee, *The King and the Kingdom of Heaven* (New York: Christian Fellowship Publishers, 1978), 195-196.

[4] Charles Haddon Spurgeon, *The Gospel of the Kingdom* (New York: The Baker Taylor Co., 1893), 263.

[5] Neil T. Anderson, *Helping Others Find Freedom in Christ* (Ventura, CA: Regal Books, 1995), 101-109.

[6] Henry Ward Beecher, *The Biblical Illustrator: St. Matthew,* ed. Joseph S. Excell (New York: Randolph and Co., n.d.), 345-346.

[7] Barclay, *The Gospel of Matthew*, 2:142-144.

[8] Ibid., 2:143.

[9] John Calvin, *Commentary on a Harmony of the Evangelists Matthew, Mark, and Luke* (Grand Rapids, MI: Eerdmans, 1957), 292.

[10] Matthew Henry, *Commentary on the Whole Bible* (New York: Fleming H. Revell, n.d.), 5:232.

[11] R.E. Nixon as cited by Neil T. Anderson, *Setting Your Church Free* (Ventura, CA: Regal Books, 1994), 272.

[12] Mark A. Downing, missionary to Brazil (Baptist General Conference) and professor in Greek, note to author, April 1997.

[13] R.C.H. Lenski, *The Interpretation of St. Matthew's Gospel* (Minneapolis, MN: Augsburg Publishing House, 1943), 630.

[14] William Hendriksen, *New Testament Contemporary Exposition of the Gospel of Matthew* (Grand Rapids, MI: Baker Book House, 1973), 651.

[15] Derek Prince, "Aggressive Prayer," *New Wine*, March 1977, 7, 24.

[16] Morris, *The Gospel According to Matthew*, 469.

[17] W.P. Stephens, *The Theology of Huldrych Zwingli* (Oxford: Clarendon Press, 1986), 273.

[18] Watchman Nee, *God's Plan and the Overcomers* (New York: Christian Fellowship Publishers, 1977), 76.

[19] Andrew Murray, *With Christ in the School of Prayer* (Springdale, PA: Whitaker House, 1885, 1981), 222.

[20] Kurt Koch, *Demonology, Past and Present* (Grand Rapids, MI: Kregel Publications, 1973), 154.

[21] *The Complete Writings of Menno Simons* (Scottdale, PA: Herald Press, 1956), 990-991.

[22] Eduard Schweizer, *The Good News According to Matthew* (Atlanta: John Knox Press, 1975), 343.

[23] McCandlish Phillips, *The Bible, the Supernatural and the Jews* (Camp Hill, PA: Christian Publications, 1995), 148.

[24] Charles B. Williams, *The Williams New Testament* (Chicago: Moody Press, 1954), 59.

[25] D.A. Carson, *Matthew*, The Expositor's Bible Commentary (Grand Rapids, MI: Zondervan, 1984), 377.

The Teacher Who Opposed God

Delbert McKenzie

In one community where we pastored, a junior high student became very enthusiastic about his relationship with Jesus Christ. He talked openly about it both on campus and in the classroom.

One of his teachers, who professed to be an agnostic, was infuriated by this witness, especially so when the student brought a Bible to class and laid it on his desk. When the teacher saw it, he launched into a tirade, then walked over, picked up the Bible and hurled it against the wall.

Following this, he marched the student down the hall to the principal's office and demanded that he be expelled from school. The student, for his part, reported all this to me and asked counsel. I met with the boy and his parents and then with the principal of the school. We were able to establish that the student had the right to bring a Bible to the classroom if he wished, but he agreed not to flaunt it before the rest of the students.

The teacher, however, continued to harass the boy for his faith. The man happened to live on a block where several families from our church also lived. A meeting was called to discuss the ongoing conflict. It was decided that we would bind the man by the authority and power of Jesus Christ. We spent a lengthy time in prayer for him and then did the binding by faith.

Two days later, the teacher died of a heart attack. All of us were convinced that he had set his heart so irrevocably against God that the Lord had, in one sovereign act, removed him from the scene.

13

THE DISCIPLES' PERSPECTIVE

BUILDING UPON THE TWO EARLIER PASSAGES, Matthew 12 and Matthew 16, we now move to Matthew's final comments on binding and loosing in chapter 18 to expand the concept to its fullest measure:

> I tell you the truth, whatever you bind on earth will be bound in heaven, and whatever you loose on earth will be loosed in heaven.
> Again, I tell you that if two of you on earth agree about anything you ask for, it will be done for you by my Father in heaven. For where two or three come together in my name, there am I with them. (18:18-20)

We are now faced with more than binding the strong man, as important as that is, and we are faced with more than a powerful apostle, namely Peter, receiving and wielding the keys of the kingdom of heaven. Here, in its most expansive mode, Jesus clearly extends binding and loosing to the disciples. The "whatever" and the personal pronouns also appear again. This is as staggering a passage as one can find in the entire New Testament.

Whatever you bind, it will be bound in heaven.
Whatever you loose, it will be loosed in heaven.
Whatever two agree on earth, it will be done in heaven.

That is powerful stuff!

The Periphrastic What?

A careful reading of the Greek tense (periphrastic future perfect again!) requires that verse 18 be understood this way: Whatever you bind on earth is that which is already bound in heaven, and whatever you loose on earth is that which is already loosed in heaven. A friend puts it this way: The believer does not exercise this authority according to his or her own reasons or whims; rather, by the Holy Spirit's leading, he or she is simply cooperating with the divine will in any matter.

Once again, we hear from D.A. Carson:

> How is the contrast between "heaven" and "earth" to be understood? Our exegesis determines the answer. . . . If our remarks on the periphrastic future perfect are correct, then . . . heaven's rule has thereby broken in. Thus Jesus' disciples, in accordance with his gospel of the kingdom, take up the ministry of the keys and bind and loose on earth what has with the coming of the kingdom been bound and loosed in heaven.[1]

The Amplified New Testament, as we have already observed in our discussions about Matthew 16, translates in a manner that reinforces Carson.

> Truly, I tell you, whatever you forbid and declare to be improper and unlawful on earth must be what is al-

ready forbidden in heaven, and whatever you permit and declare proper and lawful on earth must be already permitted in heaven. (18:18, Amplified)

Dana and Mantey, authorities on the Greek language, note that the future form of the "periphrastic was readily adaptable for expressing durative action in the future . . . " and that the periphrastic "is the regular construction for the future perfect in the New Testament. Exceptions are rare and doubtful."[2]

Like Prayer and Lightning

For these reasons, I see this reading of this Scripture as the correct one, a concept which links the teaching here with the teaching about prayer elsewhere in the Bible. For example, it was A.B. Simpson's view on Romans 8:26-27 that the Holy Spirit plants the prayer in the heart of God's child, and further, that answered prayers are those petitions which are prayed back to the Father.

> And so there is a divine and most perfect provision in the economy of grace by which the Holy Spirit adjusts our spirit into such harmony with God that we can catch His thought and send it back again, not merely as a human desire but as a divine prayer. True prayer, therefore, is not only the voice of man crying to God but the voice of God in man expressing the deepest needs of the human heart and conveying them to the throne in such a manner that the answer shall be assured.[3]

Prayer has sometimes been compared to lightning. Apparently, so the scientists tell us, an electronic field stretches toward the heavens from trees and tall buildings and other earth-bound attractors. An electronic field also exists in the skies. As it builds and intensifies, it reaches toward the earth—and its potential targets. The greatest impulse by far is from the heavens. But when the imperceptible connection is made, in a split second a lightning strike has its electronic route marked out for it, and it summarily slams into its target.

Similarly, we are told, there is a God in heaven above who desires to communicate with His attractors (believers) on earth who also wish to communicate with Him. When a person catches the divine thought—whether in prayer or in binding and loosing—then is the matter done.

John Piper strengthens this analogy in a chapter entitled "Praying for What Cannot Fail":

> God appoints prayer as the means of finishing a mission that he has promised will certainly be finished. Therefore we pray, not because the outcome is uncertain, but because God has promised and cannot fail.[4]

The Matthew 18 text plunges on, introducing the word Jesus so often used in prayer—"whatever." This extends binding and loosing beyond spiritual warfare and beyond discipline, removing it at least one step from the context of direct spiritual warfare and the actual binding of the strong man. It is because of the "whatever" that I thought this book would not focus on spiritual warfare. To limit the message to spiritual warfare alone would mean to exclude one of the most powerful teachings in the Bible.

The Church Discipline On-ramp

Also in Matthew 18, the context undeniably relates binding and loosing to church discipline. The tendency at times is to overlook the progressive pattern of discipline and focus on the most dramatic or severe forms such as binding and loosing. Let me suggest seven stages of church discipline, five of them from this passage and two from First Corinthians 5. Repentance and restoration are, of course, possible and desirable at any point in the process.

1. Go to the offender (Matthew 18:15).
2. Take someone with you (18:16).
3. Tell the matter to the church (18:17).
4. Treat the person as a pagan or tax collector (18:17).
5. Do not eat with the offender (1 Corinthians 5:11).
6. Cast out the offender from fellowship (5:13).
7. Bind and deliver over the offender to Satan (Matthew 18:18; 1 Corinthians 5:5, 1 Timothy 1:20).

Commentators regularly refer to First Corinthians 5:5 as an example of Paul exercising the disciplinary authority of binding and loosing. Zwingli also relates binding to this passage.[5] H.A. Ironside likewise refers to First Corinthians 5:5 as an example of binding and loosing:

> In First Corinthians 5, [Paul] was binding [the offender's] sin upon him until he should repent. When in Second Corinthians 2:5-11, he instructed the assembly to forgive this man upon evidence of his repentance, he was loosing him.[6]

Matthew Henry also sees First Corinthians 5:2ff as an example of the Matthew verses.[7]

But what is seldom addressed, or even recognized, is that this action of binding and loosing in the context of church discipline is not merely exercising a judgment of discipline or excommunication, but it involves a binding, supernatural transaction. The offender is literally bound over to Satan.

As mentioned earlier, A.B. Simpson believed that

> such an act on the part of the Church of God will be
> followed by the Lord's effectual dealing in all such
> cases. . . . God's hand will deal with the offender
> through temporal judgment.[8]

Instant Discipline

Ambrose, one of the Church Fathers, understood all too well
what discipline in this context could mean. In the fourth century, he disciplined a man, saying, "He must be turned over to
Satan, so that his flesh disappears, and that in the future he may
commit no such deed." The biographer Paulinus records that
even before Ambrose finished speaking, an evil spirit began to
torture the man who had become the object of discipline.[9]

Similar incidents of evil invasion for the purposes of discipline
took place when a person was delivered over to Satan through
the ministries of St. Severin and St. Eligius in the fifth century.[10]

Another example of binding and loosing in discipline is recorded in First Timothy 1:20 where Paul delivers Hymenaeus and
Alexander over to Satan. These two men apparently are backslid-
ers who have gone so far as to publicly dishonor God. Inasmuch
as this kind of discipline, i.e., binding, is not frequent in Scripture,
it should not be a first option in the life of the contemporary
Church.

A Canadian evangelist once delivered over his own wayward
and backsliding son to Satan for the purposes of the destruction
of his flesh and the saving of his soul. The young man was becoming very proficient as a hockey goalie and was, in the process, straying far from God. After the binding was done, the
young man broke his leg.

While still on crutches, but having repented of his wayward-
ness and returned to God, he was instantly healed while walking

down the street of a Canadian city. The last I knew, he was in full-time pastoral ministry.

I wish to underscore that binding and loosing is not indiscriminant. It is linked with heaven. It is God's prerogative, and even when the servant of the Lord dares to bind and loose, it is because he or she has caught the impulse of heaven and is commanding God's intent after Him.

We evangelicals are not always too consistent in our application of Scripture to life. Most of us vigorously claim the promises of verses such as Matthew 18:19—"If two of you on earth agree . . . it will be done!" We also believe where two or three are gathered together in Christ's name, He is there. By what logic, then, having read the context, do we fail to believe that whatever we bind will be bound and whatever we loose will be loosed? Part of the reason for our failure is that we stagger at the thought. Is God really putting the throttle of omnipotence into our hands? In one sense, He is! But binding and loosing is not indiscriminate any more than prayer is indiscriminate. Both functions are aligned with heaven. True binding and loosing is directed by the Holy Spirit just as true prayer is directed by the Holy Spirit.

Jesus said, "Whatever *you* bind" (emphasis mine). *You* do it. If you read this section and commence to pray, "Oh Lord, bind Satan," you have missed the point! The day is coming when God will bind Satan and he will be cast into the abyss (Revelation 20:2-3). But in the meantime, believers do the binding.

If you believe, *you* do it!

I bind. *I* loose.

These are the words of authority.

Binding and loosing needs to be verbal, preferably out loud. And it needs to be specific. Say exactly what you mean and mean exactly what you say. I once was involved with a group of Christian workers in a deliverance session where no solution seemed possible until we were willing to loose what had been inadvertently bound and then rebind it. It was a lesson in the necessity of speaking specifically when it comes to binding and loosing.

The policeman on a traffic stand does not pray, "Oh Lord, in the name of the city fathers, please stop this traffic." That is so absurd as to be ridiculous. But many Christians today are much like that policeman. They cannot bring themselves to step out and stop the traffic. They cannot bring themselves to believe that the throttle of authority is really in their hands. They cannot bring themselves to bind and loose.

There are no better words of advice than those given by Mary, the mother of Jesus, at the wedding in Cana of Galilee, "Whatsoever he saith unto you, do it" (John 2:5, KJV).

Endnotes

[1] D.A. Carson, *Matthew,* The Expositor's Bible Commentary (Grand Rapids, MI: Zondervan, 1984), 374.

[2] H.E. Dana and Julius R. Mantey, *A Manual Grammar of the Greek New Testament* (New York: The MacMillan Company, 1927), 232-233.

[3] A.B. Simpson as cited by K. Neill Foster, *Warfare Weapons* (Camp Hill, PA: Christian Publications, 1995), 23.

[4] John Piper, *A Godward Life* (Sisters, OR: Multnomah Publishers, 1997), 115.

[5] W.P. Stephens, *The Theology of Huldrych Zwingli* (Oxford: Clarendon Press, 1986), 271.

[6] H.A. Ironside, *Expository Notes on the Gospel of Matthew* (Neptune, NJ: Loizeaux Brothers, 1948), 227.

[7] Matthew Henry, *Commentary on the Whole Bible* (New York: Fleming H. Revell, n.d.), 5:234, 260.

[8] A.B. Simpson, *Christ in the Bible Commentary* (Camp Hill, PA: Christian Publications, 1992), 4:96.

[9] Adolf Rodewyk, *Possessed by Satan: The Church Teaching on the Devil, Possession and Exorcism*, trans. Martin Ebon (Garden City, NY: Doubleday, 1975), 118.

[10] Ibid., 118-119.

Bound to the Bench

William A. Paul

A missionary to India, a relative of mine, was engaged in an evangelistic campaign in Michigan. The meetings were grinding along with little evidence of spiritual response.

Finally, one night, the prayer warriors determined to bind the powers of darkness and loose the working of the Holy Spirit to minister freely in their midst. They felt in their own spirits that they had succeeded.

During the next service they noticed a new sense of freedom. Following the message there was a visible response to the gospel story.

After the service was over and people were vacating the chapel, the missionary noticed that one of the chief opponents of the work of the Lord in that area remained seated. When they went to him, they found him literally bound to his seat. It was not until they loosed him that he received Christ and was able to get up and go home.

"I Can't Move"

This incident took place in a frontier church where my dominant memory of the scene is the bare lumber on the inside of the building. The furniture, the benches—all were primitive.

The town was situated near an oil field in Alberta's north, surrounded by farms and bush and muskeg. The challenge facing us that particular evening was a young woman who had encountered bondage and demonization through the laying on of hands of an itinerant evangelist.

As we probed to identify the problem (my wife and the pastor were there also), the powers began to communicate through her. "We are going to run away. We are going to take this woman out of here."

At that point, in forbidding such an eventuality, we simply bound her to the bench in the name of the Lord Jesus Christ. Having done that, the counseling process, accompanied by some unusual exit phenomena, proceeded. Finally, we all acknowledged that the woman had gained some freedom.

However, as we got up to put on our coats and prepare to leave, we noticed that she was still sitting on the bench. It became obvious that she was not leaving with the rest of us.

"Did you want to talk some more? Are you ready to go?" we asked.

Her answer surprised us all.

"I can't move."

It finally dawned on us why she could not get up. Once we loosed her from the bench in the name of the Lord, she immediately rose to come with us.

14

LOOSING AS FORGIVENESS

IT WAS A COOL AND PLEASANT EVENING. A gentle breeze flowed through the uplifted shutters and open doors of the aging tabernacle which dominated the grounds of a large Western Pennsylvania campground. Intent on the speaker's message, my ears suddenly perked up as I heard him say something like this: "In the word forgiveness, there is included the meaning of loosing. To forgive is to loose."

I was caught. The germ ideas for this book began to expand in my soul. If the definition of loosing included forgiveness, then the whole binding and loosing theme showed vast potential indeed. Little did I dream that from this verbal aside at a camp meeting would emerge one of the major reasons for writing a book like this. Moreover, as you the reader already know, this whole theme has shown such potential for expansion that I have had to limit my excursions beyond Matthew's *deo/luo* language and the *nikao* language of Luke. This foray into "forgiveness language" is yet another departure from the *deo/luo* core of our discussion.

Great Potential

The detour takes us to the day of Pentecost where, by fairly common consent, commentators agree that Peter's first use of the keys was the extension of forgiveness to thousands gathered there (Acts 2:14-40).

The Greek word for "forgive" is *aphiemi*. Thayer suggests that the meaning is "to go away, depart," giving the idea of loosing.[1]

Strong, for his part, defines *aphiemi* more extensively, using these phrases: "to send, to go, to send forth, cry, forgive, forsake, lay aside, leave, let alone, let be, let go, let have, omit, put away, send away, remit, suffer and yield up."[2] Again the definitions merge with loosing and affirm what the speaker had casually said, "Forgiveness is loosing." Jesus made it very clear. If we do not forgive, we cannot be forgiven.

> For if you forgive men when they sin against you, your heavenly Father will also forgive you. But if you do not forgive men their sins, your Father will not forgive your sins. (Matthew 6:14-15)

The Context

The whole procedure leading up to this binding and loosing passage begins with forgiveness or the lack thereof.

> If your brother sins against you, go and show him his fault, just between the two of you. If he listens to you [i.e., forgives you], you have won your brother over. (Matthew 18:15)

The parable following this passage relates directly to forgiveness. Forgiving seventy times seven certainly means that forgiveness can never be withheld. Failing to forgive, Jesus is saying, is an illegitimate form of binding and meets with serious consequences. E.M. Bounds warns, "An unforgiving spirit is not only Satan's widest door into our heart, but it is the strongest invitation and warmest welcome."[3]

When we do not forgive, we certainly bind ourselves, and in a sense bind others, preventing them from being freed to be what God wants them to be and to see the accomplishment of God's will in their lives. Loosing them from their offenses sets them free to be used by God. Matthew notes that Jesus was loosing sins and loosing disease at the same time (9:1-8).

Struggles to Forgive

Lewis B. Smedes, author of *Forgive and Forget*, tells the story of his childhood neighbor, a Mrs. Broutmeir, whose character traits and behavior caused untold pain for his mother and himself. The detail with which Smedes writes reveals something of his struggle to forgive and be loosed. (Since the name Broutmeir sounds fictional as does the use of Amity for a street name, I wonder if the account is slightly veiled.)

"The hardest person for me—ever, in my whole life—to forgive was Mrs. Broutmeir. Mrs. Broutmeir lived in a yellow frame house across the street from the smallish house my father built with his own hands for us to live in just before I was born. This woman was unbelievably cruel to my mother, and her memory has plagued me for years.

"My parents shipped off third-class to the United States from Friesland, a province up in northernmost Holland, as soon as they were wed. My father lived just long enough to see five children born and to get his own house built on Amity Avenue in Muskegon, Michigan. Then he died, only thirty-three years old and hardly underway. I was the last of the five.

"Left alone with few skills and no money, my mother put bread on our table and clothes on our bodies by cleaning other people's houses and washing other people's clothes in a second-hand Maytag that broke down every other Monday. . . .

"Our own house stood eyeball to eyeball with the Broutmeirs'. I should explain that the Broutmeirs were our 'betters.' What made them better was partly that Mr. Broutmeir had a steady job and Mrs. Broutmeir stayed home and kept her children's noses clean. (You were a high-class kid in our neighborhood if your mother never let your nose get snotty.) But their "betterness" came out most plainly in the accent factor; they spoke English like real Americans. They were second generation people; they had been around, they knew how to live, and more than anything, they knew how to talk.

"Mrs. Broutmeir, in all her true American betterness, became a monster in my eyes. She had a co-monster next door; the two of them set up a neighborhood CIA to keep an eye on the subversive goings-on at our house. She and her fellow-monster drew straws at dusk every day to see which of them would report the delinquencies of her grubby kids to my mother as she came home from that day's scrubbing.

"One day they both came across Amity to deliver to my mother the well-considered counsel of her betters that she should give away her two youngest children—my brother Wesley and me— as orphans, the reason being that my mother lacked the money and the savvy to care for us all in a proper manner. I remember getting word once that Mrs. Broutmeir had decreed that I should not cross Amity to play with her children; I was exiled to the north side of the street on grounds of a dirty nose. It seemed to us, in fact, that the Broutmeirs had us staked out night and day.

"Mrs. Broutmeir and her confederate pressed the advantage of second-generation Americanism to the moral edge; they wore my mother down with shame. They got her to feel that it was a shameful thing for a woman with a brood of little children to let her husband die so young and an immoral thing to be talking to real Americans with a foreign accent on her tongue.

"But my mother dipped her shame into a cup of heroic wrath. Deep down, where God's gift of dignity was simmering in her soul, she raged, she seethed. She was a goddess with fire in her bosom.

"One Saturday night, done in, as if life had tied the terrible tiredness of all six working days in a bundle and given her one final blow, the latest Broutmeir slap at one of her children popped the safety valve on her fury.

"We were, all six of us, in the kitchen, waiting for a pot of brown beans to finish baking, when, driven by the furies inside of her, she left the stove and strode head down, face red, fists tight, through the dining room, the living room and out the front door. With apron strings fluttering behind her, she stalked across Amity and up the Broutmeir front stoop to lay siege on the monster. The hosts of heaven never had a chance to stop her.

"The five of us were huddled around our bay window; we could see it all from there.

"She pounded on the front door and, when Mrs. Broutmeir opened it a wedge, she pushed it aside and walked into the devil's lair. Face aflame, eyes brimming with tears, finger cocked straight at the shocked Broutmeir eyes, the widow Smedes launched a frenzied defense of her beloved brood.

"Mrs. Broutmeir retreated to the dining room and took up a protected position on the other side of the round oak table with its blue Dutch teapot holding at the center. My mother used the table as a pulpit, pounding on it with her fist as she delivered her furious, inspired, but unrecorded prophecy against Broutmeir and on behalf of her own children. Mrs. Broutmeir sputtered something about the police, about calling them, and about being attacked by a woman gone crazy.

"The word 'crazy' seemed to bring my mother to her humiliated senses. Was she crazy? Maybe she was. She didn't know. If she was crazy, she was the more to be shamed. Better get out of there just in case. She left by the front door.

"She walked, head still down, face white now, back across Amity, up our front porch, into our living room past her children clustered at the window; she didn't look at us, didn't say anything to us, but strode straight ahead, through the dining room and kitchen, into the bathroom, and vomited. Then she wept. I do not remember when she came out or what she said to us when she did. . . .

"I grew up hating Mrs. Broutmeir. I wanted her house to burn down. I hoped her children would fail in school and get into a lot of trouble. I wanted them all to go to hell. My boyhood cup of aggressive hate was full.

"Have I forgiven her? I am still in the process of forgiving her. I enjoyed my hate too long, but I started to heal a long while ago, and I am well on the way."[4]

Corporate Forgiveness

Personal forgiveness is one thing, but corporate forgiveness is yet another. In the biblical case of the man delivered over to Satan, the clear implication is that he was later forgiven and loosed by the whole church in a corporate act. H.A. Ironside sees First Corinthians 5:4-5 as an example of such binding and loosing:

"When you are assembled in the name of our Lord Jesus and I am with you in spirit, and the power of our Lord Jesus is present, hand this man over to Satan, so that the sinful nature may be destroyed and his spirit saved on the day of the Lord." In this verse, Paul is binding the man's sin on him until he repents. Then in

Second Corinthians 2:5-11, he instructs the assembly to forgive the man upon evidence of his repentance. That is, Paul was loosing him.[5]

It is wonderful to be forgiven. When we are forgiven, surely we are loosed!

Revivals

Revivals—special movements of the Spirit of God—are also closely linked to forgiveness and the loosing that results. In twenty-two years of itinerant evangelism, there were a few times when God allowed me to see revival firsthand. Those moments were divine and powerful.

One particularly memorable event occurred in a small town called Banga, on the island of Mindanao in the Philippine Islands. Pastor P. and a church elder, Brother C., had been at odds with each other for some time, even though they were members of the same church. Pastor P. was extremely frail, his wife very tiny. Conversely, Brother C. was a very large man, especially for a Filipino. Still, he would not even greet Mrs. P. in the market. Relations were, to put it mildly, strained.

In the providence of God, and in the intensity of the revival atmosphere, Mr. C.'s heart broke. He walked forward in the church and publicly kissed Pastor P. So determined was he to fully repent of his unforgiveness that the next day he threw a feast of reconciliation. Among the invited guests was a cousin with whom he had not spoken for thirty-eight years. It is the only time in my life I have ever attended a celebration of forgiveness.

Mr. C. was a man loosed!

I know of no authentic revival in the history of the Church that has ever been anything other than an explosion of forgiveness among God's people. When Jonathan Goforth, Presbyterian missionary to China, went to Manchuria, abject confessions were made by Chinese Church leaders and rivers of forgiveness flowed. The confessions could not have been dragged out by wild horses, but the Holy Spirit brought them forth.[6]

John's View of Loosing As Forgiveness

One of the key passages on forgiveness is found in John's Gospel.

> After he had said this, he breathed on the disciples and said, "Receive the Holy Spirit. Whenever you forgive sins, they are forgiven. Whenever you don't forgive them, they are not forgiven." (John 20:22-23, GWV)

Many scholars recognize this passage as John's equivalent to Matthew's record of Jesus saying, "Whatever you bind on earth will be bound in heaven, and whatever you loose on earth will be loosed in heaven" (18:18). It is my view that Matthew's commentary on binding and loosing and the repeated use of the *deo/luo* language appropriately extends to the *nikao*/overcomer language of Luke and may now extend to the *aphiemi*/forgiveness language of John. I am reluctant to embrace the "parallel" concept of these passages, as some do, in that this incident in John comes after the resurrection, whereas all the other binding and loosing passages come intermediately in the ministry of Jesus, chronologically prior to the cross.

One writer says, "Loosing is the equivalent of forgiving, binding of retaining."[7] Schweizer adds, "The opening of heaven [is] the forgiveness of sin."[8] Ambrose is also an example of the parallel interpretation among the Church Fathers.[9] And indeed, what was Peter doing on the day of Pentecost? He was preaching the good news. Implicit in that message is the forgiveness of sins. Is not every evangelist, by that definition, a forgiver of sins? I suppose so, though such wording produces an evangelical self-consciousness! What did 3,000 people receive on the day of Pentecost? The New Testament account emphasizes the receptor side of the equation—they received salvation and forgiveness.

> With many other words he warned them; and he pleaded with them, "Save yourselves from this corrupt generation." Those who accepted his message were baptized, and about three thousand were added to their number that day. (Acts 2:40-41)

Merrill C. Tenney is especially helpful on this text. His comments are reminiscent of the periphrastic future perfect tense in Matthew.

> The commission to forgive sins is phrased in an unusual construction. Literally, it is: "Those whose sins you forgive have already been forgiven; those whose sins you do not forgive have not been forgiven." The first verbs in the two clauses are aorists, which imply the action of an instant; the second verbs are perfects, which imply an abiding state that began before the action of the first verbs. God does not forgive men's sins because we decide to do so, nor does He withhold forgiveness because we will not grant it. We announce it; we do not create it. This is the essence of salvation. And all who proclaim the gospel are in effect forgiving or not forgiving sins, depending on whether the hearer accepts or rejects the Lord Jesus as Sin-Bearer.[10]

Going Even Further

I wish to go even further here to say that the extension of forgiveness in the ministry of Peter is an expression of the authority of the believer. No evangelist can convincingly present the good news today without a sense of authority, a sense of divine call and commissioning. Was Peter enjoying his completeness in Jesus Christ on the day of Pentecost? Certainly. And was he celebrating the glory of God and the consciousness and power of Christ in him, the hope of glory? Affirmative again.

There is some danger in interpreting dogmatically that the "loosing" of Matthew is the "forgiveness" of John. One arrives there by synoptic comparisons, though John is not a synoptic writer. Yet there is enough similarity between the passages that strong consideration needs to be given to such an interpretation. I will not go so far as to insist that they are parallel Scriptures, but it is, I think, worth pursuing further.

There is some evidence in the Old Testament of the loosing power of forgiveness. God instructed Job's friends to offer burnt offerings and to have Job pray for them to appease God's wrath against them. The Lord turned again the captivity of Job when he prayed for his friends (Job 42:7-10). God accepted Job's intercession, forgave his friends and blessed Job besides. In fact, the Septuagint version of Job 42:10 reads, "And the LORD prospered Job; and when he prayed also for his friends, he forgave them their sin."

Stevan Davies' research, albeit from an extrabiblical source, also shows an interesting parallel:

> A text from the Dead Sea Scrolls testifies to the fact that the connection between exorcism and forgiveness was not unique to Jesus. Called "The Prayer of Nabonidus (4QprNab)," it is a late second or early first century

B.C.E. story of the recovery of the last king of Babylon. He writes, "I was afflicted [with an evil ulcer] for seven years . . . and an exorcist pardoned my sins. He was a Jew from among the [children of the exile of Judah, and he said] 'Recount this in writing to [glorify and exalt] the name of the Most High God.' "[11]

It seems to me that the king's testimony has the ring of authenticity to it though his word choice might not have exactly been approved by the exorcist.

I remember my own son, then about five years old, giving a testimony in a Bible camp. Some of the children had been coming to Christ and I, as the evangelist, had been counseling and praying with them. Through small boy eyes, and without the evangelical jargon into which we adults predictably fall, he stood up and proclaimed to the whole camp meeting crowd, "Guess what? My dad saved three girls last night!" We later explained that Jesus is the One who saves, but in reality, the forgiveness of sins had been extended—and received.

Confessing the Sins of Others

The corporate confession of the sin of others has its own special place and power too. Job confessed the sins of his children (Job 1:5), and Daniel confessed the sins of his people (Daniel 9:16). There are times to confess the sins of others and, when done sensitively in the Spirit and void of politicizations (to which they are vulnerable), confessions can be loosing events of the first order. The following extraordinary account is about the loosing of a city from its sins.

"Helmuth and Uli Eiwen stared in amazement at the ancient gravestones mounted on the old city wall where it meandered through a local park.

"Helmuth, pastor of Ichthys Church in Weiner Neustadt, Austria, and his wife Uli, had left a prayer meeting the night before convinced that the key to a mystery awaited them at the wall. For months church members had been praying for the city, asking God to show them what was blocking revival. During prayer, the conviction had grown that the Lord had something to show them at the old city wall.

"Confronted with gravestones with Hebrew inscriptions, dating from the thirteenth and fourteenth centuries, the Eiwens were intrigued by a city plaque indicating the stones had come from a Jewish graveyard closed in 1496, when every Jewish citizen was forced to flee the city.

"For centuries it was illegal for Jews to live in this city some thirty miles south of Vienna, but they gradually drifted back, and by 1938, Weiner Neustadt contained a lively Jewish community of 1,200. In that fateful year of the Nazi *Anschluss*, there were nearly 200,000 Jews throughout the country. Those who had means and the foresight to do so escaped to England, the Americas, or Palestine. About 65,000 of those who could not leave died between 1938 and 1945. Many of those who survived the concentration camps chose not to resettle in Austria. In Weiner Neustadt, the second-oldest Jewish settlement in Austria, no Jews are left.

"Stirred by this discovery, the Eiwens and the church began to confess to God the sin of the city and to pray for God's blessing on the community. Soon, however, they became convinced that it was too little simply to ask God for forgiveness. It was necessary to go to those directly offended and face to face confess the sin of the city and ask them for forgiveness. A worldwide search was initiated for Jews born in Weiner Neustadt and driven from their homes in 1938.

"Eventually the church located about sixty-five of Weiner Neustadt's former citizens. Some were too old or ill to return for an all-expense-paid, one-week visit offered by the church and its

150 members. After intensive correspondence, however, most made plans to attend the first two gatherings. . . .

" 'We invited you,' Helmuth Eiwen told the returning Jews, 'because we want to receive you in this city in a completely different spirit than the one in which you were forced to leave.'

"During each 'Week of Engagement,' as the events were called, the Jewish guests were honored by the mayor of Weiner Neustadt. They served as 'eyewitnesses' in local schools and were invited guests at special events. Accompanied by church members, they were taken on a tour of the city's old Jewish quarters, led by the archivist.

"But the central event of each Week of Engagement occurred during a day long church gathering when Eiwen, as a representative of the church and community, asked forgiveness for the 'unbelievably great wrong done to you personally, to your family and relatives in this city. . . .'

"Eiwen told the guests, 'We are deeply convinced that the God of Israel has brought you here because He wants to show you how much He loves you. . . .'

"In the course of the week some of the Jewish guests found healing for [their]. . . wounds. 'I feel like I am dreaming. God has healed so many wounds in me,' said one guest from Israel. 'Only God can do a miracle like this.'

"Another guest, surrounded by people who cared, for the first time told of an experience that had seared her heart for nearly sixty years. Deported with her family to Vienna and longing for the dolls she was forced to leave behind in Weiner Neustadt, nine-year-old Miriam Yaron had made daily visits to the window of a toy store, where wonderful dolls were attractively arranged.

"Finally, her father promised to find a way to buy his daughter a doll. The great day arrived, and a blue-eyed, blond-haired doll with a porcelain head was laid in her eager arms. Miriam's joy lasted eight days, until the delicate china head broke when the doll slipped from her arms. Once again a sympathetic father came to his daughter's aid. 'We'll find a doll doctor,' he told her. The woman at the shop said she would be glad to fix the doll, but later began to suspect that the father and daughter might be Jews.

"When the child returned to pick up her doll, the woman eyed her suspiciously. 'You are not a Jew?' she asked. Too young to understand, the little girl replied with confidence, 'Of course.' The woman appeared confused for a moment. 'But your father is certainly Aryan. He has blue eyes.' Confidently the child replied, 'He is Jewish.'

"The effect on the saleswoman was dramatic. Grabbing the broken doll, she thrust it in the child's face. 'We don't repair dolls for Jews,' she declared.

"Yaron related, 'In this moment, as a child, my sense of self-worth was stolen from me.' She had carried the story within her for fifty-seven years and had never told it to anyone.

"One evening after Yaron had related the experience to church members, Uli Eiwen came to her with a carefully wrapped package. Opening it, Yaron found a beautiful hand-made doll. Yaron told a gathering of friends, 'With this amazing act, she closed the circle for me. In Uli's gesture, I have found human kindness and my self-worth again.' "[12]

Forgiveness, concludes Neil Anderson, is "agreeing to live with the consequences of another person's sin."[13] Jesus Christ lived and died for the consequences of our sins. When we agree through Jesus Christ, loosing—and its accompanying joy—explodes among us.

Endnotes

[1] John Henry Thayer, *A Greek-English Lexicon of the New Testament* (Edinburgh: T & T Clark, 1955), 55.

[2] James Strong, *The Comprehensive Concordance of the Bible* (Iowa Falls, IA: World Bible Publishers, n.d.), 17.

[3] E.M. Bounds, *Satan: His Personality, Power, and Overthrow* (Grand Rapids, MI: Baker Book House, 1972), 139-140.

[4] Excerpt (submitted) from *Forgive and Forget* by Lewis B. Smedes. Copyright © 1984 by Lewis B. Smedes. Reprinted by permission of HarperCollins Publishers, Inc., 99-102.

[5] H.A. Ironside, *Expository Notes on the Gospel of Matthew* (Neptune, NJ: Loizeaux Brothers, 1948), 227.

[6] Jonathan Goforth, *By My Spirit* (Minneapolis, MN: Bethany Fellowship, 1942), 26-46.

[7] Donald A. Hagner, *Matthew 1-3,* David A. Hubbard, gen. ed., Word Biblical Commentary (Dallas: Word Books, 1993), 33a:532.

[8] Eduard Schweizer, *The Good News According to Matthew* (Atlanta: John Knox Press, 1975), 343.

[9] Ambrose, "Concerning Repentance: Book 1," *Nicene Fathers and Post-Nicene Fathers*, ed. Philip Schaff (Grand Rapids, MI: Eerdmans, 1979) 2:10:334.

[10] Merrill C. Tenney, *The Gospel of John,* The Expositor's Bible Commentary (Grand Rapids, MI: Zondervan, 1981), 193.

[11] Stevan L. Davies, *Jesus the Healer: Possession, Trance and the Origins of Christianity* (New York: Continuum Publishing Co., 1995), 98.

[12] Sharon Mumper, "From Pogrom to Peacemaking," *Christianity Today,* 12 August 1996, 38, 40. Used by permission.

[13] Neil T. Anderson, *Winning Spiritual Warfare* (Eugene, OR: Harvest House Publishers, 1990), 34.

Katie's Bar

Katie's Bar was located on Florida's Route 64, the road leading to the Bradenton Missionary Village, a retirement center founded by Tropicana™ orange juice entrepreneur Anthony T. Rossi.

Bars alongside roads that missionaries travel apparently become objects of prayer. Such was the case with Katie's Bar. Each time veteran Colombian missionary Oscar Jacobson passed by, he prayed for the closing of the bar and he bound it in the name of Jesus Christ.

Prayer was increased when incidents involving near accidents relating to the bar multiplied. Matters finally came to a head when one driver fishtailed into the parking lot of the bar and nearly came right out again, in reverse direction, threatening to slash head-on into oncoming traffic that included Oscar's vehicle.

One evening at dusk, a truck driver pulled into the bar to use the phone. To get back into his lane on Route 64 he had to do a U-turn. There were no reflectors on the side of the flatbed semi-trailer. As he was turning, Waldo and Cecile Mae Schindler, former missionaries to Gabon, West Africa, hit the trailer broadside. Mr. Schindler was killed instantly. His wife survived for about a half hour.

Katie, the owner of the bar, rushed to the scene, crawled into the wreckage and cradled the head of the dying missionary.

After the accident, prayer changed. The binding continued, but new phrases were added, among them, "Lord Jesus Christ, avenge the death of your saints." More than ever the bar had become a symbol of evil.

Oscar determined to call on Katie to thank her for the succor she had given to Mrs. Schindler in her dying moments. Katie, if that was her name, turned out to be a former church attender. She had stopped attending when her husband abandoned her and their five children for a younger woman. The bar had been what she thought she had to do to provide for those children.

Oscar Jacobson, always the evangelist, convinced Katie that she ought to attend an evangelistic campaign. Out of respect for Oscar and his wife Mina, she went. Whether she ever turned to the Lord is unknown, but the bar closed. We drove by it several times in a 1997 visit to Bradenton, Florida.

A large public school is being constructed just across Route 64. Oscar is convinced that Katie's Bar will never open again

Part V

BINDING AND LOOSING:
THE PRAGMATIC FACTORS

How does binding and loosing work?

There are various perspectives which require consideration and analysis. The final days are going to be characterized by *"demonic entrenchment*, an obstacle resulting from an excess of time, and *demonic desperation*, an obstacle linked to a lack of time."[1]

If indeed binding and loosing is, in its essence, spiritual warfare, then the hows and whys need further elaboration and explanation.

Pragmatism as a word makes me uncomfortable. The philosophy of William James has been a curse (Colossians 2:8).[2] I reject its truth claims.

Anecdotes, however convincing, do not establish the truth. If the doctrine in this book is not biblically solid, forget the incidents. They may illustrate truth but can never establish it.

There is, nevertheless, a biblical pragmatism, the "Once I was blind, but now I see!" kind that must be considered. It is that kind of pragmatism we now pursue.

Endnotes

[1] George Otis, Jr., *The Twilight Labyrinth* (Grand Rapids. MI: Chosen Books, 1997), 235.

[2] William James, *The Varieties of Religious Experience* (New Hyde Park, NY: University Books, 1902).

15

FALSE AND TRUE

ARLY COUNSEL ON THIS BOOK from my lifelong friend Delbert
McKenzie was, "Don't forget the true and false." That
comment demands this chapter.

The subject of binding and loosing, when addressed in an
evangelical context, immediately creates interest—and anxiety.
The reason is that there are at least three, perhaps four, major
non-biblical ways of thinking about this subject. They unfortunately often dominate the scene and make it harder for us to
think biblically. In fact, my discussion in the Introduction of the
"friends" of binding and loosing included these theological ele-
ments as major impedances to a biblical understanding of binding and loosing.

What I am saying throughout this entire book is being colored
and framed by errors abroad in the field. If you are convinced
that Peter was the first pope and that binding and loosing is the
prerogative of only priests and bishops, then the main thrust of
this book is not receptor material for you.

Similarly, the doctrines of the Faith Movement have been
promulgated rather widely. You may feel that all the teachings
rooted in the writings of E.W. Kenyon are biblical or that believ-

ers may indeed act in God's place, even becoming as one preacher suggests, "little gods."[1] This text will not be well received if that is so.

However, for a very large body of thoughtful students of Scripture, we must address the common errors associated with binding and loosing.

The Roman Catholic Error

The Roman Catholic tradition is very ancient and, in essence, teaches that Peter as the first pope was given the keys of the kingdom. Indeed, access to the kingdom, they say, is through Peter and through his divinely empowered successors. The Catholic position on Matthew 16 declares that Jesus thereby authorized the establishment of the Roman Catholic Church, the primacy of Peter in its government and the apostolic power of excommunication.[2] The Roman Church claims "that these [Matthew] statements of our Lord confer on the priests and bishops, or primarily on the pope, special power to forgive sins."[3]

We, of course, affirm, in Protestant fashion, the priesthood of all believers. The power of the keys to bind and loose, we say, is available to all believers whose righteousness is by faith and who are thus in right standing with God. However, in seeking to be submissive to Scripture, we view the Matthew passages as a unified whole, as applying to the whole Church. As demonstrated earlier, Augustine and Chrysostom, among others of the Church Fathers, saw broader applications of binding and loosing which include not only the leadership but the whole Church.

Catholics also believe that, according to Matthew 16, Peter is the rock on which the Church is built, in what is called "Peter's Primacy."[4] Chrysostom, on the other hand, though he speaks of Peter having the keys, says that the rock on which Jesus will build the Church is "the faith of his confession."[5] As evangelicals we believe that Jesus is our Rock and the Church is built on Him and the confession of our faith in Him.

The Scriptures are clear: There is "one mediator between God and men, the man Christ Jesus" (1 Timothy 2:5). The rule of Scripture frees us from Roman Catholic tradition and interpretation. However, the pervasive presence of the Roman Church in the world means that discussion of binding and loosing, if it is to follow biblical channels, must disengage and distance itself from the teachings and traditions of a church, i.e., the Roman Church which, by its own admission, is not ruled by Scripture.[6]

The Faith Movement

Secondly, teaching about binding and loosing takes place in what is loosely called the Faith Movement. Hank Hanegraaff has written extensively against this movement, but even he admits that

> [not all] these teachers espouse is wrong. If these men and women promoted nothing but error, their audiences would quickly shrink to insignificance. It is sometimes possible to watch 15 minutes of a Faith broadcast and wonder what the fuss is all about, since we may see nothing worthy of censure. But it is what occurs on minute 16 that ought to rock us on our heels, for it is the fatal error mixed in with the truth that makes the Faith movement so dangerous.[7]

Several errors in the Faith Movement must be rejected. For example, scripturally speaking, binding and loosing may certainly be applied to money as part of our Lord's "whatever," but should it be seen as the means to secure personal riches? What has been called the "prosperity doctrine"—the concept that believers are to live like "King's Kids," that Christians are intended always to prosper and never to suffer—has likewise been advanced. My Bible says, "In this world you will have trouble" (John 16:33). Christian experience illustrates this all too well.

Another teaching espoused by some in the Faith Movement has been that believers in Christ become little gods. This is a dreadful caricature of "Christ in you, the hope of glory" (Colossians 1:27). The holy linkage of heaven to binding and loosing appears to have been lost, as evidenced in the comments of a certain pastor:

> Now this is a shocker! But God has to be given permission to work in this earth realm on behalf of man. . . . Yes! You are in control! So if man has control, who no longer has it? God. . . . When God gave Adam dominion, that meant God no longer had dominion. So, God cannot [be] doing anything in this earth unless we let Him. And the way we let Him or give Him permission is through prayer.[8]

I, along with most evangelicals, repudiate such teaching.

Similarly, a transcript of a Faith Movement evangelist's prayers creates an atmosphere that is, to put it plainly, scary.

> Satan, you demonic spirit of AIDS, and AIDS virus—I bind you! You demon spirits of cancer, arthritis, infection, migraine headaches, pain—come out of that body! Come out of that child! Come out of that man. . . . Satan, I bind you! You foul demon-spirits of sickness and disease. Infirmities of the inner ear and the lungs and the back. You demon spirits of arthritis, sickness and disease. You tormenting infirm spirits in the stomach. Satan, I bind you! You nicotine spirits—I bind you! In the name of Jesus![9]

Certainly Jesus loosed a woman from a spirit of infirmity (Luke 13:11-12), but is every sickness an evil spirit? Matthew makes clear distinctions between sickness and demonization (Matthew 4:24). Probably the most alarming part of this boisterous prayer is the indiscriminate and ubiquitous use of binding terminology. Confronted with such behavior, along with the supposition that such procedure is supposedly correct, anyone with less than a bombastic psyche will tend to be driven away from the biblically ordered and Christ-adorning doctrine of binding and loosing hopefully advocated within these pages.

And there's more. God never abdicates authority; He delegates it. God was, is and always will be in control. It is true that God will not act on some matters unless we pray and take authority in the name of Jesus, but He is still sovereign. In these pages we have been able to present strong biblical support for perceiving that what God has already bound in heaven becomes our prerogative of binding here on earth.

To some, this distinction may be but a nuance. But, believe me, it is of the essence. It is the chasm between truth and falsehood. In error-laden movements, the believer runs God. In biblical Christianity, God leads His children (Romans 8:14). We listen to heaven because God's glory must be involved. When the command is formulated in heaven, then, complete in Christ and armed with believers' authority, we bind or loose whatever has already been bound or loosed in the heart of God.

Biblical psychologists Crabb and Allender astutely recognize that the human propensity [toward error] is not confined to evangelical delusions about modern Faith teaching: "The classic error of this culture: demanding heaven now through some methodology or some person."[10]

I believe it was clearly demonstrated in an earlier chapter that binding and loosing as a biblical doctrine has enjoyed an evangelical renaissance stretching over about 150 years. It may, in recent times, have fallen into disuse and disrepute through exaggeration and error, but that should not deflect us from the pursuit of biblical truth. "Heresies must come" (1 Corinthians 11:19, author's paraphrase). One of the reasons they come is to test the biblical integrity of those who would discover God's truth for themselves.

The Enamored and Disinclined

Thirdly, there are others who, having commented upon binding and loosing, may complicate the current scene. They could be categorized as the "enamored." They simply cannot quit talking about a teaching that was never intended to replace a biblical focus on prayer. The binding and loosing they exude is a caricature of the biblical truth. They, too, hinder the plain advocacy of binding and loosing as a powerful minor theme through much of Scripture.

Similarly, refusal to believe that Matthew 18:18 might have reference not just to church discipline but to the counter-kingdom does injustice to the divine mandate to bind "whatever."[11] Who is to say that the binding of demons is not God's prerogative? Again, the commonly held belief that supernatural events and gifts have passed from the scene is held by some ardent evangelicals. This disinclination toward the supernatural complicates the issue and makes it more difficult to speak biblically about binding and loosing. Nevertheless, Jesus Christ is indeed the same "yesterday and today and forever" (Hebrews 13:8). None of His attributes or powers have ever been surrendered or withdrawn. Binding and loosing is sometimes a supernatural business—wonderfully supernatural. Jesus Christ's mandate to bind and loose has not been withdrawn.

The presentation of this doctrine, indeed a whole theology then, is a path fraught with errors on several sides. Shall we withdraw the truth because errors abound? Not at all. The biblical posture is to defend the faith once delivered unto the saints (Jude 3). I am attempting to do exactly that in this book.

The Counterfeit

The fourth kind of falsehood connected to the biblical doctrine of binding and loosing is dramatically portrayed in the early stages of Moses' contest with Pharaoh, ruler of Egypt. The back-and-forth struggle was filled with true and false manifestations, among them the staff that became a snake and swallowed up the Egyptians' staffs-become-snakes (Exodus 7:9-12) and the striking of the staff on the Nile that turned it into blood (7:14-24). It should be noted that the Egyptian wise men, sorcerers and magicians were able to perform the same miracles through their "secret arts." Should we be surprised, then, that in these latter days binding and loosing likewise has counterfeit and deceptive formats? Sometimes counterfeits are necessary to direct our attention to the authentic and true.

These last few lines I would rather not have written. But I must write them. For some of you, these may be the most disconcerting paragraphs in this whole book. It must be said: *It is possible, even in a context that seems to be overtly evangelical and biblical, to have binding and loosing from another "Jesus" who is not God Almighty.*

Paul warned against "counterfeit miracles, signs and wonders" (2 Thessalonians 2:9) through the Antichrist. He also warned the Corinthians to be alert to an alternate Jesus who would be smooth enough to go down rather well (2 Corinthians 11:4). And, indeed, Jesus Himself warned against those who worked miracles without ever knowing Him (Matthew 7:22-23).

The reality is that Deuteronomy 13 is in the Bible. One of the most severe warnings against false prophets comes when Moses advises that *even if all the prophet says comes to pass*, he is nevertheless false if he draws the hearts of the people away from Almighty God (Deuteronomy 13:1-5).

Can false binding and loosing take place in the name of an alternate Jesus? Can actual, though false, binding and loosing take place let us say, in Mormonism? Potentially, yes!

I am saying that all things need to be examined; everything must be proved, so that we may isolate and seize the good (1 Thessalonians 5:21).

Endnotes

[1] _____, "Praise the Lord" program on TBN, 7 July 1986 as cited in Hank Hanegraaff, *Christianity in Crisis* (Eugene, OR: Harvest House, 1993), __.

[2] Richard H. Hiers, "Binding and Loosing: The Matthean Authorization," *Journal of Biblical Literature*, 1985, 104:233.

[3] *International Standard Bible Encyclopedia* (Grand Rapids, MI: Eerdmans, 1979), 1:511.

[4] Bernard Orchard, ed., *A Catholic Commentary on Holy Scripture* (New York: Thomas Nelson & Sons, 1953), 881.

[5] Chrysostom, "The Gospel of Matthew: Homily 54," *Nicene Fathers and Post-Nicene Fathers*, ed. Philip Schaff (Grand Rapids, MI: Eerdmans, 1979), 10:333.

[6] Austin Flannery, gen. ed., *Vatican Council II: The Conciliar and Post Conciliar Documents* (Northport, NY: Costello Publishing Co., 1975), 755, 762-763.

[7] Hank Hanegraaff, *Christianity in Crisis* (Eugene, OR: Harvest House, 1993), __.

[8] _____, as cited by Hanegraaff, *Christianity in Crisis*, __.

[9] _____, as cited by Hanegraaff, *Christianity in Crisis*, ___.

[10] Larry Crabb and Dan B. Allender, *Hope When You're Hurting* (Grand Rapids, MI: Zondervan, 1996), 132.

[11] Hanegraaff, *Christianity in Crisis*, ___.

Anonymous Loosing

Delbert McKenzie

In discussion with the prayer group of which I am a part, we came to the conclusion that we as God's people had authority to bind and loose in our community. Not having complete knowledge about who in the community might be in bondage or who might be responsive at that time to the drawing of the Holy Spirit, we concluded that we should bind any spirits of darkness which were holding people, that we should release any who were captives and then expect and allow God the Holy Spirit to draw whom He would to our church. After doing this for a length of time, remarkable events began to occur.

One Saturday night a woman heard a voice, whether literally or in her mind we cannot say, but the voice said, "Go to church tomorrow." Having no connection with any church, she went to the Yellow Pages and fingered through the list. In the providence of God, her eyes fell on the name of our church and so the next morning she came.

An opportunity was given in the service for people to come forward to receive Christ. Evidently loosed from whatever bound her, this woman was free to respond to the grace of God. She continues to grow in her Christian faith.

16

WHEN IT DOESN'T HAPPEN

I'M SURE WE ALL MUST ADMIT that there are times when the heavens are as brass, when God's ear seems so heavy that He cannot hear, when binding and loosing, as much as one may believe that it is imperative, simply does not take place. Binding is a farce, loosing a dream.

Why are there times when it doesn't work? Let's enumerate some answers to that question.

1. Binding and loosing will not work if God has other plans. There are times when the Father says no. Jesus did not receive His request that the cup of the cross pass from Him (Luke 22:42). It is commonly understood that, in matters of prayer, God's response may be yes or wait or no. All the Lord's responses are framed to secure God's ultimate glory in whatever the results turn out to be. Tozer objects.

> The God-always-answers-prayer sophistry leaves the praying man without discipline. By the exercise of this bit of smooth casuistry he ignores the necessity to live soberly, righteously and godly in this present world,

and actually takes God's flat refusal to answer his prayer as the very answer itself. Of course such a man will not grow in holiness; he will never learn how to rest and wait; he will never know correction; he will not hear the voice of God calling him forward; he will never arrive at the place where he is morally and spiritually fit to have his prayers answered. His wrong philosophy has ruined him.[1]

If we listen to Tozer, and I think he is right, there may be some waiting, some discipline, some obedience before the answer comes, even in binding and loosing.

Earlier in these pages, I sought to make very clear that binding and loosing is irrevocably linked to heaven. All the discussion about the periphrastic future perfect tense and the various translations of the passages in Matthew 16 and 18 were intended to convey that God has never surrendered any of His prerogatives. Until God's servants catch His thought and bind because He is binding and loose because He is loosing, nothing happens. More properly, what does happen is only human effort and vain repetition in prayer.

A man we will call Paul X was a constant harassment to a ministry of deliverance of which I was a part. I clearly recall that we vigorously bound his activities in the name, so we thought, of the Lord Jesus Christ. But nothing happened, at least not that we could tell. My conclusion, after these many years of retrospection, is that in the case of Paul X no binding or loosing took place because the linkage with heaven—that indispensable impulse of the Holy Spirit—was missing.

2. Binding and loosing may not work if biblical knowledge is lacking. God's people are often destroyed for lack of knowledge (Hosea 4:6). It is certainly so in this area of Christian experience.

Indeed, errors in the field hinder the lack of biblical knowledge. How can anyone bind or loose if he or she has never been taught?

3. Binding and loosing may not work because of a flawed perception of the believer's completeness in Jesus Christ (Colossians 2:10). A devastating lack of spiritual and holy God-confidence as to one's position in Jesus Christ can and does impede activity in the area of binding and loosing. For instance, if you are not dominated by a total passion for God's glory, if you doubt that you are indeed complete in Jesus Christ or that you could ever dare, because He is in you, to act authoritatively on His behalf in binding and loosing, expect nothing.

4. Binding and loosing may not work if the concept of the authority of the believer is not understood. If you do not know that you are seated in the heavenlies with Jesus Christ (Ephesians 1:22-2:6), if you do not know that all power and authority have been given to Jesus Christ (Matthew 28:18), and if you fail to see the implication of "Christ in you, the hope of glory" (Colossians 1:27), then the possibility of behaving authoritatively, even Christologically as Paul did in Philippi (Acts 16:18), is beyond you.

Conversely, once it is understood that disciples of Jesus Christ may indeed act on His behalf, allowing His authority to flow through them, then binding and loosing is more likely to take place.

5. Binding and loosing may not work because of hindering paradigms. For example, a cessationist by definition believes that supernatural events have generally ceased in the life of the Church. With such a mind-set, no binding and loosing of the supernatural variety is likely to happen. Since binding and loosing involves the strong man in some cases and may occasionally be exhibited in supernatural events, as some but not all of the incidents related here illustrate, a cessationist viewpoint impedes binding and loosing.

Likewise, an amillennial view of Scripture, in which binding and loosing might be considered unnecessary or inappropriate in these times, would similarly be a hindering paradigm.

6. Binding and loosing does not work when sin blocks communication with God. "If I had cherished sin in my heart, the Lord would not have listened" (Psalm 66:18). Binding and loosing disassociated with personal piety and holiness can be no more than vain repetition. Conversely, confessing our sins one to another and praying one for another brings deliverance and healing (James 5:16).

The Bible is not a bifurcated book. It is all of one fabric, a whole. God's rules of purity and holiness are nowhere suspended so that we may bind and loose without the discipline and order of the kingdom. Of the hindrances to binding and loosing listed here, this is possibly the most common.

7. Binding and loosing does not work when the Lord's disciples fall into the trap of indiscriminate actions. Some folks want to bind anything and everything that moves, including, as we noted earlier, the church mouse. All prayer sessions become binding and loosing sessions. Pure intercession and adoring worship of God are replaced by a twisted focus on the counter-kingdom. It is the unhealthy syndrome which Jesus addressed when He said, "Do not rejoice that the spirits submit to you, but rejoice that your names are written in heaven" (Luke 10:20).

8. Binding and loosing may not work because it is not always the weapon of choice in the spiritual arsenal. We "should always pray and not give up" (Luke 18:1). Nowhere do you find the suggestion in the holy text that men and women ought always to bind and loose. In the Old Testament, many battles were fought by the armies of Israel, but only once is it recorded that the choir was sent forth to bind the kings and nobles with praise, to inflict vengeance on the enemies of God (2 Chronicles 20:21-29; Psalm 149:8).

Binding and loosing is a "sometimes" truth for tight corners and joined battles. I will not retreat for a moment from suggesting that binding and loosing prerogatives are for "whatever." Even the admonition to first bind the strong man can be considered a special event, as was Jesus' temptation. But this trail of binding and loosing truth, as it wends its way through both the Old and New Testaments, is a minor theme still. It is not a plank of orthodoxy nor a main tenet in the kingdom.

After listening to some prominent teachers on these matters, Jim Cymbala, well-known pastor of the Brooklyn Tabernacle, has some salient and painful observations:

> In one of the teaching sessions another speaker said: "There are three levels of spiritual warfare: battles with ordinary demons every day, confrontations with the occult such as astrology or the New Age, and then strategic-level warfare against the spirits in charge of a whole region. And even the Apostle Paul never understood this third level or exercised this kind of ministry."[2]

Cymbala is incredulous: "Imagine this clever teacher transcending the great apostle of the New Testament."[3] He plunges on.

> Did Peter ever bind the spirit over Joppa or Caesarea? Paul spent three years in Ephesus, a center of idol worship, yet there is no mention of "binding the spirit of the goddess Diana, . . ." Why is there so much evil rampant on the earth if the devil has indeed been "bound"

so many times by Christians today? One well-known preacher went to San Francisco a few years ago, rented a stadium, and "did spiritual warfare" for the night, claiming to bind and rebuke every evil spirit and principality in the city. The next day he and his entourage flew home again. Is San Francisco a more godly place today as a result?[4]

Cymbala concludes, "The Bible speaks more about resisting the devil than it does about binding him."[5] Though his conclusion on the resisting point is not correct, I must still empathize with Cymbala. The rest of his comments are uncomfortably well-aimed and all too accurate!

9. Binding and loosing may not work if discipline is lacking. The painful truth is that we may find ourselves ineffective, as were the disciples. In Mark 9:29 they were unable to cast out an evil spirit for lack of discipline in prayer. Similarly, in Luke 13:12, the woman loosed by Jesus was addressed in the perfect tense, suggesting an ongoing process in which discipline was involved. If a loosing ministry requires repetition to be effective, discipline is a factor.

10. Binding and loosing may not work if the timing is not right. During the writing of this manuscript, our publishing house was in a bureaucratic struggle with a government agency. On May 28, 1997, I began to loose us from that entanglement. Although we had been praying and working on the project for two or three years, immediately after beginning the loosing, our visit to the attorney's office was marked by an unusual event. The government official "happened" to call while we were there. A fruitful, totally unplanned, teleconference conversation ensued. Prayer had been the instrument of choice for two years or more, but now, suddenly, it was loosing. On August 21, 1997, our company was loosed! Ah, yes, binding and loosing still happens! In God's time.

McCandlish Phillips was at one time a star reporter with *The New York Times*. In a book that remains one of the most powerful ever written on matters pertaining to spiritual warfare, he recounts a personal encounter with biblical ideas and their confirming events similar to what we have been discussing.

> I lived for six years in a large building in New York City in which there were no untoward events until a series of fires began in it. For a period of a little over a month there were frequent fires, sometimes more than one in a day. Each time the fire alarm would clang throughout the building there would be a scurrying to evacuate. Then the firemen and their apparatus would come and put the blaze out, usually before any extensive damage was done. The number of these fires went up and up. They broke out on various floors, in various rooms and apartments. Their number reached 20 in not much over twice as many days. An investigation was started, but it did not produce any clear-cut leads.
>
> Twice a small number of occupants met for prayer. On the second of these occasions, a minister who had come to the building at the request of a tenant said that while he was in prayer about the fires in the building, he had seen, as in a vision, a certain individual. In the name of Jesus Christ he had bound him in the Spirit from setting any more fires. It was, to say the least, a surprising assertion. Yet he made it with quiet assurance, as a man who knew exactly what he was talking about. From that day on, the fires stopped.[6]

Phillips calls the events in the apartment complex the result of the "spiritually effective action taken . . . to cut in against this demonic prompting to touch off fires."[7]

Well said, Mr. Phillips.

In conclusion, binding and loosing is an expression of God's truth that powerfully equips His servants in the kingdom. We need to understand it, operate from time to time within its borders and use its principles, all the while remembering that it is, nevertheless, far from a test of orthodoxy, far from being a cardinal doctrine of the Christian Church.

Endnotes

[1] A.W. Tozer, *Man: The Dwelling Place of God* (Camp Hill, PA: Christian Publications, 1966), 86-87.

[2] Jim Cymbala, *Fresh Wind, Fresh Fire* (Grand Rapids, MI: Zondervan, 1997), 106-108.

[3] Ibid., 106-107.

[4] Ibid., 108.

[5] Ibid.

[6] McCandlish Phillips, *The Bible, the Supernatural and the Jews* (Camp Hill, PA: Christian Publications, 1995), 200-210.

[7] Ibid.

"Il y a une Force contre Nous Maintenant"

("There's a Power against Us Now")

Chuck Davis and Bill Trinidad

In the summer of 1992, God spoke to us on two separate occasions about the need to start a prayer meeting with the specific intent of binding the strong man in Bamako, Mali. We met weekly for two hours. The first hour was worship, the second prayer against the strong man operating in that city.

About six weeks after we began, an Islamic witchdoctor tried to conjure up a spirit and send it on an errand. It was something he did regularly, and it had always worked. But this time the demon was slow to manifest itself. The witch doctor persisted, and it finally came.

"What took you so long?!" the witch doctor demanded angrily.

It answered him, "Il y a une force contre nous maintenant. C'est les chrétiens." ("There's a force against us now; it's the Christians.") Apparently, the witch doctor's ability to conjure and send the powers had been hindered by our praying.

17

BINDING, LOOSING
AND POLITICS

Rodger Lewis and his wife Lelia spent a lifetime as missionaries on the idyllic island of Bali, Indonesia. When they returned to Bali for their second term in May of 1965, their ship sailed into the harbor under a flag bearing the hammer and sickle. Banners read, "Give weapons to the people"; "Form killing teams to deal with corrupters." The purpose of those banners was to condition the people to violence and to turn an Indonesian revolution into a communist revolution.

Several months later, on the morning of October 1, they heard via Jakarta radio that a revolutionary council had taken over the national leadership "to protect it from right-wing generals who had been found plotting against the Sukarno government." The populace, it said, was to take directions from local (communist) councils which had been organized throughout the country.

But something went wrong. Instead of a communist takeover of that vast island kingdom, a chain of events was set in motion that ended in the dissolution and outlawing of the Communist Party in Indonesia.

As Lewis tells it, "Many reasons were given for the failure of the communists' attempted coup in Bali. Their 'fatal mistake had been to try and impose an alien ideology crudely and harshly upon an island in a state of perpetual enchantment with its own mystique. The communists mocked religious observance and festivals' (John Hughes, *The Indonesia Upheaval,* 1967).

"But a more basic reason may be because of prayer. That furlough year we had repeatedly asked people to pray for Indonesia. Many Christians around the world, and especially in Indonesia, were earnestly pleading with God to spare the world's fifth largest nation from the fate of other Asian countries. Following is a report by a missionary in Irian Jaya published in *The Alliance Witness,* October 12, 1966:

> On the night of September 30, 1965, three men in Australia had been so burdened for Indonesia that they travailed in prayer for hours until God gave them the assurance that all would be well. On the following morning they heard of the coup. On the third day there was to have been a slaughter of the Christian church, but, as on the third day when Christ rose from the dead . . . giving victory forevermore, so the tide turned. The enemy was overcome and a great new opportunity given for the preaching of the Gospel.

"This report was attested to in a statement by Mr. Sirdjono, an Indonesian government official, who told a group of missionaries in Irian Jaya in December, 1966, 'If the coup of October 1 had succeeded, the communists had plans to kill 250,000 people, present company included.'

"The nephew of a Balinese pastor known to me was taken into custody as a communist. On his person was found a document listing Christians who were to be liquidated, including many pastors. But the tables were turned dramatically. In some instances, communists were buried in the very graves they had dug for their enemies. Marveling, we could only echo the words of the Psalmist: 'They dug a pit in my path—but they have fallen into it themselves' (Psalm 57:6).

"We had been delivered from the violent man, divinely delivered for a divine purpose. That purpose was revealed in the days that followed when in Indonesia there occurred one of the greatest ingatherings of souls in modern times."[1]

As God intervened in Indonesia, He also intervened in the life of Britain during World War II. Rees Howells, a Welsh educator and evangelist, along with a group of prayer warriors, waged heavenly warfare in parallel with the human battles of that great conflict. Of a public service of intercession in Westminster Abbey, in Howells' hearing Winston Churchill said,

> The English are loath to expose their feelings, but in my stall in the choir I could feel the pent-up passionate emotion, and also the fear of the congregation, not of death or wounds or national loss, but of defeat and the final ruin of Britain.[2]

During the Battle of Britain, it was Howells' declared conviction through prayer that Germany would not invade England. At Dunkirk, a whole army was evacuated by small boats in a great deliverance that had no human explanation.

At the Battle of Salerno in Italy, silence fell when there should have been no silence. Again, it appeared that by prayer God had intervened to save Britain and her military men.[3]

These incidents have political and military ramifications. Though they do not directly involve what we are here calling binding and loosing, there is no question that God intervened in the political life of both these nations in time of crisis.

Some binding and loosing incidents have obvious political implications such as the one in an earlier section describing the struggles of an evangelical church to erect a building in the Muslim city of Bamako, Mali, West Africa. We know the rest of the story: All the bureaucratic bungling and delay gave way when binding and loosing was applied to the political process.

Collisions and Conflicts

What we sometimes forget is that the kingdom of God is among us. Yet, in one sense, it is in the future. In this invisible world, there is a lot of bumping and grinding. The kingdom of God and the counter-kingdom under the jurisdiction of the evil prince are always banging into one another. In the Old Testament, there are clear kingdom intimations;[4] indeed, the kingdom of God is plainly announced in the prophecies of the Old Testament, Psalm 2:10-12 being a good illustration. It implies that God's kingdom will encompass the whole earth:

> Therefore, you kings, be wise;
>   be warned, you rulers of the earth.
> Serve the LORD with fear
>   and rejoice with trembling.
> Kiss the Son, lest he be angry
>   and you be destroyed in your way,
> for his wrath can flare up in a moment.
>   Blessed are all who take refuge in him.

By definition, the kingdom of God "is the kingly rule of Jesus Christ in the lives of men and women who have become His subjects. It will ultimately issue in a realm in which the full power of His authority will be revealed."[5]

The New Testament records that when Jesus came preaching,

He said, "Repent, for the kingdom of heaven is near" (Matthew 4:17). And Luke's account details the arrival of the kingdom at the synagogue in Galilee:

> The Spirit of the Lord is on me,
>   because he has anointed me
>   to preach good news to the poor.
> He has sent me to proclaim freedom for
>   the prisoners
>   and recovery of sight for the blind,
> to release the oppressed,
>   to proclaim the year of the Lord's
>   favor. (Luke 4:18 19)

Entry into that kingdom is through the new birth (John 3:3-7). And the ultimate triumph of the kingdom of God over the kingdom of Satan has been assured since the cross (Colossians 2:14-15).

Still, there is always conflict. There are times when the glory of God is directly challenged. It can be expected that those Christians who are insightful discerners of the times will bind and loose for political purposes. The "whatevers" of Matthew 16 and 18 mean nothing if they do not at times have political ramifications. Of course, if the strong man does not mess with politics, there is no need to bind and loose in that realm.

The direct application of binding and loosing to political processes will surprise some. But it has already been hinted at in the incidents we have narrated. The anonymous contributor of the board meeting incident (at the end of this chapter) is talking about church politics.

And what about politics in academe? in sports teams? in homeowner associations? Politics are as ubiquitous as the human condition.

Three Political Options

There are three main political applications of binding and loosing concepts to Christianity, only two of which fit well with evangelicals.

1. Depersonalization of evil. In this posture, Satan is seen as an influence rather than a personage. Evil is institutionalized; therefore, it must be overthrown in a socialistic revolution. Though this posture emerges from an eroded view of Scripture, liberal Christianity is comfortable with this stance.

2. Evangelical activism. This includes voting, campaigning and in various ways denouncing the evils sometimes perceived in the current political milieu. Evangelicals, especially ardent biblicists, are sometimes prone to this approach—binding the strong man, they hope, through visible political action.

3. Personalization of evil. Regarding Satan as a person is affirmed by a high view of Scripture and is maintained by openly binding and loosing in the spiritual realm. While I am not unsympathetic to the second option above, I much prefer this one. The depersonalization of evil does not square with the Bible. Similarly, political activism often seems quite unproductive. The best path, i.e., admitting the personalization of evil, proceeds parallel to a high view of Scripture.

A Book Too Far

Until this chapter I have found no place to mention a book one would think should be very helpful, *Binding the Strong Man, A Political Reading of Mark's Story of Jesus* by Ched Myers. It is reasonably current (1988) and thick enough (500 pages), and is published by Orbis Books, known for thoughtful though not always orthodox Christian titles. The reason I have not referenced it earlier is that I find its premise in conflict with evangelical thinking. Myers' tendency is toward the demonization of structures, toward describing societal ills as demoniacal expressions. For example, the demonization of South African apartheid and the demonization of Exxon for its environmental sins against nature and the sea.

Myers' treatise sees the binding of the strong man in leftist political terms. It is a liberal view. It is a view that resonates with those in Christianity who propose to do evangelism by marching in demonstrations and yanking shares from companies which traded with South Africa in the apartheid era. Myers would undoubtedly describe the favorite hermeneutic of this book you are now reading as imperial[6] (which it may be—Jesus Christ as King!). One of his friends describes Myers' approach to Scripture as "socio-literary" and his hermeneutic as plainly political.[7]

Voters' Guides

Curiously, a very large body of evangelicalism practices a different kind of political binding and loosing. Dr. Jerry Falwell made the Moral Majority famous before it was disbanded. In the United States, the Christian Coalition distributes voters' guides to churches on election eve with the clear purpose of influencing political outcomes.

In Canada, the Reform Party, led by Preston Manning, became the Official Opposition in Ottawa. Manning himself is known for his open evangelicalism. The Reform Party advances an agenda that coincides at many points with those who take the Bible seriously.

The Southern Baptists have waged a lengthy political campaign to bind modernism and liberalism, to eject from their midst the "moderates" who are less than ardent biblicists. For the most part, the campaign has been effective, the Southern Baptists now having become a much more conservative denomination. They are now, for the record, biblical inerrantists. Theirs was a political victory for evangelical conservatives.

A few years previous, the Missouri Synod Lutherans went through the same wrenching process. Their fight was for Scripture as well. A seminary in exile resulted—called Seminex—but eventually the church saved itself from liberalism and modernism.

In the cases of both the Lutherans and the Southern Baptists, traditional politics, albeit church politics, came to the fore. Historical drift was halted, at least for a while. Binding the corruption and apostasy of the body politic in the Christian context has been done—with voting blocks and marshaled public opinion.

And Money

The 1997 controversy in evangelicalism over the intent of the Zondervan Corporation and the International Bible Society to produce a gender-inclusive New International Version (NIV) raised a firestorm in America's evangelical community. Responding to political pressure from Western feminism, Zondervan's alleged intent had been to feminize the NIV as had already been done in Britain. But the uproar in America caused an apparent capitulation. Plans for a gender-inclusive version for North America were purportedly withdrawn.

These amazing events in American evangelicalism do not relate to doctrine alone. Those concerns might not have won the day. But millions of publishing dollars were at risk. That risk was unacceptable. (I must observe that old-fashioned, hard-nosed politics in the Southern Baptist Convention were the necessary precursors to the victory which those who love their NIV translations have gained.)

Spiritual Warfare Direct

There is another increasingly well-known and attractive option. It is also political—spiritual, yes—but also political.

Rob Reynolds, in the July/August 1997 issue of *Moody* magazine, starts the issue theme of spiritual warfare with a hypothetical introduction to an article as follows. As the account unwinds, the implications of binding and loosing are clearly evident.

> The upper Midwest isn't the first place most people would look for demonic activity. Yet at least one pastor didn't believe the devil had written the region off.
>
> Looking around at the sin in his town, "David Smith" was sure he could attribute it to the working of Satan's minions. So, instead of petitioning the zoning board or town council to shut down offending businesses, he decided to confront the "territorial spirits" he believed were assigned to ensure that the locals remained trapped in spiritual darkness.
>
> For six weeks, Smith and members of his congregation prayed for deliverance from these spirits. But rather than simply praying within their church building, they took their prayers to the streets, walking through seedy neighborhoods and asking God to tear down strongholds of Satan in their town. Within those six weeks, a bar, a porn shop, and an X-rated theater all shut their doors for good. Smith is sure there was no economic or political reason for the closings.[8]

For some Christians fed up with the moral decay all around them, such spiritual warfare techniques look increasingly attractive.

My Heart Lies with Smith

If you have noticed, there are at least three political variants in the expression of binding and loosing. The liberal model depersonalizes Satan and often seeks to bind institutional evil. Though you must not see me as a supporter of apartheid, I reject liberal or neo-evangelical models as essentially unbiblical.

Further, I am basically uncomfortable with the politicization of the Church, though at least in recent times it appears to have been successful among the Southern Baptists and before them the Missouri Lutherans. It has been less successful in the secular arena, since the voting drives seem not to have stemmed the arrogance of evil in America. Democracy, after all, is not a biblical idea. It is a cultural form to which the Church adapts. It could turn out to be a sword of destruction if and when the majority wills to apostasy. Yet, I suppose, there are times when it appears to be God's instrument. Several million evangelicals would say that.

John Piper suggests a political role for fasting, much as I am suggesting a political role for binding and loosing. When we in the kingdom of God are discouraged by the resistance of the political structures, as in the case of abortion, it is helpful to remember that the whole book of Ezra demonstrates in a remarkable way that the heart of the king is in the Lord's hands. He can and does turn it as He wills, often in response to fasting.[9]

With binding and loosing, my heart lies with the fictional "David Smith." I do not think that every case of binding and loosing proceeds with prayer walks and business closings, but David Smith, if he is a real person after all, will read this book with profit. And he may yet find other opportunities for binding and loosing which bring glory to God, celebrate his completeness in Jesus Christ, flow from his authority as a believer seated with Christ in the heavenlies and are political in nature.

Endnotes

[1] Rodger J. Lewis, *The Battle for Bali* (Camp Hill, PA: Christian Publications, forthcoming).

[2] Norman Grubb, *Rees Howells Intercessor* (Fort Washington, PA: Christian Literature Crusade, 1983), 254.

[3] Ibid., 255ff.

[4] John Bright, *The Kingdom of God* (Nashville, TN: Abingdon Press, 1953), 7.

[5] K. Neill Foster, "Discernment, the Powers and Spirit-speaking" (Ph.D. diss., Fuller Theological Seminary, 1988), 41.

[6] Ched Myers, *Binding the Strong Man, A Political Reading of Mark's Story of Jesus* (Maryknoll, NY: Orbis Books, 1988), 167.

[7] Norman K. Gottwald, cover copy for Myers, *Binding the Strong Man.*

[8] Rob Reynolds, "Is There Really a War?," *Moody,* July/August 1997, 15-16.

[9] John Piper, *A Hunger for God: Desiring God Through Fasting and Prayer* (Wheaton, IL: Crossway Books, 1997), 166-172.

Religious Politics

Name withheld

Boards and board meetings and church politics seem to be part of doing church, part of laboring in the kingdom.

I heard about one board member who introduced a resolution which would have resulted in a certain ministry perhaps literally going into a tailspin. In fact, the resolution was so disconcerting that the whole board "lost it" and confusion reigned for about one hour.

During the break, one man collaborated with another brother who was as befuddled as he was with the resolution and its effect on the board. In the name of Jesus Christ they bound the spirit of confusion and loosed the board to return to sanity.

When the group reassembled, everything was back to normal. The change was as dramatic as the difference between night and day.

On another occasion, one board member began to feel that another board member should not attend an upcoming meeting because of his often negative and disruptive views. Lacking other acceptable alternatives, while driving to a meeting he resorted to prayer. Submitting himself to the will of God in an act of binding, he forbade the man's attendance at the meeting.

Arriving at the destination, he received a telephone call and was astounded to hear, "So-and-so will not be coming to the meeting." A sudden though passing ailment had overtaken him.

The lesson we can glean from these incidents is that binding and loosing may be an important spiritual posture particularly in times of corporate decision making.

Little Amy

Deloris Sunda

As the young woman got up to leave after our counseling session, she said to me, "You know, I really feel that I should not even bother to go to Sunday school and church, because every week when we take our baby to the nursery she screams so much that the nursery workers always have to come and get me out of the class or out of the worship service to care for her. She has screamed every waking minute from the time she was born until now. It is so tiring to care for her. She never stops screaming."

Suspecting the exhausted, frail little mother of exaggerating, I assumed that the baby was colicky and decided I'd give her a break by baby-sitting the little girl during the Sunday school hour.

As we went into the hallway for the first baby-sitting session, I felt strongly that I should bind the evil spirits harassing two-year-old Amy. While the mother held the child, I asked for and received permission from her to bind the powers. After bowing together in prayer and submitting ourselves to God as James 4:7 instructs, I commanded that the tormenting spirits in Amy be bound in the powerful name of our Lord Jesus Christ. We also told the spirits to loose Amy from their clutches and further instructed them to release her immediately and go to the pit of hell prepared for them by the Lord Jesus Christ. I also loosed Amy into the loving arms of the Lord Jesus Christ to accomplish His good work in her life.

Then, taking Amy from her mother's arms, the still screaming child and I went into the nursery while her mother headed to her class. When the nursery workers saw me with Amy, they shook their heads and said, "Good luck, D. We hope you have more luck than we've had with her."

Taking a rocking chair from the main nursery into an adjacent room, I began to rock Amy and sing songs to her about the powerful Lord Jesus Christ, all repeating the name of Jesus. For ten minutes I sang to the screaming child. Then, suddenly, she spied a toy on the floor, got down from my lap, picked up the toy and climbed back onto my lap. She sniffled a bit and then the crying ceased. I think she had become aware for the first time that the torture was over.

Soon a teacher came into the room with a half-dozen children Amy's age. They sat in a semicircle on the floor for a story. Amy grew interested and eventually slipped off my lap to join them. She listened quietly and intently until it was time for the church service to begin. After advising the nursery workers that if Amy began crying again they were to come and get me, not her parents, I went into the sanctuary.

This incident took place many months ago. Amy still stays quietly in the nursery while her parents attend Sunday school and worship services.

My husband and I have had many experiences of binding and loosing, but of all of them, Amy's story is one of the most amazing. She was an innocent victim of evil powers. She never invited them, yet they had stooped so low as to torment a tiny baby so that she had never had a moment's peace from her birth until that day in the room adjacent to the nursery when the powers were bound. Jesus is Victor!

Brother Martin and the Spiritist Church

Joseph Broz III

This story took place in Florida between October 1973 and May 1974. Joseph Broz III, then just a teenager, was being mentored by Rev. Martin Elz, a minister associated with the Missouri Synod Lutheran Church.

The congregation of a metaphysical, spiritualistic church regularly held séances in which it was purported that contact was made with the departed dead. "Many of my friends in high school were attracted to the ESP Fiestas held on Sundays in hotel auditoriums and malls around town," Broz says. We pick up his account of the rest of the story.

These psychic gatherings featured counseling by palm readers and psychic healers, cold readings by "sensitives," astrology and tarot card readings and mediums that made contact with the spirit world. Each ESP Fiesta was well advertised in the ＿＿＿＿＿＿＿＿ *Times* weekend religious magazine and by brightly colored handbills displayed in prominent places.

A well-known psychic (a disciple of the famous medium Arthur Ford) hosted a radio talk show and did psychic readings on the air for those seeking advice.

My friend Martin Elz had a razor-sharp ability to discern between the works of Satan and the works of the Lord Jesus Christ. Brother Martin had served the Lord as pastor in the Evangelical Lutheran Church in Germany during the height of Hitler's power.

Around Christmastime, the papers carried ads that promised that "Mary the Mother of Jesus Christ" would speak through a medium and tell what really happened the night when, as it was being suggested, Mary's womb was impregnated by a Roman soldier. The ad challenged other churches in the city to prove that their medium message from "Mary, the Virgin Mother of Christ" was false. The radio host joined in the challenge.

Brother Martin was deeply troubled by the fact that the churches in the city seemed unwilling to take the challenge. So he asked me if I knew what the Bible said about fasting and if I would like to study Isaiah 58:1-6 with him. I agreed.

Martin then shared his concern about the false doctrine and the public challenge being offered. He told me these people needed to see that there was one true God who came in the flesh. The Lord Jesus Christ, he said, had the power to destroy the powers of darkness. He urged me to fast on bread and water for one day and then to ask the Lord to show me anything that displeased Him. Then I was to pray for peace about standing with him when we would visit the psychic church. I felt at peace about doing it, so, a few days later, we attended a midweek service.

We entered the building and sat down in the middle of one of the old church pews. I leaned over and asked Martin how many people he thought were there. He estimated between 500 and 600.

The host leader welcomed those who had come. We sang the hymn "In the Garden," which was followed by a reading of poetry, a vocal solo and an offering which would be given to the speaker. Then we were asked to stand and recite the Lord's Prayer. Martin and I stood and prayed silently. I remember asking the Lord what I had gotten myself into, but the peace in my heart was still there. We sat down.

Martin told me to stay in my seat no matter what happened and not to say a word. The atmosphere was palpably evil.

The leader came to the pulpit and asked us to be quiet while the spirit guides made contact. Several minutes of silence passed and nothing happened. The host leader went up to the pulpit. He told the audience that there were individuals present that evening who were not in sympathy with the spirit guides who were supposed to manifest themselves. He asked that those individuals leave. Neither Martin nor I moved.

More time passed. Then the leader asked the ushers to walk up the center aisle and stop at a pew he would indicate. The ushers walked up the aisle and stopped—at our pew. There were perhaps fourteen people in the pew. We were in the middle.

The leader then repeated the request that those who were not in agreement with the spirit guides manifesting themselves leave the meeting. No one moved. So the leader said, "Martin and Joe are resisting and are not in sympathy with the spirit guides who would like to manifest themselves here today. Nothing can happen until they leave." It disturbed me that this man knew our names.

At that point, Martin rose to his feet.

"We are here as representatives of the Lord Jesus Christ. He is Victor over the powers of darkness and Satan. By Christ's death, shed blood and resurrection, the head of Satan has been crushed. Because the Lord Jesus Christ has all power in heaven and earth over Satan and his evil kingdom, our leaving will not make any difference. In the name of Jesus Christ, I command that no evil spirits will speak out in this place tonight." Then, as a good Lutheran, Martin emphatically recited the Apostle's Creed for all to hear.

When Martin looked up, one of the séance leaders was flat on the platform, apparently "out cold."

We then left the meeting, with some speed, I must add. To my knowledge, this group never again published any challenges to the churches. Some who had been in attendance that night made a point of reporting to Rev. Elz that, indeed, no manifestation by demonic spirits took place. The spirits had truly been bound.

The next time I saw Martin, he sat me down and in no uncertain terms pressed this Scripture upon me: ". . . do not rejoice that the spirits submit to you, but rejoice that your names are written in heaven" (Luke 10:20).

I have never forgotten.

> There shall not be found among you anyone who makes his son or his daughter pass through the fire, or one who practices witchcraft, or a soothsayer, or one who interprets omens, or a sorcerer, or one who conjures spells, or a medium, or a spiritist, or one who calls up the dead. For all who do these things are an abomination to the LORD, and because of these abominations the LORD your God drives them out from before you. (Deuteronomy 18:10-12, NKJV)

18

FASTING AS LOOSING

F ASTING, THE DELIGHTFUL DISCIPLINE. Is this a contradiction in terms? No! The practice of fasting in the life of a Christian can be truly rewarding. Fasting is geared for results. Far from somber truth dressed in drabness, fasting is a vibrant, radiant, yes, delightful Christian discipline.

But let's begin with an uncomfortable 1789 quotation from John Wesley, the founder of Methodism.

> It would be easy to show in many respects that Methodists in general are deplorably wanting in the practice of Christian self-denial. While we were at Oxford, the rule of every Methodist was to fast every Wednesday and Friday in imitation of the primitive church. Now this practice of the primitive church was universally allowed. "Who does not know," says Epiphanius, an ancient writer, "that the fast of the fourth and sixth days of the week are observed by the Christians throughout the world?" So they were by the Methodists for several years, by them all without exception. . . . The man who never fasts is no more on the way to heaven than the man who never prays.[1]

I must hasten to say that I do not wholly agree with Wesley's statement about a failure to fast keeping one out of heaven—it cannot be backed up biblically. Nevertheless, it is fascinating that such a great man of God should make such an extreme statement. I take it that Wesley wanted no one to be in doubt about his opinion regarding this discipline. Possibly he used an overstatement to make a needed emphasis and was not concerned that all he said about fasting be taken literally.

I have also heard fasting described as "the quickest way to get anything from God." I think that is absolutely true, though I would like to rephrase the statement to say, "Fasting is the quickest way to get yourself into the position where God can do what He has wanted to do all along!"

A.W. Tozer is purported to have said, "I fast just often enough to let my stomach know who's boss."

But what of the Scripture? The Bible has a great deal to say about fasting. Some of it is exceedingly interesting and some of it differs considerably from popular notions concerning this delightful but neglected discipline.

Moses

Moses practiced fasting (Exodus 34:28; Deuteronomy 9:9, 18). On two occasions he fasted forty days without food or water—clearly supernatural fasts. The supernatural element is not the absence of food, but the absence of water. Ordinarily, a man without water will die in ten days. In addition, in Moses' case, the fasts were back-to-back, which means that if there was no real break, Moses went eighty days without food and water. If this is the case, then it was certainly supernatural. If Moses' fasting had been specified as the pattern for us, we could not hope to fast at all apart from God's supernatural intervention.

The human result of Moses' fasts was the reception of God's

law among His people, an event without parallel and nearly without equal in all of human history. And fasting played a significant part. I cannot help but wonder what great events never happen because of our aversion to fasting.

Elijah

Elijah, too, was a man of the fast (1 Kings 19:8). Forty days and nights he went on the strength of his last meal. But the same statement, by its omission of any reference to drink, implies that Elijah did not abstain from liquids throughout the forty-day period. That, in turn, presents the possibility of variations in fasting—supernatural like that of Moses or natural like that of Elijah (nearly everyone is able to abstain from food for forty days and live).

It is clear from Scripture that Elijah's ministry was dominated by the miraculous. There is no substitute for the miraculous in the life of a Christian! Fasting will unleash the supernatural!

Do you need a miracle? Fasting could be the door through which it will come.

Daniel

Daniel's experience with fasting is fascinating (Daniel 9:3; 10:3). He fasted for twenty-one days. And apparently his fast was partial—he ate no "choice food" nor meat and drank no wine. But the Scripture stops short of saying he did not eat. From other references in the book of Daniel, we may assume that Daniel continued his simple diet. But he was fasting all the same, even if he was eating. Today, we would be inclined to call it dieting.

Have you noticed that, as we have probed the Scriptures thus far, fasting has become more and more understandable and feasi-

ble? Perhaps by this point some of you are asking, "Is it not a little much to suggest that one can fast and eat at the same time?" I
don't think so. When I first noticed this possibility in Daniel, I
went scurrying to a Bible dictionary. The definition was simple
and clear: Fasting is a partial or total abstinence from food
and/or water.[2] Daniel, and others in the Bible, apparently understood this.

Perhaps you cannot fast for many days. How about a few hours
or a few days? Perhaps a partial fast will meet your needs exactly. Once you discover that it is possible to eat and fast at the
same time, you are beginning to discover just how versatile fasting really is as a spiritual weapon. Anyone can pick it up at any
time and wield it in his or her own circumstances. Better stated,
the Holy Spirit should be able to direct us to use any spiritual
weapon at any time.

Jonah

The book of Jonah teaches about fasting as well. First, observe
that the people proclaimed a fast and the king supported it
(Jonah 3:5-6). Evidently the initiative for fasting can come from
the grass roots as well as from those in authority. In the case of
the Ninevites, the fast was total—even the animals were included. It lasted for three days and three nights and it was linked
with repentance. Perhaps the greatest turning to God recorded in
Scripture follows (3:10). The result was the salvation of a nation.
And these Ninevites were not even acknowledged followers of
Jehovah!

Can fasting be effective even when practiced by unbelievers?
The Bible implies that it is possible. And if God answers the
prayers of unconverted people (compare the accounts of Cornelius in Acts 10 and 11), then why should God not honor the
fasting of repentant people?

Esther

The story of Esther demonstrates that a leader may also call a fast (Esther 4:16). Queen Esther called for a fast and all the people were obligated to cooperate. The fast was total for three days and three nights. The results? The Jews were delivered and the massacre of a nation was averted—all through the discipline of fasting.

Something similar to this may have happened in the 1973 overthrow of Salvador Allende, the Marxist president of Chile. One missionary, during the breakfast hour, had been fasting for divine intervention in the affairs of the nation. On September 11, 1973, she felt the burden lift. And, for the first time in many days, she began the day with breakfast. That day, the military coup took place. In my view, the events were related.

In the New Testament we read that Paul was in fastings plural (2 Corinthians 6:5, KJV). It is not surprising that our Christian experiences are not like those of Paul. Our fasting is not like his either. Paul also said he was in fastings "often" (11:27, KJV). Frequent fasting has an obvious connection with spiritual power. But, for most of us, it is a connection that has been broken.

Once again in Second Corinthians 11:27, a fascinating truth comes to the fore. Paul distinguishes between hungerings and fastings. If there truly is a difference between being hungry and fasting, then one of the most common objections to fasting is circumvented.

I recall looking forward with anticipation to a break in my evangelistic schedule. I wanted to fast for a few days. Can you imagine my delight when I discovered that from the very first there was no hunger? I think Paul is telling us that going hungry is one thing, fasting is another. Once we learn that, fasting becomes an even more attractive and practical discipline. On the other hand, sometimes I find that I want to fast but cannot because I am too hungry. One of the reasons could be that the Holy Spirit is not prompting the fast.

Jesus

Our Lord and Savior, like Moses and Elijah, also fasted forty days. It is significant that He did this before His ministry began and before the miraculous began to occur. The absence of the miraculous among many of today's Christians can no doubt be traced to the lack of this forgotten discipline.

I think it is also safe to assume that although Jesus did not eat for forty days, He did drink water. An indication of this is that Satan tempted Him on the point of eating, not drinking; on the point of hunger, not thirst.

In Matthew 6, three fascinating promises are given (6:4, 6, 18). Jesus says, "Give, pray, fast in secret—and God will reward you openly" (my paraphrase). Praying brings results. Giving brings results. Fasting brings results. Fasting apart from prayer? Yes, apart from prayer. The promise that accompanies fasting is not hinged to prayer. It is hinged to fasting alone. Mind you, prayer and fasting *are* repeatedly linked in Scripture. They are powerful twins in the spiritual warfare arsenal, but they are not Siamese twins. Together they multiply the release of spiritual power. But alone, as well, each one brings results.

Any Christian would be foolish indeed to argue against praying. But a word in favor of fasting needs to be inserted. A switchboard operator, for example, whose work precludes verbal prayer, could be occupied completely with his or her job and still apply spiritual force to a personal problem through fasting. And, if he or she can maintain an attitude of prayer throughout, all the better.

Fasting, in the book of Acts, played a vital role in the commissioning of missionaries and in what we might now call church business meetings (Acts 13:1-4). Today, we tend to schedule banquets when the church's business is to be done. Could that be why it is sometimes so poorly executed? Could our lack of fasting have any relationship to the lack of missionary candidates?

The Greatest Text?

Probably the greatest text on the subject of fasting is found in Isaiah 58:6. After a five-verse description of the type of fast God does *not* like, the prophet says,

> Is not this the fast that I have chosen? to loose the bands of wickedness, to undo the heavy burdens, and to let the oppressed go free, and that ye break every yoke? (KJV)

Fasting will loose the bands of wickedness. There are plenty of those.

Fasting will undo the heavy burdens. There is no shortage of burdened people.

Fasting will free the oppressed. There is no lack of oppressed peoples.

These phrases seem to refer to the liberation of those bound by Satan. Occult bondage is shattered by fasting. Sometimes nothing else will break through.

Fasting also will break *every* yoke. Thank God for that "every"! For example, an invisible yoke is often formed between a young couple, one a believer and the other not. Concerned parents talk and cajole, but arguments only drive the young people together. Fasting can break a bonding yoke like that. And fasting can be applied to a problem without the participation or even the knowledge of the principals involved. Why, oh why, have we allowed the ruin of so many of our homes and families without ever once unsheathing the yoke-splintering fast God has given us?

Christ made it clear that while He was present on earth His disciples would not fast even though the followers of John the Baptist did. But Jesus also made it clear that after He departed His disciples would fast (Mark 2:19-20). I believe that, at Christ's return, fasting by the Church will be terminated. But now, until then, fasting is God's order. A nonfasting church is out of order!

In any discussion of fasting some reference needs to be made to abstinence in the marital relationship.

> Do not deprive each other except by mutual consent and for a time, so that you may devote yourselves to prayer. Then come together again so that Satan will not tempt you because of your lack of self-control. (1 Corinthians 7:5)

The context indicates that a temporary abstinence from sexual relations within marriage is a fitting and proper self-discipline, an appropriate kind of fast. One of my ministerial friends describes fasting as "a disciplined abstinence from all that gratifies or satisfies the flesh in order to give one's self totally to seeking the Lord in the Spirit. This is the ultimate. Anything less is partial."

A fast may be undertaken in secret, as in Matthew 6, or it may be public, as in Acts 13. It may be initiated by a leader, as in Esther, or it may come from the grass roots, as in Ninevah. It may also be done carnally, with wrong motives, and without effect. The Christ who lives in His people is the same Christ who fasted forty days. We are complete in Him and He wishes to express His fasting nature through us today so that He can hone the spirituality and discernment of His Church.

Some say, "I believe in fasting, but I don't feel led." It is true that we should be led as God's children. But why is it that so few Christians are "led" to fast when it is so obviously a vital, loosing part of Christianity? Usually, we fail to fast because the whole concept of fasting has remained uninviting and uninspiring. Fasting has not been presented as the delightful discipline that it is!

My personal testimony is that I have never fasted without seeing some result. When I shared this fact with a pastor friend, he countered with, "When I fast, nothing ever happens." One day during an evangelistic campaign, we fasted together. That evening the church was full. A film was shown which had a very ordinary impact. My message was ordinary enough, though evangelistic and clear. But God was there. There were many inquirers—men, women, teens and children. So many went to the prayer room that we lost track of the actual number.

The next day I asked the pastor, "Can you still say that God never does anything in response to fasting?"

With a smile, he answered, "No!"

Enthusiasm for fasting on the part of some may be understandable. But the pitfall of regularly scheduled fasts should probably be avoided. All biblical fasts were issue-oriented. A determination to fast every Monday or the third Thursday, for example, may lead present-day believers into the kind of fasting the Bible consistently condemns. It is far better, I think, to apply the awesome power of fasting to specific issues at specific times.

The results are certain to be gratifying indeed.

> To love fasting is not only possible. In the light of the facts, I will go so far as to say that the contrary appears impossible to me to whatever degree one has truly experienced fasting. Experience fasting, and you will love it.[3]

Endnotes

[1] *The Works of John Wesley* (Grand Rapids, MI: Zondervan, n.d.), 7:288.

[2] *Holman Concise Bible Dictionary* (Nashville, TN: Broadman and Holman Publishers, 1997), 236.

[3] Adalbert de Vogue, *To Love Fasting: The Monastic Experience* (Petersham, MA: Saint Bede's Publications, 1989), 104 as cited by John Piper, *A Hunger for God: Desiring God through Fasting and Prayer* (Wheaton, IL: Crossway Books, 1997), 206. This Roman Catholic writer is certainly worth pondering on this issue. Piper's entire work *A Hunger for God* may become a classic in this field. I heartily commend it.

Loosing the Kidnapped

Paul King

On May 22, 1924, four missionaries, including Dr. Robert A. Jaffray along with two others of The Christian and Missionary Alliance and Rev. Rex Ray of the Southern Baptists, left Wuchow, China by boat. Their purpose was to effect a rescue of other missionaries in the besieged city of Kweilin. Although the countryside was "confused and disordered to a degree challenging belief,"[1] they headed north on the Kwei Kiang river. Along the way to Kweilin, their boat the *Roanoke*, was taken captive by pirates. When the missionaries were asked for booty, Jaffray as usual took over. He demanded to talk to their chief.

"We are missionaries," he told the chieftain. "You have no right to ask toll of us. We *receive* offerings to help us with our work. Come now, be reasonable. Give us an offering and let us go." The sheer brass of the man had its effect as he knew it would.[2]

Back in Wuchow, J.A. MacMillan and the other missionaries received word of the situation on May 26. On May 29, they received a wire to the effect that Jaffray and another missionary, Dr. Harry G. Mills, had been released in order to press, the robbers hoped, the ransom demands.

On June 1, Jaffray and Mills arrived back in Wuchow. MacMillan wrote that they had arrived "looking like a pair of bandits—dirty, unshaven, and with towel turbans. Both felt greatly the physical strain, and are wearied to the extreme limit."

Two missionaries were still being held captive, Rex Ray and Edgar Carne. Then on June 11, Ray escaped his captors.

That the missionary team had not been praying all along would not be true, but on June 20 MacMillan and the rest of the missionary team began concentrated prayer and intercession. That day, they received faith to declare Mr. Carne "loosed."

On June 22, a month after the ordeal had begun, two days after the particularly intense session of prayer, a telegram was received. Edgar Carne had been set free on the 20th—the very day of the loosing. MacMillan's cryptic comment called the release "a very gracious confirmation of our 'loosing' him on that day. Praise God."[3]

Endnotes

[1] A.W. Tozer, *Let My People Go* (Camp Hill PA: Christian Publications, 1990), 43-49.

[2] Ibid., 45.

[3] This account is part of the research emerging through Paul King's doctoral program. His dissertation, entitled "A Believer with Authority: The Impact of the Life and Ministry of John A. MacMillan" is focused on the life and ministry of Rev. J.A. MacMillan and will be published by Christian Publications, Inc.

19

BINDING, LOOSING
AND TERRITORIAL SPIRITS

THE SUBJECT OF TERRITORIAL SPIRITS forces its way into the binding and loosing discussion, but not because of textual evidence. Rather, the concept of territorial spirits demands attention because evangelicalism, particularly its missiologists, is fixated with it.

Territorial spirits as a concept correctly suggests that the counter-kingdom is hierarchical, but it then proceeds to suggest that various geographical regions—continents, countries, cities—of the world may be held under the sometimes observable thralldom of invisible evil superspirits, all resistant to the kingdom of God.

Dr. C. Peter Wagner writes:

> It is my view that sound missiological strategy will take responsible, but aggressive, action to bind demonic strong ones, principalities, powers, territorial spirits, or whatever they might be called, who are serving Satan by keeping large populations in spiritual darkness.[1]

Binding or overcoming the powerful spirits is where binding and loosing intersects with this concept of territorialism. I see no reason why territorial spirits cannot be bound or their victims loosed if that is the impulse of heaven. Although binding and loosing is peripheral to the concept of territorial spirits, it nevertheless is pulled into the discussion since, if a territorial spirit is discovered, what must be done with it? "Bind it, of course" would seem to be the common consensus.

Biblical Evidence

Although others argue that more biblical texts must be considered, I believe that the textual backing for this idea is concentrated in only a few places in the Bible.

Daniel, describing the conflict of Michael the archangel in the heavenlies, makes it clear that Michael was powerfully and persistently resisted by the prince of Persia. In the same Scripture, the prince of Greece is named (10:20).

The second mention comes from Paul's writings. In Ephesians 6:12, he speaks about rulers, authorities, powers of this dark world and spiritual forces of evil in the heavenly realms. While not necessarily assigned geographical territories in the Holy Spirit's words, Paul's reference to powers and authorities in Colossians 2:15 likewise suggests territoriality.

A third Pauline reference that connects with territorial spirits is Paul's commentary on the *stoicheia*—"the basic principles of this world" (Colossians 2:8), where he uses this fascinating word. In 1988 my comments were these:

> My view is that, in some cases only, Paul was referring to the powers. Wink suggests that the best treatment of *stoicheia* is to treat each occurrence as the context determines. As for the *stoicheia* being "idea" spirits or

250

powers in Colossians, Ralph Martin lists seven reasons why they should be considered personified evil powers. Patzia also argues, more from the context than the text itself, that the *stoicheia* are personalized, philosophical powers. (Colossians 2:8, 20; Galatians 4:3, 8-9)[2]

In Paul's multiple use of the word, amplifying in each case on its meaning, it is possible to conclude that the *stoicheia* might indeed be, for example, capitalism, communism, pragmatism, Confucianism, Buddhism, Hinduism, Islam or Roman Catholicism. *Stoicheia* could be referring to territorial idea-spirits holding vast sway over large parts of the world.

Fourth, the goddess Diana (also known as Artemis), worshiped throughout the whole province of Asia (a geographical designation), might be another case of a territorial spirit (Acts 19:27). That, at least, was the view of her worshipers. Whether it was the spiritual reality is not clear. Pagan people often believe pagan error.

These are but four textual sites which could refer to what today are being called territorial spirits.

Yet another way to arrive at a doctrine of territorial spirits is to embrace the reading of the Septuagint, where in Deuteronomy 32:8 it reads, "When the most high divided the inheritance to the nations, when he separated the sons of Adam, he set the boundaries of the peoples according to the number of the angels of God."

The reality is that the Septuagint is a Greek translation of the Old Testament, and the reading, some believe, is supported by the best Hebrew text. "Our first evidence is an ancient Hebrew manuscript . . . and surely original."[3] Dead Sea Scroll support for the Septuagint reading also exists. It is increasingly difficult to argue biblically against the reality of territorial spirits.

Doubtful Texts

Both Jesus and the Jews refer to Beelzebub (Matthew 12:24, 27). Some think Beelzebub was a territorial spirit, but our Lord's clear interpretation of the name is Satan. In fact, in the context of Beelzebub, Jesus uses the phrase, "If Satan drives out Satan . . ." (Matthew 12:26), the obvious implication being that Beelzebub is another name for the devil. The majority of commentators are likewise of this opinion.

Others suggest that the "python spirit" which Paul drove out (Acts 16:18) was territorial in nature, but the argument has little validity. The incident seems at most to be a clear deliverance, carried out in public with riotous economic aftereffects.

Church History

The second-century Church Father, Justin Martyr, recognized a principality over the city of Damascus:

> For that expression in Isaiah, "He shall take the power of Damascus and spoils of Samaria" [Isaiah 8:4] foretold the power of the evil demon that dwelt in Damascus should be overcome by Christ as soon as He was born, and this is proved to have happened.[4]

Justin goes on to elaborate, suggesting that this power had dominion over all of Arabia, especially through the religion of the Magi, and that Christ overcame that power by drawing the Magi to come to Him and worship.

> For the Magi who were held in bondage for the commission of all evil deeds through the power of that demon, by coming to worship Christ, show that they

have revolted from that dominion which held them captive, and this [dominion] the Scripture has showed us to reside in Damascus.[5]

This single incident would be more significant if the writings of the Church Fathers were laced with similar incidents and interpretations. They are not. Yet, this account *is* there.

Similarly, in recent evangelical history (1897), Jessie Penn-Lewis wrote that there were in her opinion, " 'principalities' who rule over various lands."[6] She advanced this concept in a missiological context at a China Inland Mission conference in London.

Tozer and Missionary Literature

There is also evidence in pioneer missionary literature that collisions between light and darkness involved what today are being called territorial spirits. A case in point from the life of the famous missionary Robert A. Jaffray is noted in his biography written by A.W. Tozer.

In January 1928, Robert Jaffray arrived at a forbidden Borneo island called Balik-papan.

> Veteran though he was of years of pioneering, the sheer spiritual frigidity of the place crept in on his spirit and pinched his heart like a killing frost. He later wrote: "While in Balik-papan, deep depression of spirit and a feeling of discouragement, doubt and fear seemed to settle upon my soul. It came upon me like a dark, thick cloud of gloom and I could not shake it off. Only His light and joy finally dispelled the darkness. It did not last long, but long enough to make me realize that I was *on the enemy's territory*. Yes, here is

a place where the supreme rule of Satan has never been disputed. The Prince of Darkness has never been challenged here."

Deep in his heart he [Jaffray] determined that *this* Prince of Darkness *should* be challenged soon.[7]

Tozer here focuses upon a certain personage, "this" Prince of Darkness. Written long before the current controversy and emphasis, Tozer's wording makes it clear that he believed Jaffray was tangling with a powerful geographical entity.

Territorial Revival Phenomena

One of the curious and little discussed features of Christian revivals is their territorial nature. I was surprised to learn in reading about the revivals of Jonathan Edwards that the territory of the revival was fourteen miles long and two miles wide. (Paul King gave me a map of Edward's revival which shows it as a carrot-like profile.)[8]

Similarly, one hears of ships entering the New York harbor during the later Great American Revival of 1858 and running smack into the revival atmosphere, with the result that conversions preceded by great agony of soul and profound repentance broke out on board the ships once the perimeter had been breached.

Ship after ship arrived with the same tale of sudden conviction and conversion. On one, a captain and the entire crew of thirty men found Christ at sea and entered the harbor rejoicing.[9]

Wesley Duewel describes "holiness zones" in the 1858 revival, and writes that a "divine influence seemed to pervade Utica and Rome during these revivals and turned them into a zone of holiness."[10]

A canopy of holy and awesome revival influence—in reality the presence of the Holy Spirit—seemed to hang like an invisible cloud over many parts of the United States, especially over the eastern seaboard. At times this cloud of God's presence even seemed to extend out to sea. Those on ships approaching the east coast at times felt a solemn, holy influence, even one hundred miles away, without even knowing what was happening in America.[11]

A friend told me about a revival that took place in Yarrow, British Columbia some years prior to our arrival there in 1959 for pastoral ministry. A railroad crossing leads into the town from the northeast. When my colleague crossed that railway and dropped down into the town, his testimony was, "You hit the revival. You could feel it."

Do these kind of subjective phenomena indicate that revivals represent the overthrow or the binding of territorial spirits? Perhaps.

The Welsh Revival, the New Hebrides Revival, the Western Canadian Revival, the Asbury Revival—all these terms have geographical modifiers. Could the presence of those modifiers be telling us something? Perhaps.

Cautionary Advice

John Dawson, who probably triggered the discussion of territorial spirits in the current era, offers advice which is, by and large, being ignored:

Very little is revealed about specific territorial spirits in the Bible, and that's no accident. . . . [The existence of territorial spirits] should not be taken as a mandate for the development of spiritual maps in which we seek knowledge for the sake of knowledge. If we gain knowledge of the name and nature of an evil spirit and publish it broadly, the enemy will only attempt to glorify himself.[12]

Negatives to Consider

The doctrine of territorial spirits is getting a lot of bad press. Serious, godly writers are advising great caution. Peter Wagner, after apparently experiencing opposition to his ideas, is unusually defensive about his advocacy of territorialism in his book *Confronting the Powers*.[13] I know him to be an optimist, but there are, he has been finding, reasons why the critics are uneasy.

The resistance to the territorial spirits concept is not directed so much at the idea of their existence as at the assumed necessity to focus excessively on these powerful and invisible entities.

Clinton Arnold has written in a similar vein,

> Although territorial spirits are not prominently featured in Scripture, there is enough evidence to say that the Bible clearly teaches the reality of evil entities assigned to geopolitical units. . . . Of even greater significance for the issue confronting us is the fact that the Bible nowhere narrates, describes or instructs us on how, or even whether, we are to engage these high-ranking territorial spirits . . . a strategy for taking on territorial spirits is absent.[14]

Error Embraced

Curiously, in the current passion to engage territorial spirits, error has already been embraced by suggestion as follows: "Few have the spiritual authority and resistance of a Daniel to handle such high level spirits on their own, by themselves."[15]

When pressed to its limit, this error suggests only a partial conquest of the counter-kingdom by Jesus Christ; it suggests a kind of elitism in spiritual warfare not found in the Bible and it makes light of the authority vested in every believer, including Daniel and the apostle Paul (as noted earlier by Cymbala). It denies that believers in Jesus Christ are both kings and priests (Revelation 1:6).[16] By implication it suggests that it is somehow inadequate just to be seated with Jesus Christ in the heavenlies and further, that the Church is less than capable of the overthrow of spirits of every size and rank.

I protest!

The Uneasiness of the Evangelical Soul

1. **Paucity of Biblical Text.** Far and away, the first major obstacle to the concept of territorial spirits is the scarcity of biblical text. Even before I delved into the writings on this subject, I was wondering how such a theory might advance among evangelicals with so little in the Bible to support it. Indeed, the fiercest opposition seems to come from the most ardent biblicists.

While I do not for a moment deny that there are territorial spirits, the preoccupation with them, the study of them, the elaboration upon them is far less than scriptural and is potentially dangerous.

George Otis, Jr. admits that the biblical basis for a detailed view on territorial spirits could be weak, but argues somewhat dangerously for a pragmatic use of the concept anyway.

In the final analysis, the current theological critique of territorial spirits must be seen as a uniquely Western indulgence—a kind of academic polo for tenured (and mostly Anglo) professors. Even if the doctrine of territorial spirits stood on shaky ground biblically, the concept so dominates the lives of non-Western peoples that it takes on a practical validity that cannot be ignored.[17]

2. Forget the Inventory. Of the making of lists there seems to be no end! In a close parallel in the Old Testament, Joshua advised Israel not even to mention the names of the pagan gods when they went in to possess their inheritance. He did not want Israel to associate with the pagan nations; they were not to invoke the names of their gods nor swear by them. And they certainly were not to bow down to them (Joshua 23:7, KJV). Curiously, he did not advise securing an inventory of the demons beforehand.

The King James Version and the New International Version have both caught the "don't worship or invoke the names of these gods" nuances. The reason these commands are not wholly expressed in English is the fault of our sometimes impoverished tongue and not the divine text itself.

In like manner, the psalmist David had no doubt about what he ought to do about the gods whom others were running after: "I will not . . . take up their names on my lips" (Psalm 16:4). The psalmist seems to quite deliberately avoid even the mere mention of such a name. Spurgeon echoes the psalmist:

> If we allow poison upon the lip, it may ere long penetrate to the inwards, and it is well to keep out of the mouth that which we would shut out from the heart.[18]

Another writer agrees: "Only the lips that abstained from pronouncing the names of foreign deities could drink of the cup of blessing provided by God."[19]

Both Joshua and David are harking back to the Torah, Exodus 23:13: "Do not invoke the names of other gods; do not let them be heard on your lips." It is apparent that there was a twofold Hebrew prohibition not just against the invoking and worship of foreign gods, but even of saying the names of those gods. It is no wonder that biblical literature and New Testament texts offer restrained reference to these powers. It is hard to imagine Moses, Joshua or David getting very interested in certain kinds of spirit inventories and spiritual mapping. When Israel is welcomed back to Jehovah in the prophecies of Hosea, the Lord says, "I will remove the names of the Baals from her lips" (Hosea 2:17). Could it be that some of us as evangelicals need to be purged of some Baal-talk?

In today's context, Joshua might be advised that spiritual mapping was obviously necessary as a preparation for gaining the promised land, but warrior that he was, he would not have listened. Yes, those nations had gods. And, yes, those gods had names. But what was that to Israel? Nothing! Baal and Beelzebub and Diana and a few others have gotten their names into holy writ—but as vanquished powers. The focus in all of Scripture is on the Holy One of Israel and His Son, Jesus Christ. Should Christ-adorning ministries ever be focused otherwise?

3. Innocent Concerning Evil. Scripture advises us that we are to be innocent concerning evil (Romans 16:19). While that should not and must not preclude awareness of the enemy's devices (2 Corinthians 2:11), there is a restraint cast on God's servants to be uninformed about the intricacies of Satan's kingdom and the patterns and structures of evil. We should rather be experts on the kingdom of God, graduate students in the extension of God's grace to all mankind and scholars of the first order in the glory of God. We must never permit the prince of darkness and his underlings to become the focus of our doctrine and praxis.

Let me make myself clear. There may be spiritual battles where

Christian workers enter into lethal combat with the powers, even getting to know in the process who those unlawful gods are. But the systematizing of that kind of information does not ring true in my own heart. Whose kingdom are we announcing after all? Surely not the realms of the dark prince!

In 1963, long before spiritual warfare became as known as it is today, my wife and I, along with a number of other Christian workers, were engaged in a lengthy deliverance. Violence and manifestations abounded, with evil powers from many parts of the world in which the victim had never been manifesting themselves. Along the way, many names of demons were elicited or revealed in the ongoing process of deliverance. We wrote down their names, even though at times we didn't know what they meant. All this information was carefully annotated in a spiral notebook supposedly to be preserved for posterity.

But as time wore on we became uncomfortable about the information and finally burned the book. In retrospect, I'm glad we did. It was good riddance to counter-kingdom rubbish. The important thing is that, after seven months of battle, the girl was delivered.

4. Discernment Needed. Much of the information about territorial spirits is gained in a subjective or pragmatic manner. If God reveals something, as He certainly has the right to do, this information is not necessarily for the whole world to know. Discernment, even discerning of spirits, is most often private illumination for later use or perhaps non-use. Surely Paul knew a long time before he addressed the python (Acts 16:18), that the girl was demonized and that eventually he would have to deal with the situation.

Evil spirits are liars. When strategy is built upon counter-kingdom utterances or observations about spirit phenomena, we are most impoverished. Origen, no orthodox hero himself, with nascent universalism in his soul, was right on this issue:

Delusion, error and heresy are not far behind if we become "listeners to and disciples of the demons."[20] The collation of information about territorial spirits derived from animistic and occult sources should be rejected out of hand.

5. A Line through Technology. Pragmatism, itself perhaps one of the territorial spirits of America and the West, or more likely, one of the *stoicheia,* one of those basic principles of this fallen world (Colossians 2:8), obviously demands the collation of materials. If missionaries around the world are encountering these *stoicheia*, these princes like those of Persia and Greece, should there not be some computerization going on? Shouldn't we be able to dial an 800 number or get a printout on our way to confront yet another frontier with the preaching of the gospel?

If ever there was a place to draw a line through technology, it is here. God's Word in printed form is circulated around the world through technology. But that same technology spews out pornography. The internet is both a marvelous boon to Christian work and a fountain of pollution. Just because information about the dark prince and his underlings *can* be collated, does not mean it *should* be.

6. The Sinfulness of the Human Soul. The focus on territorial spirits tends to shape and caricature the common view of sin and iniquity of the human heart. Implicit in the discussion is that if we can just deal with the territorial spirits, everything will be all better. The sad truth is that humanity is fallen, with hearts bent to evil. And if there were no powers of darkness at all we still would be hell-bent and iniquitous. Wherever territorial spirits are uniquely blamed, there and to that proportional degree the biblical view of the fall of man and the sinfulness of the human soul is eroded. "Man in his unregenerate state is a slave to sin and cannot turn to the light on his own."[21]

7. **The World and the Flesh.** The world and the flesh are often overlooked as enemies of the Christian when the focus gets on territorial spirits. Attitudes of spiritual laxity and worldliness compromise millions of Christians into powerlessness. Perhaps those same Christians have never heard of death to self as the real victory that needs to be won. That Paul exulted in the fact that he was crucified with Christ (Galatians 2:20) is often incomprehensible to the common Christian. And, I venture to say, more territorial spirits could be profitably ignored if Christians themselves were unspotted from the world and alive in Christ.

8. **The Pull toward Curiosity and Subjectivity.** Territorialism draws the focus of Christians away from holiness, sound doctrine, fervent devotion, godly discipline and the indwelling Christ (Colossians 1:27). It pulls them instead toward curiosity, subjectivism and unhealthy expertise. It also cultivates itching ears (2 Timothy 4:3) which, in the end, will generate error—plenty of it.

Keith M. Bailey has written as follows:

> In 1959, A.W. Tozer wrote a masterful chapter on how to deal with the devil. He wisely points out that there is only a hairline between truth and superstition. Tozer offered this counsel to the Church:[22]

> > The scriptural way to see things is to set the Lord always before us, put Christ in the center of our vision, and if Satan is lurking around he will appear on the margin only and be seen as but a shadow on the edge of the brightness. It is always wrong to reverse this—to set Satan in the focus of our vision and push God out to the margin. Nothing but tragedy can come of such inversion.[23]

How Shall We Then Proceed?

We should obviously pursue holiness without which no one shall see God (Hebrews 12:14).

We should focus on the glory of God as our chief end (1 Corinthians 10:31).

We should elevate and obey the first commandment to love God with all our heart and soul and mind and strength (Mark 12:30).

We should fervently love our neighbors and one another (Mark 12:31; John 13:34).

We should zealously pay attention to doctrine (1 Timothy 4:13).

We should carry out the Great Commission with holy passion (Matthew 28:19-20).

We should allow the overthrow of territorial spirits and all other kinds to be so common we forget to mention it in our prayer letters.

We should not be rejoicing that these evil powers are subject to us, as indeed they are through Christ, but we should be rejoicing that our names are written in heaven (Luke 10:20).

These signs, when they come, must not lead us. They are intended always to follow—and at an appropriate distance.

Conclusion

Spiritual mapping, if it takes a form which focuses on the occult or the territoriality of the various dark powers, is likely to carry its practitioners into peril. But spiritual mapping which is more akin to the old-fashioned field study, including some description of the demon powers of false religions, is the kind of spiritual mapping which could be acceptable. George Otis, Jr. has defined spiritual mapping as "nothing more ethereal than creating a spiritual profile of a community carefully based on research."[24] What needs to be understood is that although this new definition sounds very much like its old-fashioned precursor, it focuses predominantly on the spirit world.

There are powerful deputies and princes in Satan's hierarchical kingdom. It is likely that they may spiritually control geographic areas of the world. But they were, along with their prince, defeated at the cross of Jesus Christ who is the Head over every power and authority (Ephesians 1:22).

Further, they have been disarmed and made a spectacle by Christ's triumph (Colossians 2:15). God has placed all things under the feet of Jesus, our Lord, and made Him to be Head over everything for the Church (Ephesians 1:22).

Every believer is seated with Jesus Christ in the heavenlies (Ephesians 2:6), where the Son is at the right hand of the Father (Hebrews 10:12). This same Jesus is the One about whom Paul sang, "Christ in you, the hope of glory" (Colossians 1:27).

And, what's more, we should be collating these eternal truths and celebrating the glory of God. This is the reality, "For from him and through him and to him are all things. To him be the glory forever!" (Romans 11:36).

Endnotes

[1] C. Peter Wagner, *Blazing the Way: Acts 15-28*, The Acts of the Holy Spirit Series, Book 3 (Ventura, CA: Regal Books, 1995), 67.

[2] K. Neill Foster, "Discernment, the Powers and Spirit-Speaking" (Ph.D. diss., Fuller Theological Seminary, 1988), 106-107.

[3] Patrick W. Skehan, "A Fragment of the Song of Moses (Deut. 32) from Qumran," *Bulletin of American Schools of Oriental Research (BASOR)*, 136 (December 1954), 12.

[4] Justin Martyr, "Dialogue with Trypho, chapter 78," *The Ante-Nicene Fathers (ANF)*, eds. Alexander Roberts and James Donaldson (Grand Rapids, MI: Eerdmans, 1978), 1:238.

[5] Ibid.

[6] Jessie Penn-Lewis, *The Warfare with Satan* (Fort Washington, PA: Christian Literature Crusade, 1963), 20.

[7] A.W. Tozer, *Let My People Go!* (Camp Hill, PA: Christian Publications, 1990), 90.

[8] Edwin Scott Gaustad, *The Great Awakening in New England* (Gloucester, MS: Peter Smith, 1965), opposite 195.

[9] Arthur Wallis, *Revival: The Rain from Heaven* (Grand Rapids, MI: Fleming H. Revell, 1979), 51.

[10] Wesley Duewel, *Revival Fire* (Grand Rapids, MI: Zondervan, 1995), 102.

[11] Ibid., 133.

[12] John Dawson, *Taking Our Cities for God* (Lake Mary, FL: Creation House, 1989), 156.

[13] C. Peter Wagner, *Confronting the Powers* (Ventura, CA: Regal Books, 1996), 173.

[14] Clinton Arnold, *Crucial Questions about Spiritual Warfare* (Grand Rapids, MI: Baker Books, 1997), 161.

[15] Paul King, personal research, 1997, 2. King is not describing his own be liefs; rather he is summarizing attitudes held on this subject.

[16] Jim Cymbala, *Fresh Wind, Fresh Fire* (Grand Rapids, MI: Zondervan, 1997), 106. Though the Bible teacher cited by Cymbala is reiterating ideas first popularized by Peter Wagner, Wagner himself should not be blamed for suggesting that Paul was unable to cope with strategic level spiritual warfare.

[17] George Otis, Jr., *The Twilight Labyrinth* (Grand Rapids, MI: Chosen Books, 1997), 197.

[18] C.H. Spurgeon, *Treasury of David* (Grand Rapids, MI: Zondervan, 1950), 1:195.

[19] Peter C. Craigie, *Psalm 1-50,* Word Biblical Commentary, gen. eds. David A. Hubbard and Glenn W. Barker (Waco, TX: Word Books, 1983), 157.

[20] Origen, as cited by T.K. Oesterreich, *Possession: Demonaical and Other* (Secaucus, NJ: Citadel Press, 1930), 166.

[21] Csaba Leidenfrost, " 'Peretti Evangelism,' " *Christian Research Journal*, Vol. 20, No. 1, September-October 1997, 53.

[22] Keith M. Bailey, *Strange Gods* (Camp Hill, PA: Christian Publications, 1998), 196-197.

[23] A.W. Tozer, *Born after Midnight* (Camp Hill, PA: Christian Publications, 1989), 43.

[24] George Otis, Jr., as cited by Art Moore, "Spiritual Mapping Gains Credibility among Leaders," *Christianity Today*, 12 January 1998, 55.

Robert Jaffray's Battle for Kalosi

A.W. Tozer

One year while Robert Jaffray and Rev. Gustave Woerner were traveling in Borneo visiting newly opened stations they came to a place called Kalosi which up to that time had been marked by a strange unresponsiveness to the Gospel. It was as if an invisible ring had been drawn around the place and the people living inside the circle had been struck deaf and dumb. However the truth might prevail everywhere else not one convert could be made inside that circle. In addition to a total apathy toward the Gospel there was among the natives there an active hostility wholly foreign to the rest of the island. Here the two missionaries had occasion to stay over night.

Jaffray lay down at the usual time to sleep, apparently in normal health. In the middle of the night Mr. Woerner was suddenly awakened by sounds of a commotion in the room where Jaffray slept. He rushed into the room and found Jaffray struggling and groaning in agony. All his motions were those of a man wrestling with someone trying to choke him to death, an invisible antagonist who seemed about to kill him. This continued for a short time and then suddenly ceased. Immediately Jaffray came to consciousness weak and badly shaken. Mr. Woerner prayed with him and ministered to him as he was able and Mr. Jaffray's strength returned slowly. By morning he was feeling well again.

The struggle of the night before he never doubted as a personal engagement with the devil himself. He stated boldly that he had met in prayer and had conquered the "prince" who had been responsible for the strange bondage of the natives in and around Kalosi. By a quick accommodation of Scripture to his needs he saw in this "prince" old Pharaoh who was holding the people in bondage and he sternly commanded him to "let my people go!". . .

Were we to stop here the whole thing might be smiled off tolerantly as the pardonable weakness of an intensely religious man, and nothing more. But there is a significant sequel. Almost at once the whole situation changed within that previously barren circle. The indifference of the people melted like ice before the summer sun. The work of conversion that was sweeping across Borneo broke out at Kalosi and the men of the district began to turn to Christ in large numbers.[1]

Endnote

[1] A.W. Tozer, *Let My People Go!* (Camp Hill, PA: Christian Publications, Inc., 1990), 116-118.

Grandma Frida

David P. Jones

The young couple, Sergio and Regina Pinto, had just rented an apartment. It wasn't much to look at, just two small rooms in the front half of a rough, wood-framed home.

The owner, Grandma Frida, a poor, crippled German-Brazilian widow, along with her son and three grandchildren, lived in the back half. As new believers, Sergio and Regina with their infant daughter, Marta, were about to begin an adventure that would change their lives and those of many others.

The first few days in their sparsely furnished rooms were un-eventful. However, on Friday night they were dismayed to hear the haunting throb of the *batuque,* the rhythmic drum of the *pai de santos* (literally "father of the saints"; actually the leader who "calls down" the demonic spirits). Although the noise was muf-fled by the rough plank walls dividing their two rooms from Grandma Frida's quarters, Sergio and Regina could hear the man invoking the *santos.* (Literally "saints"; actually spirits of the saints. In Brazilian culture there is a corresponding spirit for every saint, an effort to make spiritism acceptable to the Roman Catholic hierarchy.) These demons gave him power, revealed se-crets and kept millions of Brazilians like Grandma Frida spiritu-ally imprisoned.

Somewhat fearfully, yet purposefully, Sergio and Regina began to pray, pleading the blood of Jesus Christ for protection against the evil spirits being called by the medium. Then they began to sing quietly and clearly, "There is power, power, wonder-work-ing power in the precious blood of the Lamb." Gradually their voices rose in volume and fervor. Then Sergio began to rebuke the enemy and to forbid the demonic spirits to "come down" at the request of the medium who was drinking deep draughts of *cachaca* (cane liquor) and puffing on a pungent cigar.

On one side of the wall, the servant of Satan was pounding his drum, calling for the spirits to appear and trying to make contact with his *guias* (spirit guides). On the other side, a young Christian and his wife were working against the adversary, binding the spirits and neutralizing the medium's power.

After several minutes, the drumming stopped and a gruff voice said, "The *santos* won't come; I'm leaving." With that, the door slammed. Sergio and Regina breathed a sigh of relief.

The next Friday night, the scene repeated itself. Again, the young warriors launched their combat strategy. Frustrated and puzzled, the medium again ceased his efforts and left.

During that week, Regina began talking with Grandma Frida about Jesus and His special love for her and her family. She told the old lady about God's power and Satan's defeat. A nominal Catholic and a practicing spiritist, Grandma Frida had never heard about God's love, much less His power over Satan.

The next Friday, the medium returned, lit up his cigar, gulped down some liquor and began his rhythmic chanting and drumming. Once again, Sergio and Regina took up their spiritual arms and began to pray, sing and bind the demonic spirits. Within a short time, the drumming stopped.

"Are there any Christians around here?" the *pai de santos* asked.

Grandma Frida replied, "Yes, there is a young couple, evangelicals, who just moved in a few weeks ago."

The man stormed out of the house. "As long as they are here," he said, "the spirits won't come down. They can't. Those believers won't let them."

Within a few weeks Grandma Frida and her family had turned to Jesus Christ as Savior and Lord. A small group began to meet

in her yard, one of the first evangelical churches in the city of
Porto Alegre.

20

BINDING, LOOSING
AND PRAYER WALKS

A BOOK ABOUT BINDING AND LOOSING seems to require comment not just about territorial spirits, but also prayer walks, for the same reason—association, not exegetical, but contextual.

The situation could not have been clearer when I received an invitation to speak about binding and loosing to a group of pray-ers who would be conducting prayer walks throughout Eastern Pennsylvania. It was obvious to me that these colleagues in ministry were associating prayer walking with binding and loosing. I shared with them some of the material included here.

Although prayer walks are nowhere mandated in Scripture and at best encouraged in certain instances, they may be appropriate for the following reasons.

Prayer Walks in the Old Testament

1. A prayer walk is a posture of prayer, as is kneeling or standing. So, why not walking? There are no Scriptures forbidding it; there are some that seem to endorse it. Abraham was told to go

for a walk in connection with possession of the land God had given him. "Go, walk through the length and breadth of the land, for I am giving it to you" (Genesis 13:17).

2. Joshua was told to enter the promised land and that he would receive all the land upon which he would set foot (Joshua 1:3). Again, since the Old Testament has meaning for New Testament Christians, this is a potentially significant event (Romans 15:4). Does it not suggest that stepping out in conquest is part of possessing any land of promise, physical or spiritual?

3. The incident in which Israel walked around Jericho six times then seven times more before the walls fell and the conquest was secured is yet another Old Testament encouragement for the present practice of prayer walking (Joshua 6:2-5).

4. The commanders of Israel were commanded by Joshua, "Come here, and put your feet on the necks of these kings. . . . This is what the Lord will do to all the enemies you are going to fight" (Joshua 10:24-25). The symbolism is powerful. The "kings" to be overcome in the life of the Christian believer submit their necks to those who will walk over and assume the position of victory and authority over them. Prayer walking, if this passage is typical, seems to have a connection to spiritual warfare and victory over the powers—in this case, enemy kings.

5. In times of crisis, Jehoshaphat inquired of the Lord, and during a national emergency "they came from every town in Judah to seek [the Lord]" (2 Chronicles 20:4). Some folks were doing some walking. In fact, Israel's propensity to worship in the high places was the result, in part, of the nation's desire to go less than all the way to worship. Dick Eastman's 6,000-mile journey to the Berlin Wall to press his hands against its bulk before it came down was a prayer walk of sorts, though done for the most part on an airplane.[1] "Going there" is a biblical idea. Symbolic events are suggestive at best.

Prayer Walks in the New Testament

1. Jesus Christ "went around doing good and healing all who were under the power of the devil" (Acts 10:38). What was the life of Jesus if it was not a three-year prayer walk? One possible exception to the pattern of walking and praying might be Jesus' ride on the colt coming into Jerusalem (Luke 19:35-38).

2. Prayer walking is what the disciples did. When the seventy were given authority and sent out, they did not have the option of piling into their vehicles and taking off. They walked, as did Peter, Paul and John in all their New Testament itineration (except for Paul's several boat rides).

3. Prayer walking is potentially missiological. It involves "going" with prayer to some part of the world. Prayer walking is not carrying out the Great Commission though it could be combined with preaching, teaching and disciple-making (Matthew 28:19).

General Principles

1. **Prayer walking is both verbal and nonverbal communication.** Scholars say that fifty-five percent of all communication is nonverbal.[2] If so, then prayer walking is an appropriate situation in which, by the very physical act of walking and being seen by others, communication is taking place. The message becomes, "These Christians have come here for a special purpose and they are doing something important and significant."

2. **Prayer walking is incarnational.** Jesus Christ came in the flesh. Every spirit that does not continually confess that Jesus Christ is come in the flesh is not of God (1 John 4:1-3). Incarnational presence is a biblical idea, so much so that God sent His Son into the world incarnationally (John 1:14). The old argument about persuasion evangelism versus presence evangelism

273

may reemerge. Though evangelicals ardently come down on the necessity of persuasion, this may be a moment to affirm presence as important in itself.

Such incarnational endeavors by the evangelical community involve physical visits to various sites, geographical locations or even buildings where prayer is offered. The prayer may be a cleansing prayer as in the case of missionary prayer over haunted houses in China. Intercessory prayer can take place anywhere in the world. Incarnational presence and prayer require going.

3. Prayer walking is confrontational, even territorial. It makes the assumption that spiritual warfare as exhibited in the prayer walk format is expected to produce spiritual results in geographic areas. Spiritual warfare weapons, all focused on Jesus Christ (2 Corinthians 10:4), produce positive results. Satan's work in the world may indeed be damaged or destroyed through prayer walks.

4. Prayer walking is an expression of obedience. The Scriptures admonish that everything be done by prayer, that prayer is to be made without ceasing (1 Thessalonians 5:17). It is, however, "in everything by *prayer*" (Philippians 4:6), not "in everything by walking."

5. A prayer walk is an act of sanctification. Those who dedicate themselves to it are separating themselves from their homes and other concerns and devoting their energies and time to the prayer walk. The prepositions "to" and "from" are the very essence of sanctification.

6. Prayer walking has been an evangelical practice for years. When Ralph Winter was claiming the ground he eventually secured for the U.S. Center for World Mission in Pasadena, California, he was only doing what generations of evangelicals before him have done—walking the property and claiming the land for God's use. (In Winter's case, the land was being claimed for a new ministry since it already belonged to the Nazarene Church.)

Similarly, Thomas Moseley, veteran missionary from China and later president of Nyack College, New York, went prayer walking along with his wife Eva on the Nyack hillside before strategic adjoining properties were acquired by the college. In the Nyack incident, the properties were clearly retrieved from the dark powers of Tibetan and Eastern mysticism and dedicated to Jesus Christ.

Ruth Dye felt that thirty-eight acres of property on Lake Nakamun near Edmonton, Alberta should be a Bible camp and conference ground. So persuaded was she that she walked over the property, claiming it for God. She also invested her own money to purchase the site. Later, she informed us that she had stopped and prayed in some places more than others. Today, the grounds are used year-round for Christian work. Those thirty-eight acres belong to God because a little lady tramped the hills and woods and lakeshore for the Lord.

While in the process of writing this chapter, I viewed a video magazine in which a marvelous work of God in a small city in Africa was described by Dr. Peter Nanfelt. It is a most unusual report. So many Muslims have turned to Christ that several mosques have closed. But the particular information that caught my attention was this: Prior to the moving of the Holy Spirit in that city, missionaries, adopting a spiritual warfare approach, went personally to the four corners of the city to stake their claim for God's intervention. They also physically encircled at least one mosque with prayer.[3] Though the exact details were not spelled out, those events were seen to relate to prayer walking.

Some Guarded Conclusions

There are "red flags" that need to be raised in the overall discussion. Prayer walking can become an evangelical "shibboleth," a kind of methodology for all situations. Linkage with indiscreet binding and loosing plus association with unwise territorialism or eccentric behavior can likewise give prayer walking a negative context. Consider the following.

Ai came after Jericho. Arrogance followed victory. In the dramatic conquest of Jericho by Joshua (Joshua 7), the Israelis sought to take the small city of Ai. They were rebuffed and defeated—defeated by a feeble enemy and their own arrogance. They had not consulted the Lord, nor had they dealt with Achan's sin in their midst. Apparently they imagined that they could just casually go up to Ai and take the town. They were wrong. Prayer-walking aficionados who make a great deal about Jericho need to remember Ai.

Ai-like Nonprayer Walking

Just as the trip to Ai by the Israeli soldiers was a disaster, prayer walking can be disastrous too. It is wrong when it is not in concert with heaven. It is wrong when separated from God's mind and heart. Is it wrong when immature persons press themselves into leadership in any ministry. If prayer walking is a legitimate expression of the kingdom, then prayer walk leaders should be mature leaders of the Church (1 Timothy 3:6).

Prayer walking can also be problematic if the hermeneutic is deviant. There is some temptation in it toward triumphalism and postmillennial thought. If prayer walkers think they are going to bring in the kingdom of God and set up Christ's millennial rule, there is something wrong with their interpretation of Old Testament events in the light of New Testament realities. They make the same mistakes the disciples made so long ago when they expected Jesus to set up His kingdom then and there (Luke 19:11).

Does anyone plan to do Jericho prayer walks where all the women and children are wiped out at the end of a physical battle? The twisted hermeneutic of the Christian crusades resulted in atrocities and centuries of shame for the Church.[4]

Sometimes, unhappily, there are peripherals attached to prayer walks which raise flags of caution. Like binding and loosing, prayer walking too has "friends" that can cause it embarrassment and can label it eccentric. Speaking evil of dignities or "scoffing at the power" of evil angels (2 Peter 2:10; Jude 8, NLT) should have no place in prayer walks. A prayer walk with swagger is from the evil one and not a divine instrument at all (James 4:6).

Sometimes too, prayer walks can become vehicles for unbiblical and extravagant theories about territorial spirits which cannot be substantiated biblically. This is not to deny that there are territorial spirits; rather, it is to say we should be simple concerning evil. Like Joshua, we should not even be mentioning (and thus promoting) the names of the gods in the land we are about to claim for God (Joshua 23:7, KJV). Our expertise should be in kingdom matters, not in the dark subterfuge of the counter-kingdom.

George Otis, Jr. observes, apparently from experience, that being uninformed, hasty and ill-prepared in certain efforts (ill-advised prayer walking?) can have negative results.

> The consequences of this parade of folly—which include dampening the enthusiasm of potential intercessors, squandering valuable supplies of time and money and granting the enemy additional cover for his work—have been severe.[5]

Although other arguments might be marshaled alongside these, in my opinion prayer walks can be advantageous to God's kingdom, can be result-oriented expressions of spiritual intent and can be properly used to advance missiological, territorial and spiritual warfare objectives. Inasmuch as binding and loosing may also occur in these contexts, I see prayer walking as a potentially and occasionally useful kingdom activity.

Prayer walking which adorns the gospel of Jesus Christ and advances His kingdom should be welcomed. When done with pure motives, under the direction of the Holy Spirit and for the glory of God, then all is well.

Endnotes

[1] Dick Eastman, *The Jericho Hour* (Orlando, FL: Creation House, 1994), 12-13.

[2] Bert F. Bradley, *Fundamentals of Speech Communication* (Dubuque, IA: Wm. C. Brenn Publishing, 1974, 1991), 224.

[3] Peter Nanfelt, "Guinea," *Alliance Video Magazine,* Vol. 11, No. 2, 1997.

[4] Kenneth Scott Latourette, *A History of Christianity* (San Francisco: Harper and Row Publishers, 1975), 383-484.

[5] George Otis, Jr., *The Twilight Labyrinth* (Grand Rapids, MI: Chosen Books, 1997), 227.

The Strong Man of Mangnambougou

Chuck Davis and Bill Trinidad

For eleven years the church in Mangnambougou, a neighborhood in Bamako, Mali, West Africa was trying to get land and put up a church building. We encountered many difficulties, and twice the government lost important papers that the church had submitted. Things were moving slowly, if at all.

We realized that we were not up against merely human opposition, but we were fighting against principalities and powers. When we started to take the spiritual battle seriously, God led us, in the spring of 1993, to take five prayer walks in the area surrounding the building site. We proclaimed the Lordship of Christ to the spirit world. We took authority over any powers who might be hindering the obtaining of the papers. We bound the strong man of Mangnambougou from working.

Within a few months, the new building was up and ready for worship. So far as we were concerned, using our authority to bind demonic opposition in conjunction with the prayer walks was the key to the breakthrough in this church.

Part VI

BINDING AND LOOSING: THE CONCLUSION OF THE MATTER

When God's glory is first,
all is in order.

21

BINDING, LOOSING
AND THE GLORY OF GOD

ONNECTING THE GLORY OF GOD with the sometimes messy procedure of binding and loosing seems at first to be a curious juxtaposition of divine truth. However, there can be no doubt this doctrine is very much connected with God's ultimate glory. For Brother Lawrence, even the most mundane of tasks was regarded this way, "If I'm washing dishes I do it to the glory of God and if I pick up a straw from the ground I do it to the glory of God."[1]

A couple of generations ago, A.W. Tozer wrote,

> Always and always God must be first. The gospel in its scriptural context puts the glory of God first and the salvation of man second. The angels, approaching from above, chanted, "Glory to God in the highest, and on earth, peace, good will toward men." This puts the glory of God and the blessing of men in their proper order.[2]

Dr. John Piper, known in this era for his passion to declare the supremacy of God and the glory of God in all things, is an ardent affirmer of God's supremacy and sovereignty. When invited to speak to the students at Wheaton College, some of his friends and colleagues went with him. They were stunned when they heard him say, "The chief end of God is to glorify God and enjoy Him forever." Concluding that he had misstated himself, they shuddered to think that he had "blown" a great preaching opportunity. But not so. Piper's intent was to declare the supremacy and glory of God in those things concerning Himself.

The ringing tones of the Westminster divines can and must be applied to all things. God Himself, man created in God's image, as well as all those obediences which may find themselves part of kingdom endeavors must in every case align themselves with the glory of God. Binding and loosing cannot be excluded from this divine agenda. Piper is disarmingly transparent.

> One of the most important discoveries I have ever made is this truth: God is most glorified in me when I am most satisfied in him. This is the motor that drives my ministry as a pastor. It affects everything I do.
>
> Whether I eat or drink or preach or counsel or whatever I do, my aim is to glorify God by the way I do it (1 Corinthians 10:31). This means my aim is to do it in a way that shows how the glory of God has satisfied the longings of my heart.[3]

The passion for the glory of God existed in the Godhead before creation (John 17:5). The atmosphere of heaven in eternity past cannot be adequately conceptualized or imagined apart from the overwhelming expression of the glory of God. There is no one who can express in impoverished human words that eternal and incomprehensible reality.

Always remember that long after your mind has given up and quit, you can feel your way through to God with your heart. God is out yonder, infinitely transcendent above all His creatures. The old Germans used to say, "The heart is always the best theologian." You can know more with your heart than with your head.[4]

Moses likewise was a leader who demanded to see the glory of God (Exodus 33:18). Moses' passion for God's glory was most unusual. It is possible that one of the real keys to Moses' greatness was his relentless pursuit of the glory of God.

Israel too needed to learn how to secure the glory of God. Leviticus 9:1-6 is one of the most powerful passages about the glory of God found anywhere in Scripture. Its express purpose was to explain to Israel how to bring down the glory. Four offerings are required: a sin offering which speaks of atonement and redemption; a burnt offering which speaks of consecration and sanctification; a fellowship offering which speaks about relationships, both vertical and horizontal; and a grain offering mixed with oil which speaks of the harvest of a lost world.

The explicit objective of the passage is the realization of God's glory by His people. It is part of the reason I dare to say that there should be no doctrine developed about any of God's works unless God's glory is the sustaining foundation. Certainly no writing should be undertaken, no book penned, unless every facet of that endeavor reflects and celebrates the glory of God. To separate Jesus' teaching about binding and loosing from heaven and the glory of God is to diminish Him and to erode His authority. All is well when God's glory is supreme.

The psalmist could not refrain from shouting the glory of God (Psalm 3:4; 24:7-10). David was excited—excited about the glory of God. His dramatic and artistic traits, his music and poetry—all in the end were directed to the glory of God. Pastoral serenity and military valor were both alike submerged in his melodic pursuit of the glory of God.

David's son Solomon likewise so cleansed and sanctified himself that finally the glory of God descended on the temple at its dedication (2 Chronicles 7:1). All of Solomon's vast preparation of the temple and his determined sanctification and separation from evil had one object in mind—the manifest glory of God.

Ezekiel too saw the glory of God depart and return (Ezekiel 10:18; 43:4). As a prophetic witness, he recounts the horror of the departure of the glory. But he is there as well to witness its return, proffering in the process hope for every people that has lost the glory of God.

Jesus' prayer in John 17 is the expression of His passion for the Father's glory (17:1-5). If Moses was passionate about the glory of God, Jesus more. If David was a shepherd for the glory of God, the Good Shepherd, more.

Paul cannot keep himself from verbal exultation when he, by the Spirit, celebrates the Church as God's glorious inheritance (Ephesians 1:18). And he is the one who introduces the glory of God's rule: "Whatever you do, do it all for the glory of God" (1 Corinthians 10:31).

In John's Revelation, God's glory is splashed everywhere. It is the canvas upon which all the events of His grand finale are painted in riotous color (Revelation 1:6; 19:1).

This passion for the glory of God is a pervasive and dominant theme through all of Scripture. Little wonder, then, that this doctrine of binding and loosing, connected as it is with spiritual discipline, spiritual warfare, aggressive prayer and the enormously expansive "whatever" of the New Testament should also be inextricably connected with heaven and the glory of God.

One of the strongest passages on binding in the Old Testament is Psalm 149. Binding the kings and the nobles is clearly a privilege of the saints. But it is more. It is the *glory* and *honor* of

God's saints (149:9). Coming as it does in a context relating to the authority of the believer, can there be any doubt the phrase "This is the glory of all his saints" hints of God's ultimate glory? If the saints may glory in God's execution of judgment through them, is not God's ultimate glory also affirmed and lauded?

The answer here is positive. "Whatever you do, do it all for the glory of God" (1 Corinthians 10:31)—binding and loosing included. "The glory of God is the health of the universe; the essential soundness of things requires that He be honored among created intelligence."[5]

When Paul describes the "riches of his glorious inheritance in the saints" (Ephesians 1:18), his prayer is a prelude to a larger agenda. He wants the saints to see who they are, what they have and where they are. To be seated with Christ in the heavenlies, to find oneself at the right hand of the Father in Christ, is the doctrinal and theological underpinning of a thousand things in the Christian life, not excluding the authority of the believer—and its consequent outworking in binding and loosing. This, too, is part of the glorious inheritance of the saints.

In both Matthew 16 and 18, Jesus links binding and loosing to heaven: "Whatever you bind on earth will be bound in heaven, and whatever you loose on earth will be loosed in heaven" (18:18). Jesus' meaning must include the glory of God.

> Who is this King of glory?
>   The LORD strong and mighty,
>   the LORD mighty in battle.
> Lift up your heads, O you gates;
>   lift them up, you ancient doors,
>   that the King of glory may come in.
> Who is he, this King of glory?
>   The LORD Almighty—

he is the King of glory.
(Psalm 24:8-10)

Jesus is relating all the binding and loosing that is to be carried out to His person and to His glory. Why? Because He is the King of heaven, the Lord of glory!

Spurgeon divides this entire Psalm as follows:

> It consists of three parts. The first glorifies *the true God,* and sings of his universal dominion; the second describes *the true Israel,* who are able to commune with him; and the third pictures the ascent of *the true Redeemer* who has opened heaven's gates for the entrance of his elect.[6]

It is Spurgeon's reference to the ascension that captures my imagination.

The Welcome in Heaven

If heaven exploded when Jesus was born, how much more when the task was done and His humiliation complete?

At Bethlehem, the song of the angels was

> Glory to God in the highest,
> and on earth peace to men
> on whom his favor rests.
> (Luke 2:14)

At the end of the journey, He is announced as the King of Glory. Imagine, if you will, the hosts of Bethlehem multiplied a million times—all around the thrones of heaven.

Banks upon banks of mighty ones.
The cherubim.
The seraphim.
The angels.
The archangels.
A thousand Bethlehems on every side.

The sound of worship and praise is thunderous beyond comprehension. Earth and heaven are rocked and shaken with the spectacle. The King of Glory is arriving home.

Off in the distance, to one side, lurk the dark powers. Demons of fear and sickness, war and hate; demons of the dark places, angels of light.

All are aghast.
All are appalled.
All are eternally ruined.

The King of Glory has vanquished them all. The cross has precipitously canceled their plans. Satan is routed at last.

This King of Glory is strong and mighty—they know that. He is mighty in battle—and they are losers all.

Then the doors of heaven open up. And, like the father welcoming home his prodigal son, God the Father rises from His throne to welcome home this sinless True Redeemer, the King of Glory.

The Father embraces the Son, and heaven erupts once more.

The work is done!
It is finished!

I see the devil and his serpent minions fade from view, slithering on their way to the abyss, over its edge in a flurry of flailing tails.

Heaven rules.
The conquest is complete.
The Son is seated,
enthroned at the Father's right hand.

And then, wonder of wonders, those who have been redeemed, those who have believed, are seated there at the right hand of the Father. In Jesus Christ. Marvel of marvels. Incomprehensible of incomprehensibles. Yet true. An innumerable host of the faithful and redeemed are crowding into the heavenly kingdom.

The King of Glory has carried them in His train. And the praises surpass the first thunder of worship and the second thunder of worship, and all heaven gives throat to heaven's Hallelujah Chorus:

Blessing and honor,
and glory, and power,
be unto him that sitteth upon the throne . . .
forever and ever and ever . . .

"Worthy is the Lamb, who was slain,
to receive power and wealth and
wisdom and strength
and honor and glory and praise!"

Then I heard every creature in heaven and on earth and under the earth and on the sea, and all that is in them, singing:

"To him who sits on the throne and to the Lamb
be praise and honor and glory and power,
for ever and ever!"
(Revelation 5:12-13)

Amen, amen and amen!

Endnotes

[1] Brother Lawrence as cited by A.W. Tozer, *Worship: The Missing Jewel* (Camp Hill, PA: Christian Publications, 1992), 25.

[2] A.W. Tozer, *Born After Midnight* (Camp Hill, PA: Christian Publications, 1989), 23.

[3] John Piper, *A Godward Life* (Sisters, OR: Multnomah Publications, 1997), 23.

[4] A.W. Tozer, "The Person God Uses," in *Missionary Voices*, eds. H. Robert Cowles, K. Neill Foster and David P. Jones (Camp Hill, PA: Christian Publications, 1996), 16.

[5] A.W. Tozer, *The Early Tozer: A Word in Season,* comp. James L. Snyder (Camp Hill, PA: Christian Publications, 1997), 19.

[6] C.H. Spurgeon, *The Treasury of David* (Grand Rapids, MI: Zondervan, 1930), 1.374.

POSTSCRIPT

Aftᴇʀ ᴛʜɪs ʙᴏᴏᴋ ʜᴀᴅ ʙᴇᴇɴ ᴡʀɪᴛᴛᴇɴ and the polishing of the manuscript was moving along, my partner in this endeavor, Paul King said, "You need something at the end."

He was right. I knew immediately what I had to say.

Running concurrently with the writing of the manuscript, we had been involved here at the publishing house in a second set of negotiations which were intense to say the least.

Then one of my colleagues, with more than forty years of pastoral and literature ministry to his credit and an author in his own right, asked me, "Why don't you do some binding in this negotiating issue?"

My answer, paraphrased here, was telling.

"I don't feel led to do any binding and loosing. It doesn't seem to me that the Lord is leading that way. This is a prayer issue. And we are pressing the matter on that level."

Thankfully, matters were resolved positively—through prayer.

In retrospect, I want nothing more than to add a postscript that affirms that we "should always pray and not give up" (Luke 18:1). Scripturally, there are many more admonitions to pray than there are to bind and loose. Scripture does *not* say, we "ought always to bind and loose." It is not "in everything by binding and loosing," but instead it is, "in everything by prayer" (Philippians 4:6).

I would like to be the brother who wrote a book on binding

and loosing and concluded it with an admonition to put prayer first, without forgetting the glory of God and our completeness in Jesus Christ, without neglecting the authority of the believer—and without abandoning for a moment the truth that there are times when God and His glory will be "most" supreme through the act of binding and loosing through His children.

APPENDIX

THE GREEK COGNATES

THE INCLUSION OF COGNATES of the various words for binding and loosing is important to this volume in that various nuances of meaning emerge when these Greek expressions are considered.

In the interest of keeping a narrow focus and limiting the scope of this volume, the cognates should be considered as leads which others may follow in the pursuit of a fuller knowledge of binding and loosing.

Deo/Luo Cognates

Sources used:

Walter Bauer, trans. by William F. Arndt and Wilber Gingrich, *A Greek-English Lexicon of the New Testament* (Chicago: University of Chicago Press, 1957).

Colin Brown, ed., *The New International Dictionary of New Testament Theology* (Grand Rapids: Zondervan, 1971, 1978).

Gerhard Kittel, ed., Geoffrey W. Bromiley, trans., *Theological Dictionary of the New Testament* (Grand Rapids: Eerdmans, 1964).

Henry George Liddell and Robert Scott, *A Greek-English Lexicon* (Oxford: Clarendon Press, 1968).

Bruce M. Metzger, *Lexical Aids for Students of New Testament Greek* (Princeton, NJ: Theological Book Agency, 1969, 1976).

James Hope Moulton and George Milligan, *The Vocabulary of the Greek Testament* (Grand Rapids: Eerdmans, 1963).

James Strong, "Greek Dictionary of the New Testament," *Strong's Exhaustive Concordance* (Tulsa, OK: American Christian College Press, n.d.).

George V. Wigram and Ralph Winter, *The Word Study Concordance* (Pasadena, CA: William Carey Library, 1972, 1978).

From *Deo*

Deo comes from the Greek root *de* meaning "bind." Metzger, 53.

There are two branches of the *deo* root, representing two ways in which *deo* is used: *Deo*—to bind and derived from that; *deo*—to be in need of, to be necessary (Liddell, 383).

Kittel, and Liddell and Scott see Paul as bound (*deo*) in spirit in Acts 20:22 an example of supernatural binding (Liddell, 176; Kittel, 2:60).

Cognates include:

Deo "to be in need of, necessary":

dei	there is a need (the sense of moral obligation), needful, must (Liddell and Scott, 372).

deon	that which is necessary, binding, right, proper, for needful purposes, ought to be (Liddell and Scott, 379).
deontos	as it ought (Liddell and Scott, 379).
deomai	pray, beseech, ask, request, need, require (extension of *dei*—necessary, expressing a need) (Liddell and Scott, 383).
deo (middle of)	binding oneself (Strong, 21).

Entreaty has developed into demand—a still stronger "expression of need" (Moulton and Milligan, 141).

The verb has a regular use in petitions addressed to ruling sovereigns, as distinguished from those addressed to magistrates (Moulton and Milligan, 141).

deesis	prayer, request, supplication (from *deomai*, binding oneself (Strong, 21).
prosdeomai	to have need of something more (Kittel, 2:42), Acts 17:24. (The idea of binding is intrinsic and implicit in this common word for prayer.) Used almost exclusively by Luke and Paul (Kittel, 2:41).

Deo "to bind":

desis	binding together, tying in bundles, joint (Liddell, 380), not in NT.
desmeuo	to be a binder, a captor, to enchain, to tie; Matthew 23:4—binding heavy burdens; Acts 22:4—Saul binding to prisons (Moulton, 142).
desmeo	to tie, shackle, bind, Luke 8:29.

desmon;	
desmos	a bond, ligament, shackle: fig., impediment, disability (Strong, Greek Dictionary, 21).

Referring to the "bound of tongue" in Mark 7:35, Moulton and Milligan explain, "The expression has a 'technical' meaning derived from the old belief that a man was 'bound' by daemonic influences. The man was not merely made to speak, but daemonic fetters were broken, and Satan's work undone" (Moulton, 142).

desmee	a bundle, Matthew 13:30.
desmophulax	jailer (one who binds), Acts 16:31.
desmotes	prisoner; Acts 27:1, 42.
desmoteerion	prison
despotes	Lord, master
oikodespotes	the ruler of the house
oikodespoteo	to rule the house and family (Kittel, 2:49); 1 Timothy 5:14.
doulos	a derivative of *deo* meaning a slave, bondservant.
ekdeo	bind, fasten (Liddell, 505)—not in NT.
hupodeema	that which is bound under [the foot], a sandal, shoe.
hupodeomai	to shod or bind on sandals, tie; Ephesians 6:15, feet shod with preparation of gospel of peace (we have bound ourselves to share the gospel).
katadeo	speaking of *deo,* "With Luke 13:16 where demoniac power 'binds' the sufferer from curvature of the spine" (Moulton, 144). (Used in NT only of Samaritan binding wounds in Luke 10:34.)
sundeomai	bind; Hebrews 13:3.
sundesmos	bond, that which fastens together, Acts 8:23; Ephesians 4:3; Colossians 2:19; 3:14.

From Luo

Luo comes from the Greek root *lu*, meaning "loose" (Metzger, 62). There are two basic branch meanings of *luo* used in two ways—to loose and to destroy (undo).

Luo "loosen":

halusis	chains (not loose), link in armor; metaphorically, bondage, distress, anguish (Liddell, 74); Mark 5:3-4; Luke 8:29; Revelation 20:1.
analuo	leave; Luke 12:36; Philemon 1:23; undo, set free (Liddell, 112).
analusis	departure; 2 Timothy 4:6; can also mean a loosing or releasing from evils (Liddell, 112).
apoluo	release (loose from), put away, dismiss (Moulton, 66); redeem (Liddell, 208). Loosed him and forgave him, released from debt, release a prisoner; Matthew 18:27; Mark 15:6, 9, 11, 15. forgive and be forgiven; Luke 6:37. loosed from infirmity; Luke 13:12. healed him and loosed him (released, let him go); Luke 14:4.
epilusis	interpretation, explanation (opening upon), 2 Peter 1:20.
epiluo	expound (to open, untie, loose upon); explain, solve (Liddell, 644); Mark 4:34; Acts 19:39. To set free, release; fig., explain, interpret (Bauer, 295).

The *lutro* "redemption" word group is derived from *luo* as a specific type of loosing (Wigram and Winter, 465).

apolutrosisa	releasing, redemption.
lutron	ransom (a loosing), Matthew 20:28—He gave His life a ransom (a loosing) for many.
lutro	redeem, Titus 2:14, "that He might redeem (loose) us."
lutrosis	redemption, Luke 1:68; 2:38; Hebrews 9:12.
lutrotes	deliver, Acts 7:35.
lusitelei	better, profitable—used only in Luke 17:2.
alusitelees	unprofitable, Hebrews 13:17.
lusiteleo	used as a contract for work (Moulton, 382).

Luo (destroy) cognates include:

luo	meaning to destroy, melt down, dissolve, break down, 2 Peter 3:10, 11, 12; 1 John 3:8; breaking law, John 7:23; ship broken, Acts 27:41; breaking wall, Ephesians 2:14; divorce or separation, 1 Corinthians 7:27.
aluo	distraught, beside oneself, at a loss, perplexed, at wit's end, fretful, restless (Liddell, 74)—not in NT.
dialuo	loosen, disperse, dissolve (Moulton, 151).
dialuomai	scatter, Acts 5:36.
ekluo	faint, Galatians 6:9; Matthew 9:36; 15:32.
ekluomai	I am unstrung, grow weary, become faint-hearted (Metzger, 62).
lumainomai	to ravage, make havoc, Acts 8:3; a broken contract (Moulton, 381), injuring (Moulton, 382).
kataluo	I dissolve, I destroy, Matthew 26:61; the intensive or stronger use of *luo* in the sense of "to put down" (Kittel, 4:338). I lodge (after having loosed the straps and packs of the beasts

	of burden as well as one's own garments) (Metzger, 62), Luke 9:12; 19:7.
akatalutos	indestructible, indissoluble, Hebrews 7:16 (Kittel, 4:338)—only place used in NT.
lusis	loosed—used only in 1 Corinthians 7:27. Can mean the discharge of bonds, debts, marriage tie (Moulton, 382).
luono (lono)	dissolve, melt (Moulton, 384)—not used in NT.
paraluomai	I am unstrung, I am a paralytic (Metzger, 62), Hebrews 12:12—weak knees.
paralutikos	a paralytic, Luke 5:18, 24; Acts 8:7; 9:3; Matthew 8:6; 9:2, 6; Mark 2:3, 4, 5, 9, 10.

Binding and Loosing in OT (LXX):

luo	meaning destroy in connection with "handing over," Ezra 5:12.
luo	to redeem from death, Job 5:20; loosing a donkey, Job 39:5.
	Joseph who was loosed can bind others, Psalm 105:20.
	Hebrews who were bound in fire are loosed with a fourth, Daniel 3:25.
	Daniel solved (*luo*) difficulties (*sundesmos*—bonds), Daniel 5:12; Judges 15:13ff—Samson bound.
	Lamentations 1:14—bound by yoke of sins, God hands over to enemies.

BIBLIOGRAPHY

Anderson, Neil T. *The Bondage Breaker*. Eugene, OR: Harvest House Publishers, 1993.

____. *Helping Others Find Freedom in Christ*. Ventura, CA: Regal Books, 1995.

____. *Setting Your Church Free*. Ventura, CA: Regal Books, 1994.

____. *Victory over the Darkness*. Ventura, CA: Regal Books, 1990.

____. *Winning the Spiritual Warfare*. Eugene, OR: Harvest House, 1990.

Anderson, Neil T. and Dave Park. *The Bondage Breaker,* Youth Edition. Eugene, OR: Harvest House Publishers, 1993.

Arnold, Clinton E. *Crucial Questions about Spiritual Warfare*. Grand Rapids, MI: Baker Books, 1997.

____. *Ephesians, Power and Magic*. New York: Cambridge University Press, 1989.

____. *Powers of Darkness*. Downers Grove, IL: InterVarsity Press, 1992.

Augsburger, David. *Caring Enough to Forgive*. Scottdale, PA: Herald Press, 1981.

Bailey, Keith. *Strange Gods*. Camp Hill, PA: Christian Publications, 1998.

Barclay, William. *The Gospel of Matthew*. The Daily Bible Study Series. Philadelphia: The Westminster Press, 1975.

Bauer, Walter. *A Greek-English Lexicon of the New Testament*. Translated by William F. Arndt and Wilber Gingrich. Chicago: University of Chicago Press, 1957.

Beecher, Henry Ward. *The Biblical Illustrator: St. Matthew*. Edited by Joseph S. Excell. New York: Randolph and Co., n.d.

Bounds, E.M. *The Preacher and Prayer*. Grand Rapids, MI: Zondervan, 1950.

_____. *Satan: His Personality, Power, and Overthrow*. Grand Rapids, MI: Baker Book House, 1972.

Bradley, Bert F. *Fundamentals of Speech Communication*. Dubuque, IA: Wm. C. Brenn Publishing, 1974, 1991.

Bright, John. *The Kingdom of God*. Nashville, TN: Abingdon Press, 1953.

Bromiley, Geoffrey W., gen. ed. *International Standard Bible Encyclopedia*. Grand Rapids, MI: Eerdmans, 1979.

Brown, Colin, ed. *The New International Dictionary of New Testament Theology*. Grand Rapids, MI: Zondervan, 1978.

Bubeck, Mark. *Overcoming the Adversary*. Chicago: Moody Press, 1984.

Bublat, H.O. Personal correspondence with author, 1996.

Burgess, Joseph A. *A History of the Exegesis of Matthew 16:17-19 from 1781 to 1955*. Ann Arbor, MI: Edwards Bros., 1965.

Calvin, John. *Commentary on a Harmony of the Evangelists Matthew, Mark, and Luke*. Grand Rapids, MI: Eerdmans, 1957.

Carson, D.A. *Matthew*. The Expositor's Bible Commentary. Grand Rapids, MI: Zondervan, 1984.

Charles, A.H. *The Apocrypha and Pseudopigrapha of the Old Testament,* vol. 2. London: Oxford University Press, 1913, 1964.

Cowman, Mrs. Charles. *Springs in the Valley.* Minneapolis, MN: Worldwide Publications, 1968.

Crabb, Larry and Dan B. Allender. *Hope When You're Hurting.* Grand Rapids, MI: Zondervan, 1996.

Craigie, Peter C. *Psalm 1-50.* Word Biblical Commentary. Edited by David A. Hubbard and Glenn W. Barker. Waco, TX: Word Books, 1983.

Croft, Jim. "Waging War in the Heavenlies." *New Wine* (March 1977): 7.

Cymbala, Jim. *Fresh Wind, Fresh Fire.* Grand Rapids, MI: Zondervan, 1997.

Dana, H.E. and Julius R. Mantey. *A Manual Grammar of the Greek New Testament.* New York: The MacMillan Company, 1927.

Davies, Stevan L. *Jesus the Healer: Possession, Trance and the Origins of Christianity.* New York: Continuum Publishing Co., 1995.

Dawson, John. *Taking Our Cities for God.* Lake Mary, FL: Creation House, 1989.

de Vogue, Adalbert. *To Love Fasting: The Monastic Experience.* Petersham, MA: Saint Bede's Publications, 1989.

Douglas, J.D., ed. *Encyclopedia of Religious Knowledge.* Grand Rapids, MI: Baker, 1991.

Duewel, Wesley. *Revival Fire.* Grand Rapids, MI: Zondervan, 1995.

Eastman, Dick. *The Jericho Hour.* Orlando, FL: Creation House, 1994.

Epp, Theodore. *Praying with Authority.* Lincoln, NE: Back to the Bible Broadcast, 1965.

Escobar, Alfonso Llano. "Piensa Dejar la Iglesia Catolica?" *El Tiempo*, Bogota, Colombia, June 1, 1997.

Fant, Clyde E., Jr., and William M. Pinson, Jr., eds. *Twenty Centuries of Great Preaching*. Waco, TX: Word, 1971.

Flannery, Austin, gen. ed. *Vatican Council II: The Conciliar and Post Conciliar Documents*. Northport, NY: Costello Publishing Company, 1975.

Foster, K. Neill. "Apologetics and the Deliverance Ministry." Paper presented to the annual meeting of the Evangelical Theological Society. Philadelphia, November 1995, 1.

_____. "The Believer's Authority." Camp Hill, PA: Christian Publications, 1995.

_____ with Eric Mills. *Dam Break in Georgia*. Camp Hill, PA: Horizon Books, 1978.

_____. *The Discerning Christian*. Camp Hill. PA: Christian Publications, 1981.

_____. "Discernment, the Powers and Spirit-speaking." Ph.D. diss., Fuller Theological Seminary, 1988.

_____. "Fasting: The Delightful Discipline." Camp Hill, PA: Christian Publications, 1995.

_____. *Lessons Learned When a Teenager Was Liberated from LSD*. Beaverlodge, AB: Evangelistic Enterprises Society of Alberta, 1974.

——. *The Third View of Tongues*. Camp Hill, PA: Horizon Books, 1975.

——. *Warfare Weapons*. Camp Hill, PA: Christian Publications, 1995.

Gaustad, Edwin Scott. *The Great Awakening in New England*. Gloucester, MS: Peter Smith, n.d.

Gesenius, Wilhelm. *Gesenius' Hebrew and Chaldee Lexicon*. Grand Rapids, MI: Eerdmans, 1949, 1974.

Goforth, Jonathan. *By My Spirit*. Minneapolis, MN: Bethany Fellowship, 1942.

Gordon, A.J. "The Ministry of Healing." In Jonathan L. Graf, ed. *Healing: The Three Great Classics on Divine Healing*. Camp Hill, PA: Christian Publications, 1992.

Gothard, Bill. *Rebuilder's Guide*. Oak Brook, IL: Institute in Basic Youth Conflicts, 1982.

Grubb, Norman. *Rees Howells Intercessor*. Fort Washington, PA: Christian Literature Crusade, 1983.

Hagner, Donald A. *Matthew 1-13*. Edited by David A. Hubbard. Word Biblical Commentary. Dallas: Word Books, 1993.

Hanegraaff, Hank. *Christianity in Crisis*. Eugene, OR: Harvest House, 1993.

Hendricksen, William. *New Testament Commentary Exposition of the Gospel of Matthew*. Grand Rapids, MI: Baker, 1973.

Henry, Matthew. *Commentary on the Whole Bible*. New York: Fleming H. Revell, n.d.

Hiers, Richard H. "Binding and Loosing: The Matthean Authorization." *Journal of Biblical Literature* 104:2 (1985): 238-249.

Hillis, Dick. "Prayer Was Not Enough: China," in *Demon Experiences in Many Lands*. Chicago: Moody Press, 1960.

Holman Concise Bible Dictionary. Nashville, TN: Broadman and Holman Publishers, 1997.

Hunt, Dave. *Beyond Seduction*. Eugene, OR: Harvest House Publishers, 1987.

Hunt, Dave and T.A. McMahon. *The Seduction of Christianity*. Eugene, OR: Harvest House Publishers, 1985.

International Standard Bible Encyclopedia. Grand Rapids, MI: Eerdmans, 1979.

Ironside, H.A. *Expository Notes on the Gospel of Matthew*. Neptune, NJ: Loizeaux Brothers, 1948.

Jackson, Samuel Macauley and Clarence Nevin Heller. "Zwingli." *Commentary on True and False Religion*. Durham, NC: The Labyrinth Press, 1981.

Jacobs, Cindy. *Possessing the Gates of the Enemy*. Grand Rapids, MI: Chosen Books, 1994.

James, William. *The Varieties of Religious Experience*. New Hyde Park, NY: University Books, 1902.

Josephus, Flavius. *The Works of Flavius Josephus*. Translated by William Whiston. Philadelphia: David McKay, Publisher, n.d.

Jung, Carl Gustav. *Memories, Dreams, Reflections*. New York: Pantheon Books, 1961.

Keener, Craig S. *The IVP Bible Background Commentary: New Testament*. Downers Grove, IL: InterVarsity Press, 1993.

Kidner, Derek. *Psalms 73-150*. Tyndale Old Testament Commentaries. London: InterVarsity Press, 1975.

King, Paul L. "A.B. Simpson and the Modern Faith Movement." In Elio Cuccaro, ed. *Alliance Academic Review*. Camp Hill, PA: Christian Publications, 1996.

_____. "Holy Laughter and Other Phenomena in Evangelical and Holiness Revival Movements." In Elio Cuccaro, ed. *Alliance Academic Review*. Camp Hill, PA: Christian Publications, 1998.

_____. "The Restoration of the Doctrine of Binding and Loosing." In Elio Cuccaro, ed. *Alliance Academic Review*. Camp Hill, PA: Christian Publications, 1997.

Kirkpatrick, A.F. *The Book of Psalms*. Cambridge: University Press, 1957.

Kittel, Gerhard, ed., Geoffrey W. Bromiley, trans. *Theological Dictionary of the New Testament*. Grand Rapids, MI: Eerdmans, 1964.

Koch, Kurt. *Christian Counseling and Occultism*. Grand Rapids, MI: Kregel Publications, 1972.

_____. *Demonology, Past and Present*. Grand Rapids, MI: Kregel Publications, 1973.

Latourette, Kenneth Scott. *A History of Christianity*. San Francisco: Harper and Row, 1975.

Leahy, Frederick S. *Satan Cast Out*. Edinburgh: The Banner of Truth Trust, 1975.

Leidenfrost, Csaba, "Peretti Evangelism." *Christian Research Journal,* Vol. 20, No. 1 (September-October 1997): 53.

LeJeune, R. *Christoph Blumhardt: His Life and Message*. Rifton, NJ: The Plough Publishing House, 1963.

Lenski, R.C.H. *The Interpretation of St. Matthew's Gospel*. Minneapolis, MN: Augsburg Publishing House, 1943.

Lewis, Rodger. *The Battle for Bali*. Camp Hill, PA: Christian Publications, forthcoming.

Liddell, Henry George and Robert Scott. *A Greek-English Lexicon*. Oxford: Clarendon Press, 1968.

Linder, William, Jr. *Andrew Murray*. Minneapolis, MN: Bethany House Publishers, 1996.

MacArthur, John, Jr. *Charismatic Chaos*. Grand Rapids, MI: Zondervan, 1992.

_____. *Our Sufficiency Is in Christ*. Dallas: Word Publishing, 1991.

MacMillan, John A. *The Authority of the Believer*. Camp Hill, PA: Christian Publications, 1997.

____. *Encounter with Darkness*. Camp Hill, PA: Christian Publications, 1980.

Martin, Ralph P. *Colossians and Philemon*. New Century Bible. London: Oliphants, 1974.

McElheran, Clifton. *Let the Oppressed Go Free*. Calgary, AB: Self-published, n.d.

Metzger, Bruce M. *Lexical Aids for Students of New Testament Greek*. Princeton, NJ: Theological Book Agency, 1976.

Moulton, James Hope, and George Milligan. *The Vocabulary of the Greek Testament*. Grand Rapids, MI: Eerdmans, 1963.

Michaels, J. Ramsay. *Servant and Son: Jesus in Parable and Gospel*. Atlanta: John Knox Press, 1981.

Montgomery, Carrie Judd. *The Secrets of Victory*. Oakland, CA: Triumphs of Faith, 1921.

____. *Triumphs of Faith*. Oakland, CA: Triumphs of Faith, 1921.

Moore, Art. "Spiritual Mapping Gains Credibility Among Leaders." *Christianity Today* (12 January 1998): 55-57.

Morgan, G. Campbell. *The Gospel According to Matthew*. Old Tappan, NJ: Fleming H. Revell, 1929.

Morris, Leon. *The Gospel According to Matthew*. Grand Rapids, MI: Eerdmans, 1992.

Mounce, Robert H. *Matthew: A Good News Commentary*. San Francisco: Harper and Row, 1985.

Mumper, Sharon. "From Pogrom to Peacemaking." *Christianity Today* (12 August 1996): 38-40.

Murray, Andrew. *With Christ in the School of Prayer*. Springdale, PA: Whitaker House, 1885, 1981.

Myers, Ched. *Binding the Strong Man: A Political Reading of Mark's Story of Jesus*. Maryknoll, NY: Orbis Books, 1988.

Nanfelt, Peter. "Guinea." *Alliance Video Magazine* (1997): Vol. 11, No. 2.

Nee, Watchman. *God's Plan and the Overcomers*. New York: Christian Fellowship Publishers, 1977.

____. *The King and the Kingdom of Heaven*. New York: Christian Fellowship Publishers, 1978.

Nevius, John L. *Demon Possession and Allied Themes*. Chicago: Fleming H. Revell, n.d.

Niklaus, Robert L., John S. Sawin and Samuel J. Stoesz. *All for Jesus*. Camp Hill, PA: Christian Publications, 1986.

Oesterreich, Traugott Konstantin. *Possession, Demonaical and Other*. New Hyde Park, NY: University Books, 1930, 1966.

Orchard, Bernard, ed. *A Catholic Commentary on Holy Scripture*. New York: Thomas Nelson & Sons, 1953.

Otis, George, Jr. *The Twilight Labyrinth*. Grand Rapids, MI: Chosen Books, 1997.

Oxford NIV Scofield Study Bible. New York: Oxford University Press, 1978.

Patzia, Arthur G. *Colossians, Philemon, Ephesians*. San Francisco: Harper and Row, 1984.

Penn-Lewis, Jessie. "How to Pray for Missionaries." *The Alliance Weekly* (12 June 1937): 26

____. *Prayer and Evangelism*. Dorset, England: Overcomer Literature Trust, n.d.

____. *The Warfare with Satan*. Fort Washington, PA: Christian Literature Crusade, 1963.

Penn-Lewis, Jessie and Evan Roberts. *War on the Saints*. New York: Thomas Lowe, 1912, 1963.

Phillips, McCandlish. *The Bible, The Supernatural and the Jews*. Camp Hill, PA: Horizon Books, 1995.

Piper, John. *A Godward Life*. Sisters, OR: Multnomah Publications, 1997.

____. *A Hunger for God: Desiring God through Fasting and Prayer*. Wheaton, IL: Crossway Books, 1997.

Plummer, Alfred. *An Exegetical Commentary on the Gospel of St. Matthew*. Grand Rapids, MI: Baker, 1982.

Prince, Derek. "Aggressive Prayer." *New Wine* (March 1977): 7, 24.

Reese, David. Personal correspondence with author, August 17, 1997.

Reynolds, Rob. "Is There Really a War?" *Moody* (July/August 1997): 15-16.

Rinker, Rosalind. *How to Get the Most Out of Your Prayer Life*. Eugene, OR: Harvest House, 1981.

Roberts, Alexander and James Donaldson, eds. *The Ante-Nicene Fathers*. Grand Rapids, MI: Eerdmans, 1978.

Rodewyk, Adolf. *Possessed by Satan: The Church and Teaching on the Devil, Possession, and Exorcism*. Translated by Martin Ebon. Garden City, NY: Doubleday, 1975.

Rommen, Edward, ed. *Spiritual Power and Missions.* Pasadena, CA: William Carey Library, 1995.

Schaff, Philip, ed. *Nicene Fathers and Post-Nicene Fathers.* Grand Rapids, MI: Eerdmans, 1979.

Schweizer, Eduard. *The Good News According to Matthew.* Atlanta: John Knox Press, 1975.

Simons, Menno. *The Complete Writings of Menno Simons.* Scottdale, PA: Herald Press, 1956.

Simpson, A.B. *The Christ in the Bible Commentary.* Camp Hill, PA: Christian Publications, 1992.

____. "Christ in Me." In *Hymns of the Christian Life.* Camp Hill, PA: Christian Publications, 1978.

____. *The Gospel of Healing.* Camp Hill, PA: Christian Publications, 1994.

Skehan, Patrick W. "A Fragment of the Song of Moses (Deut. 32) from Qumran." *Bulletin of American Schools of Oriental Research (BASOR),* 136 (1954): 12.

Smedes, Lewis B. *Forgive and Forget.* San Francisco: Harper and Row, 1984.

Spurgeon, Charles Haddon. *Faith's Checkbook.* Chicago: Moody Press, n.d.

____. *The Gospel of the Kingdom.* New York: The Baker Taylor Co., 1893.

____. *Treasury of David.* Grand Rapids, MI: Baker, 1950, 1978.

____. "Unbinding Lazarus." In *C.H. Spurgeon's Sermons on the Miracles.* Grand Rapids, MI: Zondervan, 1958.

Stanphill, Ira R. "Room at the Cross for You." In *Amazing Grace.* Grand Rapids, MI: Kregel Publications, 1990.

Stephens, W.P. *The Theology of Huldrych Zwingli*. Oxford: Clarendon Press, 1986.

Strong, James. *The Comprehensive Concordance of the Bible*. Iowa Falls, IA: World Bible Publishers, n.d.

____. "Greek Dictionary of the New Testament." In *Strong's Exhaustive Concordance*. Tulsa, OK: American Christian College Press, n.d.

Tam, Stanley. *God's Woodshed*. Camp Hill, PA: Horizon Books, 1989.

Tasker, R.V.G. *The Gospel According to Matthew: An Introduction and Commentary*. Grand Rapids, MI: Eerdmans, 1961.

Tenney, Merrill C. *The Gospel of John*. The Expositor's Bible Commentary. Grand Rapids, MI: Zondervan, 1981.

Thayer, John Henry. *A Greek-English Lexicon of the New Testament*. Edinburgh: T & T Clark, 1955.

Thompson, David C. *Beyond the Mist*. Camp Hill, PA: Christian Publications, 1998.

Tozer, A.W. *Born after Midnight*. Camp Hill, PA: Christian Publications, 1989.

____. *The Early Tozer: A Word in Season*. Compiled by James L. Snyder. Camp Hill, PA: Christian Publications, 1997.

____. "God's Greatest Gift to Man." Camp Hill, PA: Christian Publications, 1995.

____. *Let My People Go!* Camp Hill, PA: Christian Publications, 1990.

____. *Man: The Dwelling Place of God*. Camp Hill, PA: Christian Publications, 1966.

_____. "The Person God Uses." In H. Robert Cowles, K. Neill Foster and David P. Jones, eds. *Missionary Voices*. Camp Hill, PA: Christian Publications, 1996.

_____. "Worship: The Missing Jewel." Camp Hill, PA: Christian Publications, n.d.

Tuttle, Robert G., Jr. *John Wesley: His Life and Theology*. Grand Rapids, MI: Zondervan, 1978.

Unger, Merrill F. *Demons in the World Today*. Wheaton, IL: Tyndale House, 1984.

_____. *What Demons Can Do to Saints*. Chicago: Moody Press, 1977.

Wagner, C. Peter. *Blazing the Way: Acts 15-28*. The Acts of the Holy Spirit Series, Book 3. Ventura, CA: Regal Books, 1995.

_____. *Confronting the Powers*. Ventura, CA: Regal Books, 1996.

_____. *Engaging the Enemy*. Ventura, CA: Regal Books, 1991.

Wagner, Donald Alfred. *Matthew 1-13*. Word Biblical Commentary. Dallas: Word Books, 1993.

Wakely, Mike. "A Critical Look at a New 'Key to Evangelism.' " *Evangelical Missions Quarterly* (April 1995): 152-162.

Wallis, Arthur. *Revival: The Rain from Heaven*. Grand Rapids, MI: Feming H. Revell, 1979.

Warden, Bert. "In the Face of Spiritual Warfare." *Alliance Life* (12 February 1997): 15.

Warner, Timothy M. *Spiritual Warfare: Victory over the Powers of This Dark World*. Wheaton: Crossway Books, 1991.

Weborg, C. John. "Reborn in Order to Renew." *Christian History* (5:2): 29, 35.

Wesley, John. *The Journal of John Wesley*. Chicago: Moody Press, n.d.

_____. *The Works of John Wesley*. Grand Rapids, MI: Zondervan, n.d.

Wigram, George V. and Ralph Winter. *The Word Study Concordance*. Pasadena, CA: William Carey Library, 1978.

Williams, Charles B. *The Williams New Testament*. Chicago: Moody Press, 1954.

Wink, Walter. *Naming the Powers*. Philadelphia: Fortress Press, 1984.

Zwingli, Huldrych. *Commentary on True and False Religions*. Edited by Samuel Macaulay Jackson and Clarence Nevin Heller. Durham, NC: The Labyrinth Press, 1981.

SCRIPTURE INDEX

SUBJECT INDEX

STUDY GUIDE

Chapter 1

The Doctrine in a Nutshell

1. What are the weaknesses or extremes of some of the "friends" of binding and loosing (pp. 9-11)? Do you know some of these "friends"?

2. Read First Peter 2:9-10. Explain the meaning of the priesthood of the believer and its implications. How is the concept of binding and loosing built on the doctrine of the priesthood of the believer?

3. Read Ephesians 1:19-23 and 2:6. What does it mean to be seated with Christ in the heavenly places?

4. What is the difference between asking the Lord to bind and loose and *you* doing the binding and loosing? Is it presumptuous for you to do it?

Chapter 2

The Jewish Concepts

1. Read Genesis 1:26. What are the basic principles of authority in the Old Testament? Do they apply in the New Testament age?

2. Read Matthew 8:8-9. How does a person under authority have authority?

3. How did the ancient Jewish writers understand binding and loosing?

4. In what way does binding and loosing involve the supernatural?

Chapter 3

The Early Church Fathers

1. Discuss some of the various ways in which the Church Fathers understood binding and loosing, especially Tertullian, Augustine and Chrysostom. Apply to situations today.

2. Read Acts 5:1-11 and 13:8-11. In what way are the cases of Ananias, Sapphira and Elymas examples of binding?

3. How does loosing involve forgiving sins, healing bodies and permitting certain conduct as Tertullian taught?

4. How can Satan have been bound by Christ and yet needs to be bound repeatedly?

Chapter 4

The Reformers

1. How is it that Martin Luther advanced the doctrine of the priesthood of the believer and yet did not seem to understand the authority of the believer to confront spiritual forces directly?

2. How did Rationalism affect Post-Reformation views of demonic spiritual forces?

3. Read Revelation 20:1-3. Explain the differences between premillennial end-time views and amillennial interpretation of this Scripture. How does amillennial theology affect the doctrine of binding and loosing?

4. Discuss the medieval Roman Church belief that the keys of the kingdom and the authority of binding and loosing belong only to the pope and bishops vs. the Protestant Reformer beliefs of Zwingli and Simons that they belong to all believers.

Chapter 5

The Doctrine Restored

1. Describe how the concept of binding and loosing was lost and re-covered in the Church.

2. Explain the teachings of Jessie Penn-Lewis and A.B. Simpson on the authority of the believer and binding and loosing.

3. Although the modern charismatic and word-of-faith movements have taught the authority of the believer and binding and loosing, there are differences in teaching and practice from classic evangelical writers such as Simpson, Penn-Lewis, Murray and MacMillan. Can you think of some of the differences?

4. Read Matthew 12:22-29. What does it mean to "bind the strong man"?

Chapter 6

Binding and Loosing in the Old Testament

1. Read Genesis 22. What is the significance of Abraham binding and then loosing Isaac?

2. Read Psalm 105:17-22. What is the significance of Joseph being bound, then released, then having the authority to bind?

3. Read Psalm 149. What is the meaning of saints having authority to bind kings and nobles?

4. Read Isaiah 58. How does fasting relate to loosing?

Chapter 7

Binding and Loosing in the New Testament

1. Read John 11:1-45. Discuss the symbolic meaning of the loosing of Lazarus.

2. Read Matthew 21:2-7. What is the spiritual significance of Jesus telling the disciples to loose the colt? In Matthew's account of this story, it is the fourth time he uses the binding and loosing language. Why is this notable?

3. Read Luke 13:10-17. In what way was the woman bound, and how was she loosed? What were the results of her loosing?

4. Read Acts 16:23-34. What brings about the loosing in this passage? How can we be loosed, and how can we loose others?

Chapter 8

The Believer's Completeness in Christ

1. Read aloud the affirmations of who we are in Christ (pp. 93-95). Discuss their implications for your life.

2. Read Colossians 2:9-15. What does it mean for Christ to be in us?

3. In what ways are we complete in Christ?

4. What is the implication of our completeness in Christ for exercising the authority of Christ in binding and loosing?

Chapter 9

The Authority of the Believer

1. What is the difference between prayer and exercising spiritual authority?

2. Read Genesis 1:26-28 and Psalm 8:4-8. Explain man's dominion over the earth.

3. Describe the various levels of authority that God has ordained.

4. In what way have believers been elevated to a position of authority over spiritual powers?

Chapter 10

The Missiological Perspective

1. Read Matthew 12:22-29. What does binding the strong man have to do with evangelism and missions?

2. What does it mean to spoil the strong man's goods? How can the Church spoil the strong man's treasures today?

3. What is a power encounter? How does a power encounter enhance the work of evangelism and missions?

4. Why does binding the strong man need to precede loosing people from bondage?

Chapter 11

The Synoptic Perspective

1. Read Matthew 12:29, 16:16-19 and 18:18-20. Discuss Matthew's perspective on binding and loosing.

2. Read Matthew 12:22-29, Mark 3:22-27 and Luke 11:14-22. Note the similarities and differences among the three accounts and explain their meaning.

3. Discuss the weapons of Satan and how they put people in bondage today.

4. What does Luke's usage of the language of overcoming tell us about binding and loosing?

Chapter 12

The Peter Perspective

1. Read Matthew 16:16-19. Discuss the meaning of the keys of the kingdom. How can you exercise the keys of the kingdom today?

2. What are the gates of Hades? In what way can the gates of Hades not prevail against the Church?

3. Who can bind and loose—just Peter? just the apostles? just bishops? What can be bound and what can be loosed?

4. Discuss some of the real-life incidents in the book which demonstrate binding and loosing today. Do you know of some similar situations in which binding and loosing have been or might be appropriate?

Chapter 13

The Disciples' Perspective

1. Read Matthew 18:18-20. What is the significance of the "periphrastic future perfect" tense? Is God bound to bind and loose what we bind and loose?

2. How is prayer like lightening?

3. Read Matthew 18:15-20, First Corinthians 5:1-5 and First Timothy 1:20. Discuss church discipline as a type of binding and loosing.

4. Can you think of any instances in which binding and loosing as discipline would be appropriate?

Chapter 14

Loosing As Forgiveness

1. Read Matthew 6:14-15 and 18:15-35. In what sense does unforgiveness cause a person to be bound?

2. How does forgiveness cause a person to be loosed? How do revivals loose unforgiveness? Do you know people you should forgive so they can be set free?

3. Read John 20:22-23. How does this Scripture relate to binding and ·loosing?

4. In what ways can corporate confession of sin loose people? What corporate sins of your church, community or nation might you confess in prayer?

Chapter 15

False and True

1. Discuss the Roman Catholic interpretation of Matthew 16:16-19 and 18:18. Why is it in error?

2. Discuss the errors of the Faith Movement in relation to binding and loosing. Has God abdicated control to mankind? Does the authority of the believer make Christians little gods? Can anything be bound or loosed?

3. How would you respond to a person who claims binding and loosing only involves church discipline?

4. How is it possible that binding and loosing could be counterfeited by satanic powers?

Chapter 16

When It Doesn't Happen

1. Can a person exercise binding and loosing at any time for anything?

2. What occasions might not be appropriate for binding and loosing?

3. What can hinder the effectiveness of binding and loosing?

4. Discuss the quote from Jim Cymbala: "The Bible speaks more about resisting the devil than binding him" (p. 214).

Chapter 17

Binding, Loosing and Politics

1. How can prayer act as a catalyst of binding and loosing for God to intervene in political situations and the affairs of a nation?

2. Why might there be a need for binding and loosing in church politics?

3. Discuss the three political options for binding and loosing (p. 224) and their appropriateness and validity.

4. How can binding and loosing have an impact on the moral ills of society?

Chapter 18

Fasting As Loosing

1. Discuss the supernatural results of the fasting of Moses and Elijah and Jesus.

2. What does the fasting of Jonah teach us about loosing for evangelism?

3. What do the stories of Daniel and Esther fasting teach us about the impact of fasting on political situations? Discuss whether the partial fast of Daniel can be a legitimate form of fasting.

4. Read Isaiah 58. Describe from this passage of Scripture in what way fasting can be a form of loosing.

Chapter 19

Binding, Loosing and Territorial Spirits

1. What are territorial spirits? What is the biblical evidence for territorial spirits?

2. Discuss historical evidence for territorial spirits. Can you think of any similar incidents today?

3. What might be the reasons for revivals taking place in certain geographical localities?

4. What are the dangers in trying to confront territorial demonic powers through binding and loosing? How might believers confront demonic powers yet avoid those dangers?

Chapter 20

Binding, Loosing and Prayer Walks

1. What is prayer walking? How was prayer walking practiced in the Old and New Testaments?

2. The author makes the statement, "Prayer walking is potentially missiological" (p. 273). Give illustrations of how that might be true.

3. Discuss the principles of prayer walking. How can they be applied in prayer walking events through your church?

4. What are some of the "red flags" concerning prayer walking?

Chapter 21

Binding, Loosing and the Glory of God

1. Why must binding and loosing be done for the glory of God?

2. What motive might cause binding and loosing not to glorify God?

3. Give illustrations of how binding and loosing can be done for the glory of God.

4. What situations do you know of in which binding and loosing would be appropriate and beneficial?

K. Neill Foster has had a diverse career as pastor, teacher, evangelist and publisher. His cross-cultural preaching and teaching ministries have taken him to more than twenty countries of the world for missionary and national workers' conferences. An ordained minister, he holds a B.Th. from Canadian Bible College, an M.Miss. from Canadian Theological Seminary and an M.A. and a Ph.D. from the School of World Mission in Pasadena, California. His writing includes numerous academic articles, booklets and six books, including this one.

Paul L. King is an ordained minister with The Christian and Missionary Alliance. His ministries have included administration and teaching at a Christian school, several pastorates, as well as interdenominational teaching and preaching. He is currently a university professor and administrator. Already the recipient of B.A. and M.A. degrees, he has also earned doctoral degrees in ministry and in theology. He is the author of *A Believer with Authority*. The Kings live in Broken Arrow, Oklahoma.

Publications by K. Neill Foster

Books

Binding and Loosing (with Paul King)
Dam Break in Georgia (with Eric Mills)
The Discerning Christian
Revolution of Love
The Third View of Tongues
Warfare Weapons

Booklets

"The Believer's Authority"
"Fasting: The Delightful Discipline"

Books edited

Holiness Voices (with H. Robert Cowles)
Missionary Voices (with H. Robert Cowles and David Jones)
Prayer Voices (with H. Robert Cowles)
Voices on the Glory (with Stephen Adams and George McPeek)